TOURISM MARKETING

TOURISM MARKETING

B.S. Badan
Harish Bhatt

Commonwealth

Tourism Marketing

Edition : 2020

ISBN 81-311-0062-6

Published by :

COMMONWEALTH PUBLISHERS
4831/24, Prahlad Street,
Ansari Road, Darya Ganj,
New Delhi - 110002
Ph. : 23275511, 23257835
e-mail : commonwealthbooks@gmail.com

Printed at :
Roshan Offset Printers
Delhi

PREFACE

Tourism can be defined as the act of travel for the purpose of recreation, and the provision of services for this act. It is a service industry, comprising a number of tangible and intangible components. The tangible elements include transportation systems—air, rail, road, water and now, space; hospitality services, accommodation, foods and beverages, tours, souvenirs; and related services such as banking, insurance and safety and security. The intangible elements include: rest and relaxation, culture, escape, adventure, new and different experiences.

Travel and tourism is a major industry in the world and is at the top of the league of invisible earners of foreign currency. Many sovereignties, along with their respective countries and states, depend heavily upon travel expenditures by foreigners as a source of taxation and income for the enterprises that sell services to these travellers. Consequently the development of tourism is often a strategy employed either by a non-governmental organization or a governmental agency to promote a particular region for the purpose of increasing commerce through exporting goods and services to non-locals.

During recent years the tourism industry has witnessed unprecedented growth. Increasing consumer demand for educational and participatory travel experiences has resulted in a variety of specialty niche markets such as ecotourism, cultural-heritage tourism, and agritourism. New paradigms link strategic tourism planning with sustainable development.

The leisure and tourism industry is one of the leading global economic activities, a multi-billion-dollar industry with

700 million international travellers per year around the world. Tourism is a motor for employment and income creation and, especially in poor countries, a vehicle for development. But today it is not sufficient to simply create employment without regard for the quality of jobs and the social and environmental effects of tourism in vulnerable areas. A growing number of organizations, including the tourism industry leadership, are increasingly conscious of the risks and are adopting a more responsible attitude.

The present publication provides an authoritative look at how to manage travel and tourism industry in a better way. It introduces the complexities of the tourism system so that they will be better positioned to eventually assume the managerial challenges and responsibilities in a diverse and challenging industry. The latest advancements in tourism theory and thinking, retaining the thoroughness of content, diversity of applications, regional and international issues, economic significance, tourism operators and the role of technology in the tourism industry etc. are also described elaborately. Numerous regional and global case studies and examples are included to provide an appropriately broad geographic context. This work will be highly informative and useful to students, researchers, policy makers, managers and working groups of travel and tourism industry.

B.S. Badan
Harish Bhatt

Contents

1 World Tourism Today

This chapter examines the current global dimensions and patterns of, and the recent trends in, travel and tourism, in order to provide a framework within which to consider the likely future of this global industry. It highlights the main generators of tourism demand, the main destinations of tourists and the main international tourism flows. Reference is made to the three leading tourism regions—Europe, North America and the Pacific Rim—and comments are also offered on the position of Africa, Asia and Latin America. The main trends of the 1990s are examined and the chapter concludes with some indicative pointers to the issues likely to influence tourism in the coming decades.

Definitions

It is important to acknowledge at the outset that the measurement of tourism is both an imprecise science and is increasingly susceptible to definitional problems. The central source of data on international tourism, and the one upon which this chapter primarily owned is provided by the World Tourism Organisation (WTO) using data owned from government sources. These data are largely concerned with two common measures of tourism—the number of arrivals registered in each country and the levels of expenditure made by visitors. They also permit some aspects of the main generators of international tourism demand. However, as Edwards and Graham (1997) point out, destination countries use ten different measures of tourism, and origin countries use a further five, and there are often some wide discrepancies between different data sources. They conclude that exponditure measures are the most reliable in assessing tourism's magnitude, yet it is immediately obvious that most countries, in discussing, planning and promoting their tourism industries, tend mainly to refer to arrivals numbers as if these were a reliable economic indicator. Clearly, without analysing the types of arrivals, they are not.

Furthermore, international tourism traffic is the tip of the iceberg. Domestic travel, in terms of the number of trips taken, far exceeds the level of international trips. Domestic travel is rarely measured with much accuracy other than through macro-economic estimations and/or sample survey data. However, to provide just one indication of the magnitudes involved, the Prime Minister of China, Li Peng, in his opening address to the Pacific Asia Travel Association conference held in Beijing in 1997 reported that the Chinese had made 640 million domestic tourist trips in the previous year. This is 45 million more than the global total of international tourist arrivals in that same year.

It is obvious that the magnitude of domestic tourism in the industrialised world is vast – notably in North America and Europe. The oft-quoted statistic that less than 10% of Americans hold passports (despite the fact that the USA is the world's largest spender on international tourism, excluding transport costs), hints at just how massive this domestic business can be. However, the main thrust of this chapter is to focus on international tourism on which, notwithstanding data problems, information is most readily available.

Growth and Magnitudes

Todays' masive tourism industy has been driven by a number of factors – and these are the factors whose future directions need to be considered. They are:

- growth in real incomes;
- the advance in personal wealth as expressed in the ability of individuals to generate resources beyond those needed to pay for life's basic needs, food, housing, clothing, education, health and, in more recent times 'essential' consumer goods – in other words, the expanding ability for discretionary expenditure on non-essential items;

- increases in leisure time;
- peace amongst nations:
- freedom from administrative restraints on international travel;
- freedoms within international currency markets;
- expansion of fast, efficient and widely affordable public transport, coupled with wide access to private transport.

In a word, tourism depends upon economic development and open, free societies. It can be immediately seen that, measured against these basic criteria, much of today's world fares very badly. Such a comparison reveals two important facts. First, the majority of the world's population has yet to attain what we in the industrialised world would regard as a minimum level of supply of these elements. Second, and as a consequence, if the world's under-privileged can reasonably hope to attain access to these elements during the next century, the capacity for demand growth in national and international tourism is, for all practical purposes, unlimited.

For the advocates of tourism, this is wonderful news. For those concerned about wider issues of environmental integrity, it is potentially terrifying. For pragmatists, it raises issues to explore and elucidate.

The basic facts of the modern international tourism industry are well known and can be briefly stated. According to WTO data, in 1950 there were 25 million international tourist arrivals and the value of tourism receipts was US$ 2.1 billion. In 1998 international arrivals had risen to an estimated 635 millian and the value of receipts to US$ 439 billion. Over those 48 years, the average annual increase in arrivals was around 7%; in terms of (current) tourism receiprs, the average was just over 11.5%. The temptation to conclude that international tourism is subject to uninterrupted exponential growth is thus obvious but, as this chapter will show, it is also misleading, since there is clear evidence that rates of growth are now slowing down.

This chapter concentrates on the trends evident during the 1990s. As Table 1.1 shows, the rate of growth in international tourism arrivals averaged just over 4% a year between 1990 and 1998, but with very wide differences by region. The world's two

Table 1.1
International Tourist Arrivals by Region, 1990 – 98 (mn)

	1990	*1995*	*1996*	*1997*	*1998*	*% change from 1990 to 1998*[a]	*Annual average % change*
Africa	15.1	20.1	21.5	23.2	24.7	63.9	6.3
North America	71.7	80.5	85.2	84.7	85.0	18.5	2.2
Caribbean	11.4	14.0	14.3	15.3	16.0	40.0	4.3
Latin America	10.4	15.8	17.2	18.9	21.7	75.1	9.6
East Asia/Pacific	54.6	81.4	89.2	88.0	86.6	58.7	5.9
Europe	282.3	333.9	349.0	369.8	381.1	35.0	3.8
Middle East	9.0	13.5	14.1	14.9	15.0	67.8	6.8
South Asia	3.2	4.2	4.4	4.8	5.0	59.4	6.0
Total[b]	457.6	563.4	595.0	619.6	635.1	38.8	4.2

[a] Calculated on unrouned data.
[b] Totals may not all due to rounding.
Source : World Tourism Organisation.

Table 1.2
Regional Shares of International Tourist Arrivials, 1990 – 98(%)

	1990	*1995*	*1996*	*1997*	*1998*
Africa	3.3	3.6	3.6	3.7	3.9
North America	15.7	14.3	14.3	13.7	13.4
Caribbean	2.5	2.5	2.4	2.5	2.5
Latin America	2.3	2.8	2.9	3.0	3.4
East Asia/Pacific	11.9	14.4	15.0	14.2	13.6
Europe	61.7	59.3	58.7	59.7	60.0
Middle East	2.0	2.4	2.4	2.4	2.4
South Asia	0.7	0.7	0.7	0.8	0.8
Total[a]	100.0	100.0	100.0	100.0	100.0

[a] Total may not add due to rounding.
Source: World Tourism Organisation.

major tourism regions – Europe and North America – both exhibited below-average growth. The fastest growing regions were Latin America, the Middle East and Africa – all relative back-markers in volume terms.

In terms of market share, Europe remains the dominrnt influence on international tourism by the arrivals measure, accounting for 60% of al1 international arrivals in 1998, with East Asia/Pacific and North America next in importance. Together, these three regions account for almost nine out of every ten arrivals globally.

Table 1.3
International Tourism Receipts by Region, 1990 – 98 (US$ bn)

	1990	*1995*	*1996*	*1997*	*1998*	*Annual average % change 1990/98*
Africa	5.3	7.5	8.7	9.0	9.6	7.7
Americas	70.0	102.7	112.4	118.9	120.0	7.0
East Asia/Pacific	39.2	74.2	82.0	76.4	68.6	7.3
Europe	146.8	207.6	222.2	220.5	228.9	5.7
Middle East	4.4	7.5	8.2	9.1	8.0	7.7
South Asia	2.0	3.5	3.9	4.3	4.3	10.1
Total[a]	267.8	403.0	437.6	438.2	439.4	6.4

[a] Totals may not add due to rounding.
Source: World Tourism Organisation.

Looking now at tourism receipts, during the 1990s these grew in current US dollar terms at an average annual rate of 6.4% to 1998. Only Europe was below average during this period, with South Asia leading the pack, and Africa and the Middle East being the next best performers.

However, the major earners in terms of the volume of total receipts remain again Europe, the Americas (of which North America accounts, for almost three-quarters) and East Asia/ Pacific. The fastest growing regions are the small ones, and it should also be noted that the rate of growth in receipts in East Asia/Pacific until 1996 was 13.1% – by far the fastest – before the first hints of a slowdown in Asia's economies became apparent. Europe's share of total tourism receipts has hovered around the 50% mark since the mid-1990s, having eroded slightly in the face of the rapid expansion in Asia in the early 1990s but recovering slightly thereafter. Similarly, the share of the Americas

Table 1.4
Share of International Tourism Receipts by Region, 1990 – 98 (%)

	1990	*1995*	*1996*	*1997*	*1998*
Africa	2.0	1.9	2.0	2.1	2.2
Americas	26.1	25.5	25.7	27.1	27.3
East Asia Pacific	14.6	18.4	18.7	17.4	15.6
Europe	54.8	51.5	50.8	50.3	52.1
Middle East	1.6	1.9	1.9	2.1	1.8
South Asia	0.7	0.9	0.9	1.0	1.0
Total[a]	100.0	100.0	100.0	100.0	100.0

[a] Totals may not add due to rounding.
Source: World Tourism Organisation.

has remained broadly stable, the slight increase in the latter years being attributable partly to accelerated growth in Latin America, while the share of East Asia/Pacific fell back.

Europe is, of course, unique in international tourism owing to its geography. Most of its countries are accessible to most of its citizens by the simple means of taking a private car or train across borders. Where distances are too great for surface transport, air transport offers a short journey time alternative – rarely in excess of a 3-hour fight. The development of mass international tourism in the post-war era largely took place within Europe, based on these factors and assisted, of course, by the progressive liberalisation of air transport markets. This allowed charter flights to drive leisure tourism forward, coupled with the development of the inclusive tour which took care of anxieties, inexperience and uncertainties arising from taking a holiday in another country where a foreign language and customs prevailed.

No other region of the world has such characteristics, so it is of little surprise that Europe is so massively important. It is, however, worth reverting for a moment to definitional issues in tourism measurement. Historically, Europe has consisted of some 30 independent states, each with normal border controls and each with its own currency. As the European Union proceeds with economic integration, these characteristics will fade. A common currency will soon be sufficiently widely in use for foreign exchange measures of tourism expenditure and receipts with the EU to become first increasingly difficult to make and ultimately irrelevant. In economic terms, intra-European tourism is on the way to becoming a domestic market. Already, border formalities between signatories to the Schengen Agreement are negligible, making the measurement of tourism flows also increasingly difficult. If the EU continues over, say, the next half century, on its path to create a European super-state, for all practical purposes intra-European tourism will become as domestic in its nature as is already the case within the USA. The point at which this becomes widely recognised is debatable, of course, but if and when it does. Europe will no longer be the

Table 1.5
Top 12 International Travel Origin Markets by Expenditure Abroad (Excluding Transport Costs), 1997

Ranking 1990	*1997*	*Country*	*Expenditure 1997 (US$ mn)*	*% share of world total*
1	1	USA	51220	13.5
2	2	Germany	46200	12;2
3	3	Japan	33041	8.7
4	4	UK	27710	7.3
5.	5	Italy	16631	4.4
6	6	France	16576	4.4
7	7	Canada	11268	3.0
9	8	Netherlands	10232	2.7
40	9	China	10166	2.7
8	10	Austria	10124	2.7
-	11	Russian Fedn	10113	2.7
13	12	Belgium	8275	2.2
Sub-total			*251556*	*66.5*
All other			128201	33.5
World total			*379757*	*100.0*

Source: World Tourism Organisation.

dominant force in what will then be termed 'international tourism'.

The Leading Origin Countries

Looking at the level of expenditure on international tourism, excluding fares, four countries – the USA, Germany, Japan and the UK – account for aver 40% of global tourism. The ranking of these countries has not changed during the 1990s. Indeed, there has been little cabbage in the rankings of the top eight countries since then. It is noticeable that the world's largest country – the

Table 1.6
Top 15 Destinations by Arrivals Totals, 1990 – 98 (mn)

	1990	*1995*	*1996*	*1997*	*1998*	*% change 1990/98*
France	52.5	60.0	62.4	67.3	70.0	33.3
Spain	34.1	38.8	40.5	43.3	47.7	40.1
USA	39.4	43.3	46.5	47.8	46.4	17.9
Italy	26.7	31.1	32.9	34.1	34.8	30.5
UK	18.0	23.5	25.3	25.5	25.8	43.0
China	10.5	20.0	22.8	23.8	25.1	139.2
Mexico	17.2	20.2	21.4	19.4	19.8	15.3
Canada	15.2	16.9	17.3	17.6	18.8	23.8
Poland	3.4	19.2	19.4	19.5	18.8	453.5
Austria	19.0	7.2	17.1	16.6	17.4	–8.7
Germany	17.0	14.8	15.2	15.8	16.5	–3.3
Czech Republic	7.3	16.5	17.0	16.8	16.3	124.[illegible]
Russian Federation	7.2[a]	9.3	14.6	15.4	15.8	119.5
Hungary	20.5	20.7	20.7	17.2	15.0	–26.9
Greece	8.9	10.1	9.2	10.1	11.1	24.8
Sub-total	*296.8*	*361.8*	*382.3*	*390.2*	*399.3*	*34.5*
% of world total	64.9	64.2	64.2	63.0	62.9	—

[a] Former USSR.

Source: World Tourism Organisation.

Peoples' Republic of China – has leapt from fourtienth to ninth place in 7 years, with newly liberated Poland (not shown in Table 1.5), also rising from forty-sixth place to fourteenth in the rankings over the same period.

The Leading Destination Countries

The ranking of tourism destination countries is different according to the measure used. In terms of international arrivals,

Table 1.7
Top 15 International Tourism Destinations by Value of Receipts (Excluding Transport), 1990 – 98

Ranking 1990	*1998*	*Country*	*Receipts 1998 (US $ mn)*	*% share of world total*
1	1	USA	71116	16.2
3	2	Italy	30427	6.9
2	3	France	29700	6.8
4	4	Spain	29585	6.7
6	5	UK	21233	4.8
5	6	Germany	15859	3.6
5	7	China	12600	2.9
7	8	Austria	11560	2.6
9	9	Canada	9133	2.1
21	10	Turkey	8300	1.9
8	11	Switzerland	8208	1.9
65	12	Poland	8000	1.8
10	13	Mexico	7897	1.8
11	14	Hong Kong, SAR, China	7109	1.6
23[a]	15	Russian Fed.	7107	1.6
Sub-total			*277 834*	*63.2*
All other			161 559	36.8
World total			439393	100.0

[a] Former USSR.

Source: World Tourism Organisation.

France, Spain, the USA, Italy and the UK form the top five and account for 35% of all international arrivals. Again, China and Poland have made rapid progress up the league table since 1990 to take sixth and ninth place respectively by 1998. The UK has moved from seventh to fifth place, while Austria and Hungary have lost ground.

Ranked in terms of tourism, receipts, however, the order at the top of the league table is different. The USA emerges as the largest earner of non-transport tourism revenues (as well as being the largest spender on international tourism), followed by Italy, France, Spain and the UK. These top five - the same as those in arrivals terms – accounted for 41% of global tourism receipts in 1998, and it is noteworthy that the USA earned over twice the level of receipts of Italy in second place. The main winners during the 1990s by this measure were China, Turkey and Poland, and the main loser in the rankings was Switzerland, albeit falling only from eighth to eleventh place.

Country-to-country Flows

Analysing the principal bilateral travel flows again raises some problems of definition. For example, China records 24 million arrivals in 1997, but most of these were related to cross-border travel from Hong Kong, often work-related, and can lead to misleading conclusions. What might be considered as 'genuine international tourists' to China may not number many more than 5 million. Day trips are sometimes included in countries' arrivals counts and sometimes excluded. The potential for distortions in the data in the case of contiguous countries is high in such cases.

Although some of the data in Table 1.8 are a little out-of-date, they indicate the broad magnitude of current tourism traffic (including the day trip/excursionist business in some cases, such as France to Spain). Nearly all of these massive bilateral tourist movements are between countries with a common land border, Where they are not, they either require transit through a third country or, in one case (UK to France), demand a short sea crossing.

This analysis underlines some very important points about international tourism. First, in volume terms it is relatively highly concentrated between a small number of countries. Of the 240-odd sovereign territories in the world, the 15 largest

Table 1.8
The World's Leading Country-to-Country Tourism Flows (mn)

	Arrivals	*Year*
France to Spain	20	1995
USA to Mexico	18	1997
USA to Canada	15	1998
Germany to France	13	1996
Canada to USA	13	1998
UK to France	12	1998
Germany to Spain	12	1998
UK to Spain	12	1998
Germany to Austria	10	1998
Mexico to USA	9	1998
Switzerland to Italy	8	1997
Germany to Italy	8	1997

Source : Travel & Tourism Intelligence, *International Tourism Forecasts to 2010;* World Tourism Organisation data; International Passenger Survey, UK; Direction du Tourisme, France.

tourism origin countries account for around 75% of all spending on international tourism and for seven in every ten trips. On the destination side of the equation, the top 15 destination countries receive almost 70% of all international tourism receipts. In arrivals terms, the 12 bilateral flows listed above account for almost 25% of all international arrivals worldwide.

We are accustomed to refer to and think of the international travel and tourism sector as a global economic activity. While that is true in one sense, the reality is that it is dominated by relatively few countries and could be quite accurately described as an activity open to an elite only – those at the top of the global income tree, living in relatively open, prosperous, stable and secure societies generally travelling to similar societies either for leisure or business purposes. International travel is out of the reach of the great majority of the world's population. The 1998s arrivals of 635 million account for only around 11% of the world's population and obviously many within that 635 million make more than one international trip a year.

Regional Issues

The great majority of international travel takes place within rather than between regions (although long-haul travel has shown some tendency to increase its overall share of the leisure market during the 1990s). Edwards and Graham (1997) estimate that 92% of trips from European countries are to European destinations, that 65% of North American trips are to North American destinations (including Mexico), and that 73% of Asia/Pacific trips are also intra-regional. Thus the recent downturn in travel within Asia which has accompanied the economic difficulties in the region cannot easily be replaced by traffic from extra-regional long-haul origin markets.

Europe is, as we have seen, the centre of international tourism and it is hard to see how it will ever be less than the regional leader, other than by changes in the definition of 'international' as already mentioned. *North America* is the next most dominant region, and together these two account for almost three in every four international arrivals, four in every five tourism dollars received and generate seven in every ten tourism dollars spent.

The *Asia-Pacific* region's explosive growth in international travel from the late 1980s until the onset of recession in the latter half of the 1990s in part reflected the immaturity of Asian origin markets – countries in which international travel had not previously featured in anything like the same degree as in Europe or North America. The leader in volume terms has been Japan. Elsewhere in the region, destinations such as China, Thailand, Australia, Hong Kong and Indonesia forged ahead during the 1990s. While some have been badly hit by economic and political upheavals in the past two years, others such as Australia and China still have great growth potential and can be expected to continue to expand their tourism sectors. China is, of course, also an increasingly important origin market.

The rest of the world as yet accounts for little volume in international tourism, either inbound or outbound. Africa, despite its above-average rate of growth in arrivals since 1990, remains tiny in its global tourism share, with less than 4% of arrivals and just over 2% of receipts. In the *Middle East* the key element in leisure tourism remains the issue of regional peace.

South America is perhaps the continent with the greatest potential to become a more important player on the international tourism scene. Although volumes remain small (Latin America – including the Central American republics, accounted for only 3.4% of global international arrivals in 1998 – a smaller share than that of Africa), the rate of growth in arrivals during the 1990s was the fastest in the world.

Finally in this rapid global tour, mention should be made of the *Caribbean*. Although the region receives less than 3% of global arrivals and accounts for a similar share of global tourism receipts, it is unique in its economic dependency on international tourism (individual countries such as the small islands of the Indian Ocean and the Pacific share similar features). Without tourism, the West Indian economy would be in serious trouble; no other region in the world, is so dependent for its future on making the right policy decisions for the tourism sector.

Some Broad Conclusions

Of necessity this has been a whistle-stop tour of the subject against which issues can be examined in much greater detail. This chapter has avoided any mention of tourism forecasts since that is the province of other authors. None the less, some broad conclusions can be drawn before considering some of the issues that will determine the industry's future.

It has been shown that international tourism has yet to touch the lives of the majority of the world's population. While countries such as Austria and Switzerland have already achieved very high levels of travel intensity – defined as the number of foreign trips made per head of population, where both countries already make well in excess of two trips abroad per person per year – others have scarcely begun. The world's most valuable origin market, the USA, has a travel intensity of around 0.15. Europe's biggest origin market of Germany has achieved an intensity of around 1.3, the UK's figure is 0.85 and that of France is 0.68. Japan's travel intensity, for all its burgeoning growth during the late 1980s and early 1990s, has only reached 0.13. China, which offers perhaps the greatest potential are which has certainly shown rapid growth, has an international travel intensity of just 0.002.

To all intents and purpose international tourism is confined to a relatively small elite. A handful of countries account for the lion's share of the industry, both as origin markets and as destinations. To regard international tourism as a global activity in which every country has a major stake is misleading. Yet almost every country in the world, given peace with its neighbours and a rational approach to development, would like to see tourism play its part in their economies. This is mainly because tourism offers a ready source of employment demands a wide range of skills, has the capacity to earn often scarce foreign currency, and the potential to fund conservation where few alternative sources of income exist.

While tourism, both domestic and international, is driven by many factors, the economic and environmental ones are of central importance. By the same token, examining the activity of tourism in the context of the behaviour of markets can help to focus attention on the determinants of demand and supply in future, and highlight some of the main issues involved.

Rising real incomes, expanding discretionary spending, increasing leisure time, faster and cheaper transport and the spread of global awareness through the printed and broadcast media and increasingly now through the Internet all fuel demand for travel. Most individuals in most countries, given the means and freedom to travel within their own countries and then to other countries would wish to take up the opportunity to do so.

At the same time, given the extreme inequalities in travel participation rates and travel opportunities, the potential for growth country-by-country is highly variable. In countries where travel intensities are already high, the scope for further growth is limited. This is not just a feature of the proportion of discretionary expenditure that individuals might wish to devote to travel, but is also affected by leisure time limitations. Travel is time-intensive, and there is growing evidence that leisure time ceilings have been reached in many of the industrialised countries – or even that available leisure time is shrinking. There are also other calls on leisure time and it cannot be taken for granted that travel will remain high on the priority list.

Another central influence on international travel demand has been the reduction in relative travel costs, especially in air transport. The progressive decline in seat-mile costs in air transport which has been achieved by step increases in the size, range and fuel efficiency of aircraft may be harder to maintain in the next 50 years of aircraft development than in the past 50. However, there are on the horizon some greater challenges to the maintenance of or further reduction in international travel costs.

Air transport and road transport infrastructure in the industrialised world, and especially in Europe, is showing signs of capacity constraints. While it may be possible to achieve the same level of flight intensity within Europe's air traffic control system as has already been achieved in the USA (and current limits are once again driving up average flight delays in Europe), the supply of airport facilities may prove much harder to expand. A free-market approach would show that, where there is a risk of excess demand, new supply will be introduced to meet it. Airport capacity, however, is driven by environmental and political concerns as well. If such concerns did not apply, Tokyo's Narita airport – an excellent example of unsatisfied demand for airport infrastructure – would have a second runway by now, and London's Heathrow might well have a third, but we all know that things are not that simple.

Ground transport is similarly under increasing threat of hitting capacity constraints. As well as influencing the airport debate directly, since ground access is integral to successful airport operations, rising congestion on the roads is reducing average speeds, raising average journey times and imposing additional time costs on travellers as a result. For the business traveller, these costs are relatively easily measurable and thus rational price-based solutions can be applied (such as the greater use of non-travel solutions like conference calls). For the leisure traveller these costs, although not so easily valued, manifest themselves in a willingness to travel to the chosen leisure destination, whether that is a seaside resort for a weekend, or an historic castle or a theme park for a day trip. Each individual will reach his or her own judgement on the point where the time costs involved in a given journey outweigh the benefits of the destination visit; at that point, behaviour will change and other, non-travel activities will be substituted.

The issue of congestion and excess demand may be thought to be a problem solely of the industrialised world, but this may not prove to be the case in tourism. For example, there are physical limits to the number of people who can have access to a given location at any one time - whether that is an ancient tomb, a natural beauty spot, a beach or an historic house. Left to market mechanisms, the solution is obvious – cause or allow the access price to rise to a point where excess demand is choked off. However, the proposition that access to desirable tourism destinations should be determined solely by the ability to pay might win few friends. Some kind of administrative limits would probably have to be imposed (countries such as New Zealand, for example, already limit access to national parks on a simple quantitative basis by setting annual visitation maxima).

The wider environmental issues implied by these problems might well turn out to be the most important influence on the future of international and domestic tourism in this new century. It is entirely conceivable that access to air transport, which has been so enormously widened in the past 30 years or so by a combination of rising wealth and falling relative prices, may soon go into reverse in some markets due to absolute limitations on transport infrastructure. While access to a national park on the sole basis of ability to pay may be unacceptable, access to international air transport on the same basis may be more acceptable, especially if seen in terms of meeting some of the costs of the negative externalities which are already part of the debate on road and private car pricing. There is much *a priori* evidence to suggest that relative travel costs may start to rise again in the coming years; if so, this would invalidate substantially some of the assumptions on which current travel forecasts are based. Continuing reductions in relative travel costs can no longer be taken for granted; it is possible that the same may apply in one form or another to access costs to leisure and tourism destinations.

The effect will be to invalidate today's tourism forecasts, and curtail tourism growth quite severely in certain regions – of which Europe is likely to be most affected. While there remains plenty of scope for vigorous tourism growth in some parts of the world – and South America seems to be the least constrained at present – in other parts the industry may well have to revise its objectives. In a nutshell, the emphasis will shift from counting numbers to assessing the net financial, economic and social benefits, including order environmental considerations; from the business of accommodating and entertaining visitors from other countries to accommodating and entertaining visitors from and other regions of the same country.

Thus there are close with a few key questions to address:

- If physical and/or environmental capacity limits do arise in major destinations or in essential tourism infrastructure, how will tourism authorities deal with excess demand?
- What criteria should be applied to measure tourism's benefits?
- How can stakeholders in the tourism industry continue to produce growth?
- What policies should countries that depend on tourism for their livelihood adopt?
- Is it inevitable that international tourism will become more elitist, open in practice to a smaller percentage of the world's population than now?

The World of Today and Tomorrow–the Global View

During the past decade, the tourism and hospitality industry flourished, even as it struggled to cope with difficult challenges. This is a taste of things to come. In the years ahead, the global population will continue to grow and change, science and technology will tighten their hold on business and society, and the world will knit itself ever more tightly into a single market. As a result, both opportunities and trials will abound.

In general, I am optimistic about the next ten years. The global economy may be troubled, but it remains fundamentally sound. The recent economic union of Europe, evidence that Japan at last may be willing to address its financial troubles effectively, and many other indicators suggest that it will be even stronger in the future, and thus that the demand for tourism and hospitality will grow. Yet a number of issues are crucial to the world's future. Three stand out:

- Japan's economic crisis clearly is not over. A healthy Japan will spur global trade, while a crippled one could drag at the world's economy for years. It now appears that Japan has begun a solid recovery that dogged it for most of the 1990s. I believe that necessary reforms in banking and business practices will continue and that the current improvement will begin another long period of growth for Japan.

- Russia's economy is the second imponderable. Moscow must find some way to pay its military, to support its pensioners, and to pay the coal miners who keep the nation alive in the harsh Russian winter. And it must do so without creating money at a level that would trigger uncontrolled inflation. Thus far, it reels from one crisis to the next, staying on its feet only with the help of international lenders. Russia will be looking for no less than $ 50 billion over the next few years from the International Monetary Fund. I believe that this situation will improve only slowly, but I do believe that it will improve.
- Finally, Brazil must set its economic house in order. If Brazil can achieve slow, steady growth, the Latin market should provide a much-needed boost for world trade. If not, it could be the final straw for a troubled global economy. The International Monetary Fund is giving the government money to cover Brazil's $ 67 billion debt. Again, I believe this task of economic reform is well in hand.

Overall, I feel reasonably confident that these potential problems will be solved, and I have made my forecasts accordingly. However, the course of the next years depends heavily on how successfully Japan, Russia and Brazil solve their current problems. Anyone with even a passing interest in the future must follow events in these lands closely.

With this caveat in mind, what follows is a summary of the most important forces I now see at work in the world. Whatever else happens, these trends will shape the environment in which the world's tourism and hospitality industry will prosper in the next 20 years.

Increasing Affluence in the Developed World

In the developed world for at least the next five years, widespread affluence, low interest rates, low inflation and low unemployment will be the norm. Real per capita income in the United States is rising at its strongest rate in decades. At the same time, wages and benefits have remained under control, consumer inflation was less than 2% in 1999, and as a result, long-term interest rates in the US are among the lowest since 1977.

GDP of the EUI5 will continue to expand for the foreseeable future. National debts were brought under control throughout much of Europe when countries there prepared for monetary union Establishment of a common currency among most EU member states will continue to stimulate trade within Europe. Relaxation of borders within the European Union should bring new mobility to the labour force and make for a more efficient business environment in Europe.

Japanese banks are finally writing off their bad debts and merging the nation's 800 banks into four banking groups. Thereafter, Japan should provide a much healthier trading partner for both the US and Europe. This will also shore up other beleaguered Asian economies, as Japan provides 50% of the money loaned to its neighbours. In all, 70% of the 'Asian flu' is related to Japan.

Many nations of the former Soviet Union are bringing order to their economies. As they do so, they are proving to be very viable markets for goods from Western Europe.

Implications for Tourism and Hospitality

Global travel will continue to grow rapidly for at least the next 20 years. Worldwide international arrivals are growing from 660 million in 1999 to an estimated 700 million in 2000, 1 billion by 2010 and 1.6 billion by 2020. Improving balance of trade means more business for European and Asian tourist destinations. Europe will remain the strongest magnet for tourism, with arrivals growth holding between 3% and 4% annually.

Low Asian currency values will continue to promote travel to the Far East, for so long as they last. Growth of the new middle and wealthy classes in Russia and other former Eastern bloc lands has created a profitable new market for vacation and business travel to the West. Demand from this quarter should grow for many years to come.

Technology Dominates the Economy and Society

Discovery grows exponentially, as each new finding today opens the way to many more tomorrow. Thus the single greatest force for change in the 20th century can only grow more powerful in the 21st. The only factor slowing this process will be a shortage in trained, creative scientists, engineers and technicians to exploit all the opportunities available to us – and technologies such as computers and the Internet are reducing the impact of even that basic handicap. Advances such as more powerful computers, robotics and CAD/CAM directly affect the way people live and work. Information appliances that combine a computer, fax, duplicator and telephone – with automatic language translation functions – with a large, flat screen will usher in the truly global economy.

The World Future Society identified ten technologies as most important for the next ten years: genetic mapping, super materials, high-density energy sources, digital high-definition television, miniaturisation, smart manufacturing, anti-ageing products and services, medical treatments, hybrid-fuel vehicles and 'edutainment'.

Robots will soon do mundane commercial and service jobs. Net connections, and soon satellite-based portable telephone systems, simplify relocation, speed new installations and ease communication with distant personnel.

Biotechnology offers the prospect of wholly new foods. Witness the 'quicken,' a transgenic hybrid of quail and chicken, high-protein trout, ultralean meats, and coffee beans 'naturally' low in caffeine, all proposed for future development by genetic engineers. Disease-resistant crops, crush-proof tomatoes and other such products already are making their way to market. 'Nutraceuticals', food products formulated or genetically engineered to combat stress, provide specific nutrition, or prevent or cure disease, will be the fastest growing new product area in the next 15 years.

Implications for Tourism and Hospitality

As technology knits the world into one electronic marketplace, business travel will not decline, but will grow rapidly. In a high-tech world, executives increasingly need the 'high-touch' (press the flesh) reassurance of personal relationships with their colleagues. The Internet changes the way consumers purchase goods and services. Cashless credit/debit systems of payment will continue to proliferate. Expect the use of 'smart cards' to provide detailed customer information for use in more efficient target marketing. Resorts, conference centres and other destinations are finding it increasingly easy to market themselves directly to consumers, rather than relying on intermediaries. So will air charter services and other transportation providers.

Travellers are also buying their airline seats and hotel rooms on the Internet, sometimes bidding for them through online auction services such as priceline.com. Over the next five years, this will sharply reduce the number of travel agencies required, as Generations X and COM increasingly make their own reservations online. Tourism will benefit as video – and eventually Internet 'movies' – replace printed brochures in promoting vacation destinations. Programmes include current, detailed information on accommodations, climate, culture, currency, language, immunisation and passport requirements.

The Internet makes it possible for small businesses throughout the world to compete for market share on an even footing with industry leaders.

The Population of the Developed World is Living Longer

In the developed countries, healthier diets, more exercise, the decline of smoking in the United States and the trend toward preventive medicine are extending later life. Life expectancies in Japan are entering the nineties, and those in parts of Europe are not far behind. Medical advances could well help present-day middle-aged Baby Boomers to live far longer than can be predicted even today.

The elderly population is growing fastest throughout the developed world. In Europe, the United States and Japan the aged also form the wealthiest segment of society. These 21st century old folks are much healthier and more active than the elderly of previous generations. At the same time, nostalgia also is a strong influence on them. Many older people still want to indulge in the same activities and entertainment they enjoyed in their youth, and they now have more disposable income to spend on them.

Implications for Tourism and Hospitality

With above average wealth and relatively few demands on their time, the elderly will make up an ever-larger part of the tourist and hospitality market. This industry will prosper by catering to their needs for special facilities and services. More retirees will travel off-season, tending to equalise travel throughout the year and eliminate the cyclical peaks and valleys typical of the industry. Resorts that combine extra comforts for the elderly with an adventure-vacation theme will be in especially high demand.

Time is Becoming the Worlds Most Precious Commodity

Forecasters once imagined that computers would make it possible to cut the working week and give us more leisure. Instead the opposite has happened. Companies have cut employee rosters, often dramatically, leaving more work to be done by fewer people. Rising costs and stagnant wages have driven former stay-at-homes into the labour force. Entrepreneurs, whose numbers are growing rapidly in the United States and have begun to expand elsewhere, work even longer hours than the rest of us. Time that once would have been spent shopping and taking care of household chores is now spent in factories and offices, and leisure is becoming ever more scarce. There is no sign that this trend will slow in the near future.

In the United States, workers spend about 10% more time at work than they did a decade ago. European executives and other non-unionized workers face the same trend. On average, two-thirds of European women from age 25 to 59 work outside the home. This sharply reduces the time available to them for cooking, cleaning and other household tasks. In this high-pressure environment, single workers and double-income couples are increasingly desperate for any product that offers to simplify their lives or grant them a taste of luxury.

Implications for Tourism and Hospitality

Brand names associated with high quality come to seem even more desirable, especially far from home. Two-earner households especially want and can afford the small satisfactions of buying what they perceive to be 'the best'. Small, affordable luxuries, such as hotel restaurant meals, increasingly are substituted for absent leisure.

Multiple, shorter vacations spread throughout the year will continue to replace the traditional two-week vacation. Demand for luxurious 'weekend getaways' will grow rapidly, especially in cultural centres and at destinations nearest large cities.

Value and Lifestyles are Changing

Technology brings new opportunities, but conflicts with tradition, Telecommunications bring news from around the globe. Western ideas infiltrate conservative cultures in Asia and the Middle East, often triggering a 'fundamentalist' backlash. These and many other pressures are eroding the values and lifestyles of previous generations. In their place, a new, opportunistic, technology-oriented eclecticism is beginning to appear throughout the developed world, among the intellectual and economic elites of some developing nations, and especially among the under-40 generations.

Consumer needs are changing under this pressure. For business and pleasure, international and intercontinental travel and tourism are becoming a normal part of life for most well-to-do workers and their families. Growing numbers of adults say their lives are too stressful, so convenience and a relaxing atmosphere will be the order of the day.

Implications for Tourism and Hospitality

The trend is toward ultra-high quality, authenticity and convenience-luxurious accommodations, fresh meals that seem like labours of love, and constant pampering of customers – all done at a price that will not make consumers feel guilty.

Two-income couples increasingly take several short, relatively luxurious weekend getaways rather than a single longer vacation.

Older, wealthier travellers also fly business class in preference to coach, but save money by travelling in off-peak periods and at odd hours. Unlike members of Generations X and . COM, who are relatively tolerant of impersonal service, however, they want to feel that they are recognised (especially if they are repeat customers) and respected. Xers could almost be addressed by their credit-card number; older patrons appreciate being addressed by name, as 'Mr' or 'Mrs'.

Life-long Learning Will Become Essential

Technology and communications are rapidly changing the way we live. New discoveries in science build at an exponential rate, while consumer products based upon them proliferate even more rapidly. Within a few years, new technologies create entire new industries, while the industries they replace wither and disappear. As a result members of the generation now entering the labour force can expect to have an average of five entirely separate careers before their working days are over. At each new turning, our old skills become obsolete, and we are forced to learn anew. In the high-tech industries, this is already a fact of daily life: we work at one job while preparing for the next, which may be wholly unrelated to our previous experience. Over the next decade, this demand will affect everyone who hopes for a career of more than unskilled labour.

Implications for Tourism and Hospitality

New technology will greatly improve life-long learning. Video conferencing, probably based on the Internet and on corporate intranets, will make it possible to train and monitor workers at locations around the world. Large chains can use Net-based education to ensure product quality and uniformity by giving chefs and other personnel at the front and back of the house the same training around the world.

In the United States, corporations such as Motorola, IBM, Arthur Andersen and McDonald's have opened their own 'universities' to ensure that employees remain current with state-of-the-art technologies and business practices. Other industry leaders may wish to adopt this practice to help them remain competitive.

Concern for Environment Issues Continues to Grow

As rain forests disappear and evidence of global warming builds, it is becoming ever more difficult to ignore our impact on nature – and its impact on us. At this point, the question is not whether we will change our industries and lifestyles to accommodate the environment, but how radically we must change, how quickly we must act, and how much it will cost us. This will not be an easy transition. As the United States continues to resist changes that could retard its economy and Third World countries assert their right to the same energy-consuming, polluting luxuries the West has long enjoyed, the controversy over environmental issues can only grow in the years to come.

Topics for attention include air pollution, acid rain, loss of forests, depletion of the ozone layer, waste disposal, toxic chemicals in our food and water, soil erosion, mass extinction of species and pollution of beaches, oceans, reservoirs and waterways.

Concern for the indoor environment will spread. New regulations will control the quality of indoor air, the effect of building materials, asbestos and radon gas.

Implications for Tourism and Hospitality

Demands for still more environmental controls are inevitable, especially in relatively pristine regions. 'Ecotourism' will continue to be one of the fastest growing areas of the tourism industry. The increasing dominance of high technology in our daily lives also promotes this trend, Rain forests, wilderness areas, the ocean and other unpolluted regions provide a unique and necessary chance to escape from keyboards and cell phones.

Recycling, air quality, waste disposal, kitchen safety and other aspects of the workplace environment will be increasingly regulated and will require greater management attention and investment.

Generations X and '.COM' will have Major Effects in the Future

There are approximately 50 million people in Europe between the ages of 15 and 24. Another 30 million are between 25 and 29. The under-30 cohort represents about 22% of the European population. They have grown up with computers, mass media and advanced telecommunications. As a result, their values often differ sharply from those of their Baby-Boom parents. They will present unique and difficult challenges for both marketers and employers in the years ahead.

The under-20 cohort is remaining in school longer and taking longer to enter the workforce than before. The age at which at least half of young Europeans either have a job or are seeking one rose from 18 in 1987 to 20 in 1995. EU-wide, 59% of all 18-year-olds in 1995 were exclusively in education or training. The number varied from 27% in the UK to 88% in Belgium.

Generation X should be renamed 'Generation E', for entrepreneurial. Throughout the world, they are starting new businesses at an unprecedented rate. Twice as many say they would prefer to own a business as opposed to being a top executive. Five times more would prefer to own a business rather than hold a key position in politics or government.

They have little or no loyalty to their employers, to their bosses, to established political parties, or even to branded products. They are extremely sceptical of all claims, and especially those of large institutions, whether in politics or in business. Compared with the Baby-Boom generation, they can be a marketer's nightmare. Perhaps as a result, they are extremely experimental, willing to try new products, foods, and attractions, but rarely patient enough to give a second chance to less-than-stellar offerings.

Implications for Tourism and Hospitality

Generations X and .COM will be major customers for tourism and hospitality services in the future and the industry will have to learn to market to them. This requires a light hand, with strong emphasis on information and quality. Brands credibly positioned as 'affordable luxury' will prosper.

They also will be the industry's future employees. This is both the good news and the bad. They are well equipped for work in an increasingly high-tech world, but have little interest in their employers' needs and no job loyalty at all. They also have a powerful urge to do things their way.

Institutions are Undergoing a Bimodal Distribution

In one industry after another, the big get bigger, thanks to economies of scale. The small prospers by providing high levels of service in niche markets. The middle-sized, lacking either advantage, are either squeezed out or absorbed by larger competitors. This has been the single most powerful trend in business for the past 20 years, and the consolidation has yet to run its course. This trend is seen among hotels, retail stores, restaurants, private banks, hospitals, airlines and many other industries.

Implications for Tourism and Hospitality

Few companies, if any, are too large to be potential take-over targets. Hotel industry consolidation will be fastest in Europe, the Middle East and the Pacific Rim and Third World countries, where market-share leaders own less than 3%, 2% and 1% of rooms, respectively.

US corporations, blessed with record profits and easy access to capital, will be among the busiest players in the global acquisitions game.

Service, Service, Service Replaces Location, Location, Location

Competitive pressures are making it ever more difficult to distinguish one hotel or chain from the rest, especially at the level of the global chains. As soon as one offers a product or service that attracts customers, its competitors match it and try to improve upon it. The result is a generally high standard in basic products and services. Increasingly, what distinguishes one provider from another is attention to detail. This is the battleground on which hotels and restaurants will fight the competitive wars of the early 21st century.

Personal service and attention to detail set the best hotels, restaurants and resorts apart from the rest.

Implications for Tourism and Hospitality

Unique locations or facilities are the major exception to 'commoditisation' in the tourism and hospitality industries. The only inn at a major ski resort has no effective competition. The altenative is for hotels to become destinations in themselves. known for luxurious surroundings, fine food, special amenities for repeat visitors and the best possible service.

As customers grow more open to new experiences, unique facilities and attractions, cuisines offer a growing opportunity for hotels and tourist destinations to distinguish themselves from the competition.

2

What is Tourism Marketing

What is One-to-one Marketing?

One-to-one marketing encompasses a set of marketing techniques aimed at selling to the individual. Instead of selling one product at a time to as many consumers as possible, it is about selling as many products and services as possible to one customer using databases and interactive communication. What is important in the one-to-one marketing is not how much you know about all of your customers that counts but how much you know about *each* of your customers. This means you no longer have to be a giant to win against one. Relationship or one-to-one marketing applies to everyone in the 'people' industry, especially that of tourism. It involves getting to know your customer by asking questions of your existing and potential clients. The answers are the key to learning about the individual and must be remembered, recorded and used to give customers new ideas and create new sales. Often the client does not know what he wants or what is available so it is up to the one-to-one marketer to listen to the customer's requirements and adapt the product to his or her needs by making suggestions, guiding the customer and adding a personal touch. It is the logical progression from mass to segment to direct and then to one-to-one marketing.

Why Implement One-to-one Marketing?

- One-to-one marketing allows you to take advantage of new technology. It is a concrete way to capitalise on the benefits of new technology. Technology is evolving at an amazing rate and is becoming more and more interactive. A few years ago the Internet was an unknown commodity to most people but the rate of its adoption into the home has been enormous. The adoption and utilisation of new technology and therefore new commerce should not be ignored or under-estimated. Modern technology can lead to quick and powerful marketing; it ignores country boundaries and effectively contracts the size of the world. Traditional methods of mailing have become expensive and slow when compared with the inexpensive, fast and effective new technology of e-commerce. All over the world cyber travel agencies are being developed whereby the customers do the work and have direct access to tour operators and airlines to book their own holiday.

- One-to-one marketing gives you the chance to create new markets, markets of individual customers with diverse needs, which allows you to acquire new customers, but more importantly, sell a wider variety of new products and services to extend to the newly discovered needs of existing customers.
- You will be able to improve customer retention and loyalty dramatically and increase the amount of business you receive from each individual, despite the acquisition campaigns of competitors.
- One-to-one marketing gives you the opportunity to protect and increase unit margins. Let us take, for example, the subscription to a magazine. The second year of subscription cften costs more than twice as much as the first. Why? Because presumably you like the magazine. As a result the unit margin of an existing customer is higher than that of a new customer as the company is using profit margins to create customers. Charging regular customers more is a natural consequence of trying to acquire new customers by using discounts but by bettering the product and tailoring it to the customer's specifications the company can retain the existing customers and therefore add to unit margins.

So it becomes clear that one-to-one marketing entails a need o compete using a different set of rules. How does it apply to tourism? Tourism incorporates a wide range of organisations, from destinations (countries, regions, cities and resorts) to private operators such as airlines, hotel chains, theme parks and so on. The need for one-to-one marketing methods applies to all organisations. In the past, it was only travel agents that had any meaningful sales contact with the final consumer. However, owing to the changing structure of the tourism industry and the development of new technology, the destinations themselves, through destination management organisations (DMOs) and tour operators, are encouraging a direct business relationship with the end user.

More and more destinations are using Destination Management Systems (DMS). DMS allow the centralisation of all information, including customer information, into one central database. This information can then be used through various channels. Tour operators are also developing their own call centres and using travel agents' databases for a more direct approach. Even transport companies and airlines are going straight to the end consumer; for example, seats on that Eurostar can be booked through on-line sales. All organisations have similar challenges, those of anticipating and responding to the customer's needs, increasing the customer's value and loyalty and encouraging repeat business. As a result, all organisations must adopt a one-to-one marketing strategy to maximize the benefits of their contact with the customer.

The Principles of One-to-One Marketing

Meeting Customer Needs Individually

Two customers can outwardly seem to be very similar to each-other, they may both want to go to Italy for two weeks, stay in a three-star hotel and have a budget of a thousand pounds but may still want different things from the destination. Nightlife may be important to one visitor whilst the other may only be concerned with museums and art galleries. No two customers are completely alike and this is why one-to-one marketing is especially important to tourism. Differentiating customers by their needs and then catering for those needs individually is a new tendency showing a move from mass marketing to segmentation, to a focus on the individual. In the past customers were put into groupings and marketing towards the clusters was standardised; however, now tourism is moving towards a de-grouping and treatment of the customer as a single entity. One-to-one marketing is also a powerful step towards increasing customer loyalty and as a result, unit margins.

Knowing Your Customers and Their Value to You

Customers have different, individual needs, which hold different values to a destination. The collection of customer information is a means to discovering the customer's needs and therefore value. To compete in this, the interactive age we have to treat different customers differently and to do this we must understand customer differences. The value determines how much time and investment should be allocated to that customer, and a customer's needs represent the key to keeping and growing that customer.

Aggregate marketing treats all customers the same. They all receive the same product benefits, are all charged the same price and are not in individualised interactions. However, each customer is unique and some are more valuable than others. The actual valuation of a customer is his or her 'Life Time Value' (LTV), the stream of expected future profits, net of costs, on a customer's transactions, discounted at some appropriate rate back to its net present value. Remember that the profit on a customer's relationship with a destination is not solely derived from the future purchases the customer makes. Customers also benefit the destination or product in other ways such as referrals of other customers, knowledge of other customers' tastes and preferences and help in designing new products or services. Maintaining any sort of relationship with the customer will involve cost – phone calls, faxes. e-mails, personal sales calls and setting up information systems necessary to track and remember; interaction all cost money. Those who call in to customer service the most will cost the company more money to serve. However important LTV is, it is essentially a forecast based on probabilities and we can never know precisely what a particular customer will do in the future. However, what is certain is that keeping existing customers is more profitable than trying to turn new prospects into customers.

The benefits of calculating LTV are not just to understand the *average* customers valuation but to create an accurate ranking-order system, allowing a company marketing a destination to *differentiate* its customers by their individual valuations and to add more marketing time and effort to retain the most valuable customers. Because one-to-one marketing treats its customers as individually as possible, it aims at understanding the relative valuation of each of them. Customers are individually different, and have individually different values to a company, and the most accurate picture of a customer's value is LTV. It is important to decide which are the most valuable customers and establish a maximum amount of money to be spent on retaining these customers. Those of high value must be invested in; those of medium value must be encouraged to buy other products and services from the company. Customers of low value should either be dropped or made to pay for the services they receive.

Defining the Right Strategy

A customer base is characterised by customers who have a diverse set of values and/or a diverse set of needs. The customer base can be highly differentiated on both counts or on neither. The nature of the customer differentiation of a company is a guide to an appropriate marketing strategy. By comparing a company's capabilities with its customer base a new strategy can be mapped out, aimed at improving those capabilities needed to turn the business into more of a one-to-one enterprise. If a business bus customers with widely varying tastes and preferences, they must be differentiated by their needs. The more the customers differ from one another in needs, the more benefit can be gained from offering a variety of products and services and customising right down to an individual level.

Let us take the example of the tourism destination once again. The needs of the customer are incredibly diverse. A back-packer is going to have completely different preferences to an elderly couple, just as honeymooners are not going to want the same package as a family with young children. The destination remains the same but the package must be varied to become customised to the individual's needs. It is a case of examining the customer's needs and tailoring that product to suit those needs, whether it be offering a family hotel with children's activities or a weekend city-break incorporating city tours and cultural visits. Equally in tourism customers are bound to have different values for the destination. Obviously backpackers on a shoestring budget are worth less than honeymooners who may have been saving for years to fulfil their dream holiday. However, it is important to remember that the backpackers may be opinion leaders, they are often students and will travel again in the future, probably with a larger budget, and therefore have a high potential valuation. Thus, if one-to-one marketing is implemented, contact can be maintained with these potential customers throughout their travelling life.

Implementing One-to-One Marketing

One-to-one marketing can be put into place by using several simple capabilities:

Customer Tracking

This can be done through databases, which allow a vendor to tell its customers apart and remember them individually. As much information as possible must be obtained about the customer and his or her purchasing habits and needs. The customer's history would be recorded through his or her previous interactions and with each interaction the company will learn more about the client. The customer and company can then collaborate jointly to detennine the appropriate product or service for that customer.

It is important to make it easy for customers to specify their needs by asking the right questions and then remembering and recording the specifications so that the customer does not have to re-specify. That way, customers have to go to less effort next time they wish to use the service. For example, most call centre operators will have in front of them the complete history of a particular customer's previous transactions, thanks to sophisticated databases.

Interactive Dialogue

Some kind of feedback link is necessary for the destination to learn about the customers individually and therefore make them loyal and improve the company's unit margin. It is absolutely essential to open channels of communication between the consumer and the company. Sometimes it can be as simple as printing a web-site address on the packaging of the product or, in the case of tourism, on the destination brochure. As the computer penetrates more and more homes, and as the various interactive tools available to consumers cntinue to increase in utility, web-sites that allow the customer to buy on-line will attract the most enthusiastic and therefore valuable customers.

Interaction by telephone is often the first point of contact with the customer. To incorporate one-to-one marketing the company must simply ask one or two questions about the customer's needs and map the customer into a needs-based category. To implement this, the company would need to do research to create the correct needs-based groupings and give its phone sales representatives the necessary script.

Written questionnaires are another way of interacting with customers. However, it obviously involves the customer making an effort. An increased use of coupons in order to obtain more information in destination brochures is a way of finding out about the type of client who is really interested in the destination. Another idea is a questionnaire inside a destination brochure. for example, which needs to perform some service for the end user that is actually connected to the user's need for the product. Filling in the questionnaire must also involve as little effort as possible for the customer and all barriers preventing the customer from sending it in must be removed.

Here are some suggestions for removing those barriers:

- Offer a postage-paid envelope.
- Assure the customer that returning the questionnaire will not result in any undesired additional mail or solicitations, or allow the customer to 'opt out' by ticking a box.
- Put the questionnaire at the beginning of the brochure so it is the first thing the customer sees after opening it.
- Allow the customer to reply by mail, e-mail, fax or a free-phone number.

Even after making it as convenient as possible it may still be necessary to offer some sort of incentive to the customer, perhaps a discount at a certain hotel, or on car hire, more information on the product or a free gift.

The collecting of customer information is aimed not at creating summary research but developing a better understanding of each *individual* customer's needs. Every communication and response from a customer has the potential to tell a one-to-one company more about exactly what a particular customer wants. Every single interaction is a priceless opportunity to learn more. Only recently, as information technology has improved, has it become possible for a company to identify and act on customer differences in a cost-effective way.

Customisation of Products and Processes to Customer Needs

Tourism products are ideal to customize due to their flexibility. One destination can be combined with another, different hotels can be chosen, and all sorts of activities can be decided upon depending on the customer's preferences. Tailor-made holidays are becoming more and more popular due to the amount of choice the customer enjoys. Even the way the product is presented can vary depending on ways of payment, promotion and booking (last minute deals are also increasing in popularity).

Loyalty Programmes

Customer loyalty is vital for numerous reasons. It costs more to serve new clients than it does old but surprisingly most companies do not even try to diminish the costs of trying to attract new customers as they are already budgeted. One-to-one marketing aims at reducing these costs by keeping customers instead of constantly looking for new ones. Costs involve advertising, mailings, information packs and, especially, time. The faithful customer is stable, predictable and knows the purchasing process of the company, therefore saving the staff time and bettering the service. The satisfied customers tend to recommend the product to their friends and acquaintances. Recommendation is the best form of advertising to acquire new customers. This is especially the case for tourism, when people talk about the destination they have visited and encourage others to go there. The idea of information days when happy customers meet prospective customers is developing already in the world of tourism. Word of mouth is by far the most convincing advertisement a holiday destination can have as it comes from satisfied customers whose opinions are trusted by their friends. Personally recommended customers tend to be of better value, meaning more profitable and longer lasting than those attracted by advertising or promotions. Loyal customers allow the company to provide them with a more personal product due to the fact that the company has had the chance to learn about the clients' needs and adapt to them – this is what one-to-one marketing is all about. However, despite the obvious benefits of customer loyalty, many companies focus more on gaining new clients than keeping old ones.

Loyalty programmes worked differently depending on the company; however, the essential is for the consumer to benefit by repeatedly using the service or company provided. Loyalty programmes can be very sophisticated or very simple, for example the tour operator No Limits has put into place a loyalty system whereby each time customers book or introduce a friend to No Limits they receive 'miles' which equal reductions on travel. The hotel chain Los Paradores has a card system called La Carte Amigos de los Paradores giving regular customers free nights in the hotels as well as numerous other advantages such as the option to choose their room. An example on a larger scale is Club Mauritius, a group of tour operators, hotels and airlines who have come together with the aim of offering a loyalty programme whereby the cardholder receives benefits such as regular information about special travel offers to Mauritius, free parking in the airport car park, free afternoon tea, reductions on sports activities, car rental and in certain shops, and a bouquet of flowers on departure. Depending on the number of visits the customer makes to Mauritius the benefits become more attractive. Eurostar offers a similar system with blue, silver and gold membership cards.

Many airline companies have also implemented 'frequent flyer' loyalty programmes, easily put into place due to the fact that they already have the necessary information in the reservations system. Benefits include easier check-in procedures, use of a private lounge and access to newspapers etc.

It must be remembered that, of course, other companies can set up similar loyalty programmes but the key to retaining the customers is the learning process which will have been undertaken by the company to ensure that the customer is receiving exactly what he or she wants and expects.

Conclusion

In conclusion, one-to-one marketing is about listening to customers, remembering them and providing them with the service each consciously or sub-consciously requires. It is about adapting your marketing strategy to the future and exploiting modem technology to achieve a more personal approach. After a period of mass marketing, globalisation, segmentation and lifestyle grouping in tourism, today we have to follow the tendency towards individualisation.

3

Tour Guidance

Current Perspectives on Tour Guiding

Guided tours vary widely with respect to the following:

- Length (e.g. a few hours, all day, or several days)
- Seasonality (one-season or year-round)
- Location (e.g. site- or attraction-specific, city, rural or a combination)
- Type (e.g. cultural, environmental, industrial, educational, adventure)
- Transportation (walking, non-motorised, vehicle-based, land-based, water craft-based, bicycle)
- Terrain (land-based, fresh water-based, ocean-based)
- Clientele (general, particular socio-demographic group, special interest group).

As a result, the nature of tour guiding and the skills required by an individual guide can vary widely. For example, specialist ecotour guides require minimal impact skills, while city guides may have less need for these skills. Guides leading extended tours require more complex leadership and group management skills, and may require high-level navigational skills, knowledge of remote area first aid and evacuation procedures. Many guides have activity-specific skills, licences and qualifications that complement their guiding expertise.

However, there are some elements that are common to all types of guided tours, such as:

- Presentation, communication and interpretation skills.
- Customer service skills (ability to work with colleagues and customers).
- Cross-cultural awareness and communication skills.
- Ability to follow health and safety procedures.
- First aid qualifications.
- Group management and leadership skills.
- Knowledge of local tourism resources and the tourism industry.
- Ability to research, develop and update tour content (Canadian Tourism Human Resource Council, 1996; Tourism Training Australia, 1999).

Trends in tourism generally seem to indicate a growth in more specialised tourism products aimed at more focused target markets. There is also evidence of increased environmental and cultural consciousness among travellers, including in some cases willingness to pay more for tourism products that are environmentally responsible (Blamey, 1995; 111–131). If these trends continue, growth areas are likely to be in tours targeted at special interest groups, tours focusing on particular experiences or products (e.g. adventure, nature-based, cultural and indigenous tours), and tours marketed as being environmentally friendly. There may also be a growth in customised tours, in which individuals or groups can hire a guide (or operator) and specify exactly what they want with respect to each of the above.

The current geographical distribution of tour guiding largely mirrors the distribution of tourism, generally. Where there is growth in tourism and an increase in numbers of tourists, there is growth in organised tours and therefore an increase in the demand for quality tour guides. However, the demand may be somewhat greater where there are significant barriers to independent travel, such as in China. Russia and certain countries in the Middle East, Africa, Southeast Asia and Latin America. Some of these barriers include a native language different from that spoken by the majority of visitors to the region, threats to safety and personel security, political barriers and lack of tourism infrastructure. It seems the more exotic and unfamiliar the natural and cultural environments of a destination, the more likely that a visitor will engage the services of a guide.

The regional demand for tour guiding may be affected by many other factors such as the prevalence of visitors who can visit only for a short time, and therefore require the assistance of a guide in order to sight-see. For example, cities that cater to business, educational and conference travellers tend to support a larger number of tour guides.

In the future, guided tours to remoute destinations such as Antarctica and some of the new travel destinations opening up in Asia seem likely to continue to thrive because most or all of the visitors to these destinations need a guide to visit the region. Given that first-time travellers seem more likely to seek the comfort and security of a guided experience, destinations near to new tourist markets such as China and India are also likely to experience growth in tour guiding. However, destinations that are experiencing growth in tourism but are not perceived to be 'difficult' to visit may have a stable or declining demand for guided tours. Unless particular actions are taken it is possible that nature destinations and those in decline will experience a decline in the demand for guided tours.

What's Wrong?

Images of Guided Tours, Tour Guides and Tour Guiding

The image of guided tours and clients of guided tours is stereotypical and homogeneous, and at present represents a self-fulfilling prophecy.

Many of us who work or teach in the tourism field and those who have travelled extensively are aware that tourists may choose from a wide range of guided tours that vary in scope, length, group size, target market and so on. However, prospective tourists are often not as informed as they could be. Thanks in part to mass media, the dominant image of the guided tour is often one of a large group of elderly tourists, or perhaps middle-aged Japanese couples, travelling by coach, on a fixed itinerary, with scheduled stops and with a virtually uninterrupted commentary by a tour guide, usually *via* a microphone, talking about the various sights and features along the way. While reality may be quite different, it is the image that sells or doesn't sell, the product, and this particular image poses a significant barrier to diversifying the client base and the product range. The image is reinforced partly by tour product marketing, including not only the brochures and other promotional materials used to entice clients, but also by the places and mechanisms by which guided tours are packaged and marketed, e.g. concierge desks at hotels and tour wholesalers. The visitor gets little sense that he or she might have some influence over the content and style of the tour, the size of the tour group, the tour length, or the time of departure. It is little wonder, then, that those who do not feel a 'need' for a guided experience choose to travel independently. Simply put, their stereotypical image of a 'guided' tour does not match their notion of a desirable recreation experience: it is seen as neither voluntary nor enjoyable.

Changing this image could significantly alter tour guiding and the future of guided tours. The perception of flexibility, variety and the option of customisation with respect to itinerary, tour content, tour guide and tour clients would widen their appeal. This would eventually lead to an image of tour clients in the future who choose a guided tour not because of need or convenience, but because of an expectation of a quality experience. The product must, of course, also change with the image, becoming more flexible and responsive to client interests and preferences.

Client Motivations and Expectations about Guides and Guided Tours

Visitors have few expectations of guided tours and tour guides. Generally tour clients expect to spend the day (or hour, or week) safely and with a minimum of discomfort together with some level of information and entertainment. Their expectations are often dictated by what they read in the tour brochure, which is usually to 'see' and may be to 'hear' something rather than to 'experience' or learn something or to come away moved by that experience. Not surprisingly, then, most research measuring the satisfaction levels of visitors on guided tours has found that visitors claim to be satisfied with their experiences (Geva and Goldman, 1991; Blamey and Hatch, 1996).

At present, it is assumed that guided tours largely cater to inexperienced travellers who are attracted by the safety and security of travel within a guided tour experience. However, some visitors are motivated by the opportunity to sample a new experience for which they lack either the specialised skills, the local knowledge, or a suitable vehicle and/or equipment (Blamey and Hatch, 1996; Weiler and Crabtree, forthcoming). Examples include guided snorkelling tours, white water rafting, indigenous cultural tours, and boat-based whale-watching tours.

Visitors on specialised guided tours have also indicated that they are motivated not only by the ease and convenience of travelling with a guide, but by the opportunity to learn something (Weiler and Crabtree, forthcoming). In these cases, the reputation of the company and qualifications of the guide may be important factors in tour selection. And finally, as mentioned earlier, some target markets are motivated by the desire to purchase an environmentally responsible and or culturally sensitive tour.

In the future a wider diversity of products could extend the client base of experienced travellers who want a high-quality tour experience with a knowledgeable and capable guide, or who want to sample a tour experience outside their normal range of experiences and interests. In other words, visitors would choose a guided tour, not because they have to, but because they perceive the guide and the tour as offering something better than they can experience on their own. This will require target market research, sophisticated product development, packaging and marketing, and an overall shift in consumer and industry perceptions of a guided tour experience, as was discussed in the previous section. In addition, clients may need to be educated to make more informed decisions when choosing a guided tour.

Teaching and Research on Tour Guiding

Guided tours have a negative connotation for many people, including professionals in the industry, educators and the 'enlightened' traveller.

Tour guiding has been the subject of very little scholarly enquiry, let alone rigorous research. This may be due to the tour guide's lack of profile and status and therefore visibility to researchers, in comparison to the impacts of large-scale tourism developments, which are conspicuous and therefore widely-debated by academics, industry and the general public. Similarly, there has been considerable research on tourist accommodation, tourist attractions and, more recently, tourism events. The contribution and impacts of tour guides and tour guiding are usually glossed over by researchers, planners and managers.

Tour operators have certainly been the subjects of research, but often in the form of surveys and inventories of where they are based and what they deliver, rather than any critical analysis of the experiences that they offer (cf Cotterill, 1996). Some research has been conducted on the marketing of guided tours and on specific guided tour market profiles (Wight 1996a, 1996b). As discussed in the previous section, there has been some research on the motivations and expectations of tourists on guided tours and, more recently, the tourist experience. Again, however, it has tended to be descriptive rather than explanatory or predictive. As a result, the concepts and models used to educate tourism students about tourist motivations and the tourist experience are largely untested and may serve to reinforce stereotypes and possible misconceptions of the guided experience. For example, Pearce and Caltabiano (1983) argue that as the tourist becomes more experienced as a traveller, he or she moves 'up' what they call the *travel career ladder* and away from certain needs. There has been a tendency to assume that packaged tours and guided tour experiences fulfil the needs of travellers on the 'lower' rungs of the ladder. Without strong data to support this theory, educators who use this model may thus teach implicitly that those who join guided tours are somehow lesser travellers than those who travel independently. An alternative view, which is grounded in research on guided interpretive activity attendance in US parks (Ham, 1982; Mullins and Hanna, 1981), is that selecting a guided activity merely represents a regularity or pattern in tourists' leisure tastes and preferences. Extended to tour selection decisions, those who select guided tours over independent travelling may do so not because of uncertainty or the need for a 'chaperone' , but simply because a guided tour promises to deliver the type of experience the tourist desires. More research is needed in this area.

Another example is the concept of authenticity, with considerable debate in the literature as to what exactly constitutes an authentic experience and how much of modern tourist behaviour is a quest for authenticity (Dann, 1996). As with the travel career ladder, there is a tendency to want to over-simplify and compartmentalise tourists and touristic experiences. Here independent travel is labelled as something more 'authentic', an ideal to strive for, and at the opposite end of the continuum the guided tour is seen as a contrived and therefore lesser form of travel. Some view the use of a local, as opposed to a foreign, guide as a step in the right direction, providing a more authentic experience for visitors. Empirical testing of what constitutes a quality experience and an authentic experience for the visitor, and the role of the tour guide as a cultural broker and facilitator in that experience, is required in the future.

And finally, most educators know of and teach about the impacts of tourism, but how many recognise the pivotal role that a guide plays? Particularly important in this role is the interpretive function of guiding. A central defining principle of sustainable tourism is its focus on conservation and perpetuation of the natural, cultural and physical values inherent in a place. How tourism achieves this lofty goal is often debated, but there is increasing evidence that what a guide *says* to her or his clients can influence how they think and behave with respect to the places they visit. In other words, what messages a guide imparts to a group of tourists relative to the natural and cultural values of a place may in large part determine what they will think, feel and do both in the short-term (on-site) and possibly even in the long-term (once they have returned home). According to Ham and Krumpe (1996) and others (see, for example, Knapp and Barrie, 1998), one of the most important things guides can do is to facilitate a bonding between their clients and the places they lead them; connecting people and places in powerful ways that nurture respect and caring about those places. As we have argued elsewhere (see Weiler and Ham, 2000), the guide's role in this process is central. If research begins tc document this role, it is likely that a clearer understanding of the guide's importance in sustainable tourism will be achieved.

Professionalism in Tour Guiding

Tour guiding is a low-status profession; characterised by low pay, poor working conditions, and seasonal and casual employment conditions.

Tour operators and tour guides vary with respect to a number of attributes:

- Size of company, number of offices, number of employees.
- Commercial (private) *vs*. non-profit vs. public-sector funded operation.
- Generalist *vs*. specialist operators and guides.
- Paid *vs*. volunteer guides.
- Freelance *vs*. contract vs. regular employees.
- Local *vs*. foreign guides.
- Professional *vs*. casual *vs*. part-time guides.

In most cases, qualifications are not required, those with qualifications are not remunerated or rewarded in any special way, and there is no career path, so that in time good guides may be inclined to move on to something else. In Australia, for example, the tour operations industry has no industrial awards, i.e. there are no industry-wide legal specifications regarding the rights and obligations, qualifications, working conditions and rates of pay, for either tour operators or guides. Some of the larger tour companies have enterprise agreements, which specify such conditions, but there is no government or regulatory body requiring an individual to be qualified or licensed in order to work as a guide.

For practising tour guides, there is also little incentive for individuals to actively upgrade their skills or qualifications or improve the quality of their tours. To date there has been no evidence that qualifications or skills lead to preferential treatment either in gaining employment or in career advancement. It then falls to the wider tourism industry, educational institutions, protected area managers and other government bodies to find ways, first, to raise the awareness of what is 'good practice' in tour guiding, and secondly, to provide incentives to improve the standard of guiding practice throughout the industry. To date, this has been mainly by way of professional associations and codes of conduct. The future may bring accreditation and certification of guides, if not initiated by industry, then imposed by governments. If linked to education or training programmes, these could have significant repercussions for those already working in the industry, especially those without formal qualifications.

A final mechanism for recognising and rewarding good practice is by way of an employee or tourism industry award scheme that recognises outstanding guiding. These can co-exist with some of the other initiatives already mentioned, and are truly 'best practice' awards that complement the minimum standards approach of the other initiatives, while simultaneously serving to motivate and educate guides as well as to regulate the practice of guiding.

Tour Guide Training

Tour guides and guided tours are falling short of what they could be delivering, a high quality experience that excites, changes people, motivates and rejuvenates them, while maximising the benefits for operators, host communities and the environment. Although marketplace competition has sometimes led to innovations designed to give a company a competitive edge, aggressive; experimentation will new guided tour products seems lacking. This may be due to a degree of complacency in the industry that derives from tourists' low expectations, as well as from an inherent lack of imagination on the part of guides themselves, and the companies they work for. To some extent, such forces may stem from the preparation of professional guides.

Guides, like many professionals, can be prepared for their work in several ways. First, they can be *trained technically* with skills presumed to be germane to delivering the kind of products and services needed and wanted by clients. Secondly, they can be *educated* as to the *how, why and what if* of applying their knowledge and skills to the workplace. And finally, they can be *socialised* into their profession *via* formal and informal processes that mould and shape how they see themselves, and how their employers, clients and peers see them. Current prevailing perceptions and self-perceptions of guides sometimes conjure up images of semi-robotic message repeaters who carry out rigidly orchestrated itineraries and faithfully regurgitate carefully memorised scripts, leaving little to the guide's creative imagination and ingenuity. These perceptions are, in turn, reflected in unimaginative technical training programmes that are designed to produce guides who match the perceptions. Training and education in how guides can use their skills to excite and motivate visitors, and in how their work can produce benefits to society, is lacking.

4

National Tourist Offices

It is quite feasible to regard tourism as a kind of theatrical performance, directed by National Tourist Offices (NTOs) and played out on a stage called 'destination', but in a relationship between host and visitor which pays regard to human dignity, as it is not the role of the host to play the part of the 'dancing bear' for the benefit of tourists. Nevertheless, the question must be asked: will Europe still be attractive enough to be able to count on a faithful audience for its tourist performance in the 21st century? Hill Europe have the courage and creativity to face up to its ever-more aggressive competitors throughout the world? What will be the role of the NTOs in this context? A millennium turning point is an invitation to every kind of prophecy and hypothesis. In the 19th century Europe invented tourism and in the first 70 years of the 20th century, achieved world leadership in tourism. Since the 1970s it has more or less been on the defensive. The 21st century will effectively be the moment of truth for 'Destination Europe'.

Amongst a number of defining factors there are four to which I will especially draw attention here and which, in my opinion, will decide whether Europe can – or indeed must – continue to play in the Champions' League and even take the lead again. The question is whether this is to be achieved with or without the contribution of the NTOs.

The European Union Route

I imagine it to be generally agreed that the political, economic, monetary and defence unification of Europe must not be equivalent, to unifomity of European cultural and gastronomic identity. McDonalds may be present everywhere but that does not mean that we want to convert Euroland into Hamburgerland. However, if we still believe that a product is easier to market the more clearly it can be defined and the more it possesses the attribute of becoming an instinctively recognised brand, then it is obvious that the development of ever-closer ties within Europe offers considerable advantages for marketing tourism. Here I am mainly thinking of marketing tourism overseas. The European Travel Commission (ETC) credo to position Europe as 'One Destination' is thus increasingly seen as a matter of course. The awareness of Europe's internal and external clientele in this respect is significantly enhanced by the fact that European political development features constantly in the international media. The publicity effect of this presence is greater than the sum of all reports on individual countries.

A further positive factor for European tourism is the creation of the Euro and the growth of the European Monetary Union (EMU). This makes travel easier, makes tourist offers more transparent, and acts as restraint on prices. One can envision a future, therefore, when it will be possible to visit every corner of the world without constantly having to change money and with only two currencies: the US Dollar and the Euro (at a rate of 1: 1?).

The progressive unification of Europe strengthens its presence in world tourist markets and basically makes the destination more attractive. But in the presence of the customers' unstable behaviour, this message is only effective if it is supported by decisive marketing within individual markets, by an excellent quality product, acceptable prices (meaning not low prices but value for money), plus continuing and coherent public relations and advertising using modern information technology. Technology must, however, remain an auxiliary and not replace people as providers of services and sympathy. Today all too many promoters of tourism make the mistake of treating technology itself as a strategic objective instead of an instrument for achieving objectives.

Therefore, if Europe follows the path from a confused multiplicity to a comprehensible variety within unity, it is obvious that this change also requires an adjustment to advertising strategy. This means that the ETC will tend to become ever more indispensable and that its role as an umbrella organisation for European destination marketing should be considerably strengthened. It is ironic that this fact is perceived more clearly by tourist professionals outside ETC than by the ETC itself. Dr. Ralf Carsten, President and CEO of Turistik-Union International, has made a plea recently for a much stronger ETC, which ought to become the marketing agency for Destination Europe. He was even bold enough to say that national marketing could be reduced in importance overseas and should be replaced by increased European activities. It would appear that some of the Eumpean solidarity, which was the driving force in founding the ETC in 1948, has faded to be replaced by a more strongly nationalist perspective.

Sustainability – The Moment of Truth for Tourism

'Sustainability' has become for me a negative provocation, the label for a culture of dishonesty, the ultimate in lip service. No speech, no article, no statement from politician or tourism professional does not repeat this word over and over again – though not unfortunately in accordance with its real meaning and content. It serves as a fig leaf to disguise the continuing and dominating observation with quantitative growth on the principle of *'apres moi le déluge'*. In the 21st century we who work in tourism must find our way back to a policy of 'qualitative growth'. This means that we must once again recognise that the capital assets of European tourism consist of elements that are easily destroyed, namely our human capital, our culture, nature and the environment. We must learn to use these assets – but not to use them up. It must be a strategic objective to live on the interest from tourism but not to consume the capital. Tourism can only create long-term employment if the environment is tolerable for the local inhabitant and the visitor alike. In this who other than the NTOs can dare to play the role of the 'devil's advocate"?

Sustainability is a long-term concept, which creates added value by the law of optimisation, and not maximisation of income, that is to say, it does not want the hen to lay the eggs and at the same time to be served up on plate as *'poulet rôti'*. Europe's volume share of world tourism is not so important as its share of the worldwide potential of good and cultivated visitors who realise that a good product cannot be required at dumping prices. Europe is too small to maintain its relative share of what appears to be an unstoppable growth market. Let me say once again: we must improve the quality of our market share so that the following definition of mass tourism will not apply to Europe: 'Mass tourism is the occupation of a country by an unarmed army for a limited period.'

A New Tourism Ethos for the 21st Century

Tourism is not one but all industries. This indicates not only tourism's high multiplication factor, but also that tourism is the substratum of many policies - economic, regional, social and cultural. Not everything that seems profitable to the individual businessman is desirable for the national economy. Shareholder value taken to the extreme is poison for the social contract and is the cultivation of mere egoism. George Soros (who certainly cannot be described as a follower of Keynes!), recently said: 'The markets are obsessed with greed and fear and therefore react to all economic theory not rationally, but emotionally.' What does this mean in relation to tourism? The globalisation of the economy is a reality and this calls for a global framework of order based on a globalisation of ethics. Obviously I don't want a flood of regulations; that just exchanges one evil for another. Whatever is desirable in the fundamental supporting pillars of the state and the economy must to an ever-greater degree be valid for tourism. Tourism is in fact an emanation of culture and one of its vehicles of transmission. I link a new ethos for world tourism to the following hopes in the form of a realistic vision:

- The last traces of the 'master and servant mentality' in tourism must vanish.
- Every guest is a king – but every king is only a guest.
- The relationship between supplier and customer must change to a partnership with parallel interests. In this way, it will be possible to arouse support on both sides for genuine sustainability and to convert exaggerated hedonism into a rational pleasure in consumption.
- The interests of shareholder and stakeholder must not conflict, but must be complementary.

- Tourism should not only talk of the visitors' rights, but also of their duties.
- Friendliness is not just something to be expected on the hosting side. Visitors, too, should show more respect for other people, cultures and identities.
- Development policies for tourism must be discussed from the start with the local population so that they too support them Representatives of hospitality are not just the professionals but the whole population. This will avoid tourism becoming a ghetto culture.
- The social standing and conditions of employment of workers in the European tourist industry must be improved.
- The necessary improvement of the ethics of tourism will unavoidably result in a competition of ideas in the 21st century. Concept marketing will be more important than product, marketing.

And What about the Future of the NTOs?

Soon after the first NTOs were established more than 80 years ago, sceptics were questioning what the chances of survival were. The mere existence of any business or organisation, such as an NTO, gives it no right to survive. Whereas human life has a value in itself, an NTO must face up to the constant challenge as to whether its usefulness to society, the state and the economy gives it the right to exist. This is all the more the case since the budgets of European NTOs are still financed to between 50 and 100% by the taxpayer. So the question can only be answered in the general context of political interests.

From the beginning and until very recently the mandate of many of the NTOs was approximately as follows:

- *Phase 1* – To promote a general awareness of its own country, of its historical and cultural strengths and the beauties of its landscape etc. with the objective to create a climate of sympathy. This also led to non-commercial collaboration with groups within the export economy who were similarly interested in an active presence in the markets – which was a first, if unconscious step toward destination marketing.

- *Phase 2* – To arouse tourist interest. Phase 1 was only a first step towards the objective of arousing a concrete interest in travel, to convert the 'friendly' country into a target destination for tourists. This was done with the classic means of advertising and public relations.
- *Phase 3* – To make the potential visitor decide to convert his or her wish into reality. Customers were brought to this point by sales promotion and targeted information.
- *Phase 4* – The task of the NTO ended with Phase 3, and reservations and sales were in, principle to be left to the industry.

It was also thought that this procedural concept provided a clear division for financial responsibility: phases 1 and 2 were to be financed out of public funds, phase 3 was to be financed from both public and private sources, and finally phase 4 was the responsibility of the private sector.

This was the basic model in that happy world, now past, where there was no globalisation, deregulation, shareholder value and so on! Today we are confronted by new parameters without there being a final and reliable new model for action available. NTOs are more than ever searching for a new definition of their task and their identity: they vacillate between the demands of the public sector for strategic return on investment and the private sector requirement of immediate operating profit.

As already mentioned, the share of the public sector in the financing of NTOs is substantial and without this funding they could not exist. Their continued existence is, however, dependent on future state economic policy and the further development of the separation between tasks that will continue within the public domain and those that are to be left to the private sector. This is a dynamic process which is far from being complete, whereas the arguments involved are in part ideological. Many governments are still not sure whether it is sensible or necessary to pursue a strategic policy for tourism in order to optimise the exploitation of economic growth potential. If so, then NTOs are essential. Nor can you do without them in countries where the creation of tourist demand is a means to develop economically disadvantaged regions – few private investors would be prepared to invest money for reasons of social and regional policy.

Conceptual Destination Marketing

As part of location competition between countries, regions and cities conceptual destination marketing will have a much greater significance than in the past. Conceptual destination marketing implies the summation of all the characteristics that give a location or a region a positive profiles: culture, political stability, the economy, natural beauty, population, education, but also non-quantifiable aspects such as reputation, image, sympathy, reliability etc. It goes without saying that the strong positioning of a destination, which must be accompanied by the creation of a brand image, can only succeed through long-term measures based on consistency, coherence and continuity. It is in this aspect of strategic targeting that the NTO is an appropriate institution to achieve strategic effectiveness at national level for tourism as a whole. In the rapidly changing environment of supply and demand, the resources of the private sector are too quickly absorbed in the fluctuations of day-to-day tourist business. The growing prominence of the Satellite Account System for assessing the multiplication effect of tourism shows more clearly than ever before that tourism is very much a cross-section discipline for which destination marketing at national level performs an umbrella function.

The criteria cited here to justify – indeed to demonstrate the necessity of – the NTOs existence, are similarly valid for maintaining the effectiveness of the European Travel Commission (ETC), which must also fulfil an umbrella function for Destination Europe.

If we agree that tourism:

- is part of national and regional and local area planning,
- is often the only effective instrument for the economic improvement of disadvantaged regions.
- is a strategic linking element within national economic policy,
- is a factor for job creation *par excellence*, particularly, for young people, in an environment of high rates of unemployment,
- is an excellent image builder and sympathy-promoter for a country, unparalleled by any other industrial sector,

- is a conduit for cultural exchange between one country and another,
- smoothes the path for the entire export economy.

then there should be no dispute that in this new century NTOs will not just play the part of the Sleeping Beauty or the stop-gap, but will take a leading role in tourism strategy. The public sector will certainly not be able to abandon its role as principal shareholder and stakeholder.

Nevertheless, shareholders lose interest in their company when it fails to yield a return. For this reason, the political pressure on NTOs to re-position themselves is increasing and governments will subject them to a permanent fitness programme. In the age of globalisation, tourism finds itself in a situation of hyper-competition. Not too long ago, both the number of destination countries and the number of people who could afford travel and holidays were small. Today every country on earth is a national destination and in the year 2000 some 700 million international tourist arrivals are expected. Such a growth in extent and, alas, in bulk makes it increasingly difficult for customers to keep their heads above water and choose sensibly. Modern information technology is a help, but it too could well drown itself in the flood of information. The NTOs are challenged to take on a new leadership role in an environment of innovatory and creative marketing methods – in the New Information Technology Age they must act as information brokers and contribute to the intelligent sifting of information that shows customers the way to go from trash that stifles and blinds them. We have to overcome the fact that tourists are 'over-newsed' but under-informed.

The result of this trend will be that NTOs have to get even closer to the market and collaborate more closely with the private sector, but always with the backing of the public sector in order to preserve them from becoming completely dependent and losing their ability to act at the strategic level. NTOs must become particularly professional with regard to more effective support of small and medium-sized enterprises (SMEs), since in Europe some 80% of tourism turnover is earned in small and medium-sized businesses, who also account for more than 85% of all jobs. A specially challenging task is the improvement of profitability in this sector, which today is frankly unsatisfactory – added value is just too low.

It is my conviction that the NTO has a future. Its role as nothing more than a PR instrument in the hands of governments and politicians is, however, over: on the other hand, it must not become merely the messenger boy of the tourist industry and lobbyists. The 21st century NTO will be an organisation operating in the public interest but run as a business. Through closeness to, and knowledge of the market, it will achieve quantifiable results by retaining old customers and attracting new ones. Its marketing must become more selective, because it is not just the tourist statistics that count, but the effect of tourism on the profitability of the economy as a whole. The successful supplier is not blinded by statistical growth, but impressed by the increase in the member of satisfied visitors and by adequate added value return from each overnight stay.

5
Public and Private Sector Tourism

Introduction

The intention of this chapter is to examine the origins and development of public-private sector partnerships in England, with particular reference to the tourism industry. The chapter puts forward the challenging proposition that, based on the English experience, public-private sector partnerships in tourism are best undertaken at the local level, where 'arms-length" local destination marketing bureaux provide a model organisational form to address the challenges and opportunities raised by tourism. This argument for the primacy of the local level runs counter to the conclusions that others have reached (e.g. Thomas and Thomas, 1998). Differing academic and practitioner perspectives were aired at a seminar organised by the Confederation of British Industry (CBI, 1999). My views reflect over a quarter of a century's work, both as an academic specialising in UK tourism and latterly as the head of city and tourist promotional agencies for Sheffield and for Coventry and Warwickshire. The primacy of the local level is something for which, over the years, I have consistently argued (see, for instance, Heeley, 1981).

Context

> We are in a field of co-operation and co-ordination . . . there are, if anything, far too many cooks concerned with tourism and I would like to say that there always will be, and so our biggest problem is how to resolve the old difficulty that when you have too many

interests and too many helpers, each one of whom can contribute a little, how do you get them all to work together? (Leonard Lickorish, British Travel Association, 1968; cited in Heeley, 1975)

Tourism, as an industry, has its public and private sector components. This has always been the way of things, as detailed in several excellent historical texts (e.g. Neale, 1981). There is an inevitability about the involvement of both sectors – even if there are shifts of emphasis over time (see, for instance, Cannadine, 1980), as well as widespread variations between and within nation states. As a generality, however, private sector bodies are central to the provision of hospitality, transport and entertainment services, and they also support the marketing of destinations, as can be seen, for instance, with tour operators and airlines. Public sector intervention is brought about by a variety of sectors, foremost amongst which are the needs to regulate private sector activities, to provide non-remunerative infrastructure and superstructure, to remove obstacles to more effective private sector performance, and to redress market failures. Walton's account of the historical development of Blackpool, for example, exemplifies all four modes of intervention as they gained palpable expression in promenades, illuminations, print and bylaws, and much else besides (Walton, 1978).

Over and above intervention, the rationale for public sector involvement in tourism has another, important dimension, that of leadership. For everywhere, tourism administration provides a conundrum. Whether looked at from the vantage point of the national, regional or local levels, the tourism sector is fragmented, being dominated by small firms, and is ill defined, inasmuch as many operations, public and private, do not depend solely on tourism. A chronic need therefore exists for some or other institutional mechanism to represent, co-ordinate and advance the interests of the sector. The above quote from, Lickorish captures this exigency. Nearly always, it is the public sector that steps into the breach.

A feature of the past 40 years has been the creation of 'hybrid' public-private sector mechanisms. These mechanisms are referred to here as public-private sector partnerships, defining them formally as organisations which are constituted, managed and funded as 'independent' partnerships to exercise the classic intervention and leadership roles of the public sector. Within the English context, such agencies are alternatives to traditional and by no means extinct forms of tourist organisation, namely, the central department, the quasi-non-governmental organisation (quango) and the local authority.

The public-private sector partnership in tourism is premised on the public sector 'letting go' of some or the whole of it traditional intervention and leadership accountabilities. Crucially, in 'letting go', it seeks to increase the participation of other key players and stakeholders, particularly the private sector. Not surprisingly, however, the participation of all stakeholders in the new partnerships venture is premised on 'pay-back'. In exchange for financial and other support, each public and private sector stakeholder is looking for its *quid pro quo,* which invariably is an ability to influence the policies and programme of the partnership agency and ultimately to benefit from its operation.

'Letting go' and 'pay back' therefore exist side by side in the public-private sector partnerships. Independence is woven into the philosophy and constitutional fabric of the public-private sector partnership. In contrast, independence of operation in policy and managerial senses is negotiated against a backdrop of expectations about payback, and as such is unlikely ever fully to obtain.

Despite or in spite of this ambiguity, and notwithstanding that conventional forms of tourist organisation still predominate, there is now no doubt that the growth of public-private sector partnerships is a world-wide trend, manifest at all territorial levels – international, national, regional, sub-regional and local.

The World Tourism Organisation (WTO, 1996) cites numerous examples, from Penang to Amsterdam, and ranging across Partnership Australia, the Polish Tourist Authority and the Canadian Tourist Commission, through to the privatisation of US state tourism departments and the Maiscon de la France project. Fundamentally, the WTO report relates these initiatives and experiments to a political climate of disengagement, in which a mixed but related set of considerations have come to the fore – from 'best value' to concerns over 'displacement' effects and 'red tape', to a doubting of continuing subsidy and a passion for the 'free' market.

As well as disengagement, other important politics-administrative trends alluded to in the WTO report are those of decentralisation, regional policy and regionalism. What it would all seem to boil down to is that however much the precise form and content of a particular public-private sector partnership may reflect its unique historical, political and cultural setting, an overacting template is set by the sometimes conflicting forces and demands of disengagement, decentralisation, regional development and regionalism. So how does England fare in all of this?

The Genesis and Development of Public-private Partnership Arrangements in England

> In Plymouth, the Marketing Bureau is seen as the vehicle to provide the solution. It acts as a catalyst between the City Council and the myriad of large and small companies that make up the tourist industry. The mutual mistrust has been overcome. (Roger Matthews, Director Plymouth Marketing Bureau, 1989)

Traditionally, in the period up to 1970, local authorities in England were pivotal to meeting the public sector intervention and leadership challenges to which tourism gives rise. They did so at the local, destination level, where so much of tourism take place. The development of tourism in England has traditionally been delivered by a combination of local government and the private sector (Heeley, 1980). This has been true of the physical and marketing requirements, as well as the policy and planning dimensions. Typically, utilitarian motives of private gain and wider economic benefit to the community have underpinned this coming together of commercial and local government agencies.

What utilitarianism has in practice meant is captured in this statement by the Chairman of the Harrogate Wells and Baths Committee in his evidence to a Parliamentary select committee at the turn of the century: 'although we have a loss directly in working the undertakings, the indirect gain to the town in attracting the additional number of visitors is sufficient to compensate us for any direct loss on the establishments. Of course, as a corporation we can do that whereas under private companies it would be altogether impossible' (cited in Heeley, 1980).

The above quote illustrates how tourism development took place at the local level, with local government helping trader interests to promote and develop the tourist product. In the case of Victorian and Edwardian Harrogate, this amongst other things meant the Royal Hall, the Pump Room, the Winter Gardens and the manicured lawns of the Stray and Valley Gardens. Trader interests and local government complementing one another in this way implied that a genuine 'community of interest' existed one in which local government regulation and provision of non-productive infrastructure and superstructure sustained private sector wealth production. This, is turn, gave rise to local prosperity and employment gains.

Against the backdrop of this classic model (and ultimately as a departure from it), public-private sector partnerships in tourism have unfolded in two successive and overlapping waves. The first wave occurred in the wake of the 1969 Development of Tourism Act which established a national tourist organisation, comprising the British Tourist Authority (BTA) and separate country tourist boards for England, Scotland and Wales respectively. Soon after its formation, the English Tourist Board (ETB) resolved to set up a nationwide structure of regional tourist boards, taking advantage of enabling powers contained within the 1969 Act.

Interestingly, in shaping up the Development of Tourism Bill, mandatory statutory regional tourist agencies had been rejected by national government on the grounds that 'tourism will only make progress in an area in which the interests involved really want to work together' (cited in Heeley, 1975). Again, classic 'community of interest' stuff is here being reflected, and an indication of why ETB were to encounter difficulties in establishing regional agencies for areas where little such community of interest was apparent.

In the event, it took ETB some two years to set up a nationwide system of 11 regional tourist boards (RTBs), during the course of which the Board's original motive of administrative decentralisation and its ideal of 'tripartism' were diluted to accord with political realities, especially the winning of local authority support and involvement. ETB's 'tripartite' model for the regional tourist boards was premised on equal one-third funding and representation by the constituent local authorities, private sector operators within each region and the 'parent' English Tourist Board. Tripartism, as such, foundered on the rock of accessing financial support from the private sector, so much so that a decade after their creation only about 10% of RTB funding derived from commercial members.

So the RTBs became 'independent' (but in reality local authority dominated) regional marketing consortia, thanks to a combination of the power and influence of the local authorities, of sales and marketing-minded chief executives, and of minimalist private sector funding. This contrasted sharply with ETB's original intentions, which had seen the Boards as regional offshoots, mechanisms to facilitate the discharge locally of ETB national campaigns.

The second wave of public-private sector partnerships can be dated to the late 1970s, unfurling in the 1980s and 1990s. It reflected an upsurge of interest in tourism by local authorities, coinciding with a period when local government itself was experiencing radical change. While some authorities responded in the traditional manner to the opportunities and problems raised by tourism by setting up committees and departments, others (especially the larger cities) took to creating arm's-length destination marketing bureaux, drawing on some of the terminology and practice of US visitor and convention bureaux.

These joint ventures of the local public and private sector interests were pioneered in Plymouth, where in 1978 the Plymouth Marketing Bureau was established as a company limited by guarantee, governed by a Board of Directors of whom six were nominated by the local authority and nine elected from local tourist trader interests. A decade later, nearly half of the annual expenditure of the Bureau was derived from non-local authority sources and cost effectiveness was being trumpeted (Matthews, 1989).

Similar financial and efficiency imperatives, as well as the need fully to capitalise on investments in the National Exhibition Centre, led to the formation of the Birmingham Convention and Visitor Bureau (BCVB) in 1982. In Liverpool, an urban development agency, the Merseyside Development Corporation, was the catalyst and core funder of another 1980s experiment in joint venturism, the Merseyside Tourism and Conference Bureau.

In this decade, the perceived success stories of the Liverpool and Birmingham bureaux, and of the Greater Glasgow Tourist Board and Visitor and Convention Bureau (established 1983), constrasted with failure elsewhere, especially in the so-called 'heritage towns'. Here, local authority indifference to the tourist industry meant that marketing bureaux were essentially private sector forums. Denied the succour of local authority support and core funding, such bureaux tended to have a chequered history, with more failures (e.g. Chester) than successes (e.g. York). The York Visitor and Conference Bureau, formed in 1987 and backed by local firms such as Portakabin, Rowntrees and Terry's, could in 1990 boast that all of its £200,000 annual turnover was derived from commercial membership and trading activities (York Visitor and Conference Bureau, 1990).

Into the early 1990s Birminghum, Liverpool and Glasgow were used as role models for the creation of local destination bureaux in Manchester (1990) and in Sheffield (1991), the latter styling itself Destination Sheffield and the former revamping and re-launching itself some six years later as Marketing Manchester. Both Destination Sheffield and Marketing Manchester were notable as prototypes of the integrated destination marketing communications exercise. Here, in addition to the normal visitor and convention bureaux (i.e. tourism) functions, were the related fields of city imaging and festivals management. This wider remit was also evident in the establishment of subsequent bureaux, e.g. Leicester Promotions in 1993, Coventry and Warwickshire Promotions in 1997, and in the BCVB's re-emergence as Birmingham Marketing Partnerships. Elsewhere, the narrower tourism remit remained (e.g. the South Warwickshire Tourism Company, established in 1997). Profile Nottingham, launched this year, combines tourism and city imaging programme areas, but not festivals.

However, discharge of destination marketing accountabilities direct by the local authorities is still common in England. It characterises spa and seaside towns, and remains the favoured delivery mechanism in many provincial cities, e.g. Leeds and Newcastle. Indeed, regions and sub-regions of the country typically exhibit a mixture of the 'arm's-length' and local authority modes of tourism administration, set within the official regional and national tourist board framework.

This is exemplified for the 'old' county of Warwickshire in

Table 5.1, it can be seen that there are four local destination marketing bureaux, with combined budgets of approximately £ 5 million pounds per annum. In addition, two borough councils (Solihull and Rugby) have dedicated tourism officer, while the councils of North Warwickshire and of Nuneaton and Bedworth assign tourism responsibilities to a leisure officers and to a marketing manager respectively. The existing county has excluded Birmingham since a nationwide reorganisation of local government, which look place in 1974.

In Warwickshire the work of these tourism structures is supported by the Heart of England regional tourist board, and by the tourist-related inputs of several other agencies, including the county council, the government's regional office, regional arts boards, and the new regional development agency, Advantage West Midlands.

Strengths and Weaknesses of Public-private Sector Partnership Arrangements in England

> The regional level is not one that relates well to either tourism demand or to the suppliers of tourist services. (Airey and Butler, 1999).

Any tourism structure – be it national regional or local – is effective only inasmuch as it produces customers. Only by doing so will the structure generate significant and sustained levels of industry support. Public-private sector partnership arrangements in tourism should ultimately be evaluated by reference to these criteria of visitors and industry support generated. However, conclusive assessment of public-private partnerships in this way is constrained by several factors.

Performance assessment has been an unknown term and practice for much of the 30-year period that these bodies have been undertaking their pioneering partnership roles. In a more general sense, measuring the impact of marketing work is notoriously difficult because of the complexity of the customers' decision-making processes, the multiplicity of causal factors at play, and the need to disentangle discretionary visits and spend from those that would have in any case occurred. On the industry support side, comparative analysis of private sector contributions throws up major computational issues and imponderables. What is the best measure of industry support? Is it commercial

Table 5.1
Tourism Organisations in Warwickshire : Budgets and Main Sources of Funding

	Annual income (£000)[a]	*English Tourist Board (%)*	*Local authorities (%)*	*Commercial sector (%)*	*Earned (%)*	*External (esp. EC) (%)*
Heart of England Tourism Board	2759	20	9	8	63	—
Brimingham Marketing Partnerships	2956	—	36	3	46	15
Conventry and Warwickshire Promotions	1065	—	61	4	21	14
South Warwickshire Tourism Co.	929	—	51	11	38	—
Rugby Tourism	13	—	67	15	18	—
Total	7722					

a Annual income given for financial years as follows:

Heart of England Tourism Board 1997/8

Brimingham Marketing Partnerships 1996/7

Coventry and Warwickshire Promotions 1998/9

South Warwickshire Tourism Company 1997/8

Rugby Tourism 1997/8

subscriptions and/or media advertising revenues and/or exhibition partner income? How do we treat in-kind. 'off-the-balance sheet' contributions? At the present moment, industry support is difficult to interpret in any statistically meaningful, comparative sense.

All these anomalies, caveats and qualifications notwithstanding, there is a *prima facie* case to conclude that the operation of regional tourist boards in England from 1972 to 1999 has been by and large unsuccessful in attracting tourists and industry support. Taking a lead from Airey and Butler, the regional level is manifestly unsuited to marketing, and is not one that is conducive to the development of close working relationships with the tourist industry. The Tourism Society, a prominent forum of industry academics and practitioners, has even gone as far as saying that promotion should only be undertaken at the national and local destination levels, and 'never at the regional level' (cited in Airey and Butler, 1999). Regional tourist boards, the Society says, 'have performed very patchily'.

The view here echoes those of the Tourism Society. The regions the RTBs represent provide insufficient marketing focus and are not themselves brands, while the Boards themselves have been bureaucratic as opposed to entrepreneurial, erring to the lowest common denominator as opposed to the competitive strength. They are coherent tourist destination areas neither in name nor reality and are not genuine communities of interest.

Localised joint venture arrangements, on the other hand, have in the main arisen to represent real communities of interest. Their respective territories are more or less the basis on which customers visit and the industry is organised. Working to full potential, they enable a destination to be presented in a co-ordinated way engendering a flexible and entrepreneurial approach. Typically, they operate within a framework where targets are set and the success or failure of every project is measured and reported upon.

'Arm's-length' bureaux have proved adept at enlisting the support of large and small private sector operators and at winning external grant income, especially the European Regional Development and European Social funds. The weaknesses of destination marketing bureaux are that they can be parochial, and that they do not readily embrace inter-destination partnerships. Moreover they can all to easily become the victims of their own success. The vagaries of local authority tourism finance are such that a bureau's ability to lever trade monies and external grant may lead to core funding being withdrawn! Functions inappropriate to a bureau's core business(es) may also be off-loaded on to the 'successful' bureau.

Finally, arm's-length can quickly become off-shore and unloved, unless there is painstaking communication back to the stakeholders (especially the local authority), supported by influential champions of the bureau's cause drawn from the ranks of local government and the business community. The secret of success for an arm's-length bureau is all about communication and championing.

6

Tourism in Coastal Resorts

Introduction

This chapter offers a framework for the analysis of climate change impacts on tourism in coastal resorts: How can a change in climate affect tourism? Where are the 'interfaces' between climate change and tourism and how do they work? Which kind of information do we need on climate change and its effects (e.g. from meteorology, biology, geography) in order to assess the impact on tourism? How do social processes (sucial perception, impact of media, political decisions) in a society facing a climate change process modify the pure effect of climate change?

In October 1999, the 5th UN conference on climate change met in Bonn, Germany. One of the main topics was how to organise a reduction of, for example, carbon dioxide emissions in a way that national economies will not suffer. Looking at this discussion, there seems to be little doubt that there is a significant risk for society connected with climate change.

Climate Change and Climate Change Impacts

Results of climate change research (Houghton *et al*., 1996) show that man has intensified the greenhouse effect by increasing the concentration of carbon dioxide in the earth's atmosphere. According to the prediction of climate models, this development is accompanied by a rise in global average temperature. This has a number of further consequences, which are the subject of climate change impact research. Possible effects are, for example, the rise of sea level or changes in vegetation. As far as the magnitude of these effects or regional effects is concerned, no reliable data are yet available. In addition to physical, geological and ecological changes, it is also necessary to consider sociological and psychological aspects, such as *who* perceives climate change, *how* individuals and/or societies perceive climate change, and how they respond to their perceptions of changes (for example, adaptive behaviour, avoidance strategies), in order to assess societal effects of climate change (cf. Stehr and von Storch, 1995). In order to gain some insights into how this complex system may influence tourism, we need a model of how tourism works to see where climate change impacts can affect tourism.

How Does Tourism Work?

Five factors are a prerequisite for tourism: attractiveness amenities (or facilities) and accessibility on the side of the destination (cf. Holloway, 1994: 6-9) and ability to travel and motivation to travel on the demand side (Lohmann *et al.*, 1998).

Attractiveness refers to physical features (e.g. the beauty of mountains), but may also be used in connection with some kind of event. Amenities are those essential services the tourist needs such as accommodation, food, local transport etc. Finally, accessibility refers to means of transportation to the destination as well as the psychological distance (to be reached easily) and the possibility of booking a trip to that specific destination (distribution channels). The assumption is that a region becomes a potentially successful tourist destination (i.e. is able to attract a large number of tourists) only when the region has all these three characteristics. On the other hand, a person becomes a potential tourist only if he is able to travel (usually a question of time, money and health) and if he has the motivation to do so.

We have developed a simple structural model to describe which central factors determine whether and how tourism takes place (Figure 6.1) (Lohman, *et al.*, 1998).

How can Climate Change Affect Tourism?

Naturally, climate change will first have an impact on the tourist supply, e.g. through changed weather patterns (Lohmann and Kaim, 1999) or through impacts on the 'hardware', like reduction of landmass, destroying infrastructure. The supply of goods and services may also change through reactions of the

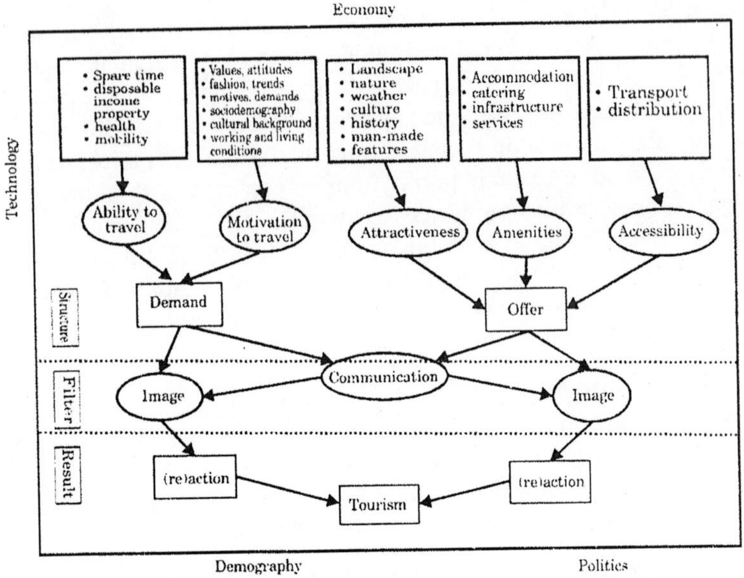

Fig. 6.1 : Tourism–framework and prerequisites.

tourism industry with respect to a real or feared climate change (e.g. more indoor facilities offered for bad weather conditions). In a second step, all this may lead to a change in tourism demand for a given area.

Nevertheless, as tourism is an economic activity mainly defined by demand (cf, Smith, 1995: 35), we will look at climate change effects on tourism starting from the demand side. One crucial aspect is the way in which climate change effects can influence the ability and the motivation to travel (cf. Figure 5.1) in general and more specifically, for a certain coastal area. In view of the uncertainties in climate research ((cf. Krupp, 1995; Hasselmann, 1997; Maxeiner, 1997, Tenbrock, 1997), something like a prognosis cannot be expected.

We have identified three possible 'interfaces' between climate change and tourism (Fig. 6.2).

1. Regional weather patterns (temperatures, clouds, amount of precipitation etc.), including change of landscape due to changed weather, (e.g. dry summers, floods).

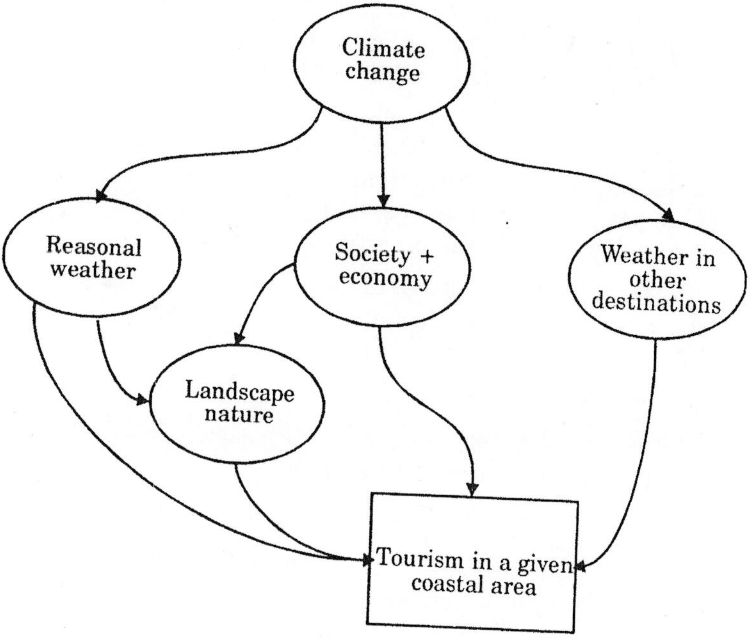

Fig. 6.2 : The interfaces between climate change and tourism.

2. Perception and evaluation of climate change in society and political administrative and economic reactions (like environment politics, attitudes of politicians, leisure time and its distribution over the year, disposable financial means, prices, e.g. for transport and insurance).

3. Weather conditions in competing destinations.

Thus, we distinguish between direct and indirect effects of climate change impacts on tourism demand.

Direct Effects

One of the most important factors influencing the attractiveness of a destination and the motivation of people to go there is weather (i.e., the perceived weather or the psychological representation of some of the meteorological/ physical variables defining the weather). Both the industry itself and tourists give this factor – the weather – some explanatory value for success or failure in tourism (e.g. Braun and Lohmann, 1989; IHK Kiel, 1998). Other relevant studies include Clawson (1966), De Freitas (1990), Adams (1973). Lohmann and Kaim (1999).

Another important factor influencing tourism directly is the weather in competing destinations. A change here may alter the relative position of a given coastal area and thus lead to a new ranking of destination preferences of tourists.

Referring to the described model in Figure 6.1, weather as a 'materialisation' of climate change may change the attractiveness of a destination and influence the motivation to go there.

Indirect Effects

Among indirect effects are the 'classical' climate change effects like rising sea level, infrastructure destroyed by storms, etc.; the kind frequently talked about in the public media (Christiansen, 1997; Hansen, 1997; Hasselmann, 1997; Lean, 1999; McCarthy, 1999; Anon., 1998; Reynolds, 1999). The impact of these on the destination is a decrease in attractiveness, on the supply side the difficulty (or impossibility) to continue the business, and on tourism demand a weaker motivation to travel to the destination.

Less frequently mentioned, but probably rather powerful, are impacts on tourism demand *via* social and economic effects. For example, in a society showing high public awareness concerning environmental issues. The possibility of a future climate change may result in rather strict environmental legislation which influences the costs of mobility (making among other things travelling more expensive). This may lead to reduced production of cars with a consequent reduction of the number of jobs and reduced incomes (decrease in tourism demand), Considering the close relationship between economic situations and beisure travel (Aderhold, 1999; Lim, 1997) such processes can influence – *via* ability to travel (Figure 6.1) – tourism to some extent.

In order to determine possible impacts of climate change (and related effects) on coastal tourism, these are the important questions:

- Do climate change effects affect a coastal area in such a

way that tourism in the traditional locations is no longer possible?

- Does climate change include changed weather patterns and how do they affect the natural and man-made environment on the one hand and tourism demand for this coastal area on the other?
- Do climate change impacts affect the ability to travel, e.g. by generating social and economic processes, which may be part of an avoidance or adaptation strategy?
- Does climate change influence the situation in competing destinations and how will this affect tourism demand for a given region?

A development perspective of tourism in a destination under climate change conditions has to incorporate different approaches and sciences. In most cases, it will be close to impossible to arrive at a valid and reliable forecast, besides perhaps some extreme cases like disappearing islands in the Pacific Ocean (cf. Lean, 1999). However, even in these cases one cannot be sure whether it should be considered a climate change effect or a natural variability. Uncertainty seems to be an escort of climate change. Therefore, social research (with tourism research being a part of it) on climate change issues has to incorporate uncertainty in its research programme, as a barrier and challenge to decision-making.

The Case of North German Coastal Resorts

Coastal areas on the North and Baltic Seas in Germany are among the most important tourist destinations in Germany (Aderhold, 1999; Lohmann *et al.*, 1998) and tourism is the most important source of income for the region (Feige *et al.*, 1999: 61).

NIT, the Institute for Tourism and Recreational Research in Northern Europe, Kiel, in co-operation with the Meteorological Institute at the University of Hamburg, the DWIF (Deutsches Wirtschaftwissenschaftliches Institut fur Fremdenverkehr) in Berlin and the Department of Psychology at the University of Koblenz-Landau conducted a multidisciplinary research project as an extensive social scientific research programme 'Coastal Tourism and Climate Change', commissioned by the German

Ministry of Education, Science, Research and Technology. The focus of this research was on the question of which direction tourism in the German coastal regions would take under various climate change development scenarios (fictitious, but possible and in line with the International Panel for Climate Change (IPCC) data; cf. Bray, 1998: 19, 52).

In the course of this research project we have developed a preliminary conceptualisation of how climate change can influence tourism in general and gained some insights with specific relevance for the destinations in Northern Germany (Bray, 1998; Feige *et al.*, 1999, Lohmann *et al.*, 1998; Braun *et al.*, 1999; Lohmann and Kaim, 1999); similar research has been carried out for other types of destinations, e.g. the Alps (Abegg, 1996, Buerki, 2000).

A complex set of methodological approaches was used in this project: scenario techniques, representative surveys of the German population, focus groups with representatives of the tourism industry and administration, psychological experiments, and others. These are described by Lohmann *et al.* (1998).

To give an example of the empirical parts of the project: within a series of psychological studies (cf. Braun *et al.*, 1999) we researched the possible impact of climate change scenarios and of the reactions of the tourism industry on the expressed destination preferences of tourists. Scenario 1 described a moderate warming accompanied by both more hours of sunshine and stronger precipitation. The industry reaction was a combination of air-conditioned hotels and more outdoor activities. In Scenario 2 the climate was described as significantly warmer, with much more precipitation, sometimes sultry and – during the wintertime – heavy storms; higher dikes and reduced fauna and flara completed the picture. The industry reaction consisted of more and better indoor facilities, both cultural and sports activities/events, shopping malls etc.

We presented these scenarios to possible tourists and then asked for their interest in spending a holiday at the German coast. The results showed a decrease in the number of interested people, especially under the conditions of Scenario 2, which can be partly (Scenario 2) or more than (Scenario 1) compensated by appropriate industry reaction.

These are some of the main findings of the project as a whole:

1. *Tourism at the German seaside* is *sensitive to climate change and its effects* – Sensitivity is high in those cases, where climate change impacts lead to a substantial change in attractiveness, facilities and/or accessibility on the supply side or the ability to travel on the demand side. But even then climate change will be only one factor among others influencing tourism.

2. *The evaluation of the effects as positive or negative depends at least partly on the developing philosophy of tourism* – Climate change effects may lead to a stronger or a weaker demand or to a high variability in tourist flows as well. In every case the tourism industry will try to adapt to the new situation, but the reactions will be quite different under the different condition.

   Thus, climate change impacts are not necessarily harming tourism in the coastal resorts. In some cases – depending on the amount and the direction of climate change itself and on the prevailing development philosophy *('Leitbild')* of tourism in the area - they may even be helpful. For example, a tourism strategy of growth may find support through climate change leading to warmer daytime temperatures during summer, whilst a tourism strategy of limitation/restriction will face a challenge under the same climate change condition.

3. *Environment policies for slowing down/reducing climate change and its impacts will influence coastal tourism as well, independently of the 'real' climate change* – Induced by economics and/or policies these effects may be the result of rising costs, lower wages, higher unemployment rates or restrictions in transport, heating or others.

4. *Climate change effects and political (re)action may be an additional challenge for the tourism, industry;*

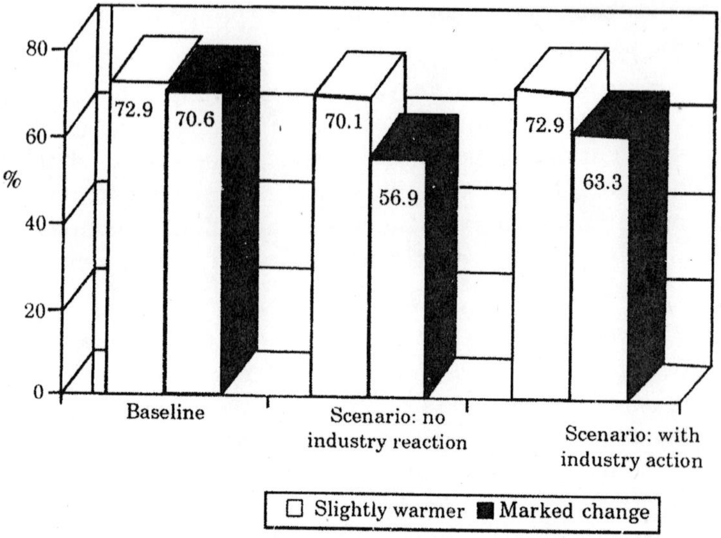

Fig. 6.3 : Change of interest in spending a holiday at the North German coast under different climate conditions.

however, within the next 30 years tourism at the coast will still be possible – Within the next two decades climate change and its impacts in the North of Germany are supposed to be not too dramatic (cf. Bray, 1998: 96). The development of tourism will be more dependent on the (global) activities of the industry. Climate change will play the role of an additional, modifying factor.

5. *In some cases, adaptation strategies may be useful or necessary,' including a repositioning of the destination*–The related activities have to be appropriate; for example an over-reaction using the new opportunities of a slight warming to attract lots of new tourists may turn into a boomerang effect, with a reduced demand due to overcrowding at the end.

6. *Adaptation can be expensive* – This is a crucial aspect: Tourism will still be possible, but someone has to pay for the adaptation to the new circumstances.

7. *Climate change is a process* – What in some of the scenarios looks like a not too uncomfortable situation in the next few decades may be nothing but a transition stage to a less desirable future.

Discussion

Our results show – in line with the international literature (e.g. Buerki and Elsasser, 1999) – that as long as a destination is able to satisfy the basic needs of the tourists and as long as the tourists have sufficient financial means, the tourism industry in a region will be able to adapt to climate change effects.

We could not identify a specific need for immediate action for the coastal resorts in northern Germany related to climate change. More interesting is the question of the possibilities of action. Are there any 'no-regrets' strategies (cf. Abegg *et al.*, 1997 : 110) at hand? That is, could actions be taken to improve the position of the coastal tourism in Germany regardless of which way climate change may turn, for example, better and more reliable financing of tourism allowing for a flexible response whenever needed, less bureaucratic structures in tourism administration and marketing and a flexible consumer-oriented product design. Such strategies would create a sound basis for a rather uncertain future.

We must face the fact that we will have to live and plan with a great deal of uncertainty. In order to reduce this uncertainty to a manageable amount, future research is needed. Our approach, described here briefly, may be an additional tool to many others to gain a clearer picture of the possible future of tourism in coastal areas under climate change conditions. For a better understanding we need more detailed data on possible weather characteristics. The availability of climate change data on a smaller geographical scale would also be very helpful. And finally, we urgently need more research on the role of social processes (perception impact of media political decisions etc.) in a society facing a climate change process with a great deal of uncertainty.

The somewhat limited threat of direct climate change impacts for tourism at the coast in northern Germany within the next two or three decades is a result not to be transferred to other places in the world without checking the specific situation there. Other destinations, with a different geographical situation and a different structure of tourism, may be hit by climate change much harder. But our methodological approach may serve as a guideline for future research projects in other areas.

Tourism as a whole, a global phenomenon, is a field that will be easily influenced by climate change, but will not be made impossible. Tourism can switch to other destinations if one is swept away, dried out or hit by some other severe impact of climate change. Tourism is more flexible than the local population.

7

The World of Today and Tomorrow

Introduction : The Travel Industry in Europe

Europe's domestic and inbound travel and tourism industry is a vital and dynamic part of its economy. As an industry it is particularly responsive to cyclical economic change and consumer volatility, and is affected by the dual pincer effects of globalisation. On the one hand, consumers have become increasingly sophisticated, with higher expectations. Lured by lower prices, they are increasingly looking to more exotic destinations. On the other, international players are taking advantage of liberalised markets and the lower transaction costs new technology has brought to move into Europe in order to escape their own mature, saturated markets. Less economically favoured regions are under particular threat, given their dependence on the sector.

Its role as an engine of growth for employment is not in question – the industry accounts directly and indirectly for 200 million jobs world-wide – that is, 8% of total employment, with an additional 5.5 Million jobs a year forecast to be created until 2010 – but many jobs created are temporary, seasonal and part-time. Women are disproportionately represented in employment in this sector, so collectively more at risk if it weakens.

Small and Medium Sized Enterprises (SMEs) are strongly represented among travel and tourism companies in Europe, and contribute to the sector's rich diversity – and fragmentation. They are frequently undercapitalised and with a rudimentary or non-existent information technology infrastructure.

The Travel Industry and Technology : Current Status

It used to be the case that for business and domestic purposes, Europe lagged behind the United States both in penetration and sophistication of technology. If we generalise greatly, it is tempting to say that Europe now only lags on penetration – global distribution systems, for example, are as sophisticated the world over – and that, even here, Europe is catching up. But this generalisation masks an unequal picture if we apply it to the tourism sector in Europe:

- There are technology 'haves' and 'have-nots' across the board – large and small companies, north and south.
- Larger companies tend to have more of their internal processes automated, while having uneven use of IT for their external communications.
- Micro businesses, when they embrace technology, do so with great zeal and often to great effect, recognising that new technology can create a 'level playing field' for the smaller company, providing an 'open all hours' professional interface at a low cost and offering access to a global market-place.
- Many niche players reason that their current client bases are not in the consuming segments which use new technology in any case.

Travel and Hospitality : Drivers for Change

To understand the drivers of change in the travel and tourism industry in the future, we should first understand the changes in consumers' lives and the changing ways in which they are prepared to do business. Consumers are becoming more affluent and they are increasingly cosmopolitan in their consumption and experience. (According to recent research by the Future Foundation, in 1999 39% of respondents said they felt closer to people of their own national background, as opposed to 60% in 1979.) With this in mind, in the following sections we concentrate on those wider changes in consumer behaviour and lifestyles which we think will most heavily impact the travel and hospitality industry in the years to come:

- Demographic shifts: an ageing population.

- Technology.
- Changes in working patterns.
- Time pressure.
- Changing modes of consumption in the travel and hospitality industry.

Demographic Shifts: An Ageing Population

In Europe the population is increasing and ageing. By 2011 there will be an additional 2.8 million consumers in Britain, but the proportion of younger people has been steadily declining for years.

The travel industry will be obliged to take into account this structural shift in the population – not just with specialist services for the infirm elderly, since in the near future many of us will be hale and hearty well into our eighties and nineties. The whole area of travel motivation will shift – with increasing numbers of elderly travellers, the proportion of travel for visiting friends and relatives will grow. This shift will almost by definition increase the number of travellers who are flexible and who have the time and patience to seek out the best deals. It might well blunt the edges of seasonality, with travellers taking advantage of off-peak prices and milder weather conditions in many traditional sunshine resorts.

The travel industry customarily relies upon the services of young employees and as a sector will find itself impacted heavily by this demographic change. Already grappling with the implications of the minimum wage, it will have to face the challenge of taking on a larger number of older workers who may expect greater remuneration, and who may not be prepared to work unsocial shifts.

Technology

Technology Penetration

Perhaps the single most important element in the future of the travel and tourism experience will be the impact of technology across the distribution and delivery chain. Across the board, consumers' access to technology is increasing and as prices plummet, this trend will deepen. The Future Foundation forecasts that by 2010, 80% of UK households will have access to interactive TV *via* PC or set-top box. This means that all but the most technologically excluded, including the very poorest in society, will have access to on-line booking and the means to search for cheap deals and consume advertising massages.

Consumers already venture onto the Net to purchase airline tickets in substantial numbers. Industry sources estimate that 11% of all world-wide transactions in 1998 were travel related, and that this will leap to 35% by 2002, with some 4 million Europeans shopping online by this year, creating a European travel market worth 6.4 billion Euros, up from 155 million (£ 99.7 million) in 1998.

Willingness to Use Technology to Conduct Travel-related Searches and Transactions

The number of travel and tourism websites is booming and there are many on and off-line information sources to help travellers navigate in real and cyber space. Consumers are in favour of a seamless automated process, which would enable them to obtain information about a holiday, and book tickets and accommodation at one go. The younger the consumer, the more enthusiastic they are about this possibility, with 74% of 15 – 24-year-olds agreeing they would find it interesting to be able to organise a complete trip on the Internet.

The Implications for Travel Agencies and Other Intermediaries

As Simon Calder says, 'The Internet does something much more profound than simply allowing me to book a ticket by pressing a few keys, it empowers me as a traveller by revealing many of the secrets of yield management'.

The threat to the agency business – and any other intermediary – is very real. Travellers already clearly regard air tickets as a commodity purchase, involving an undervalued skill in seeking out the cheapest and most appropriate deals. But exhaustive web searches take time and patience and it is often only the most flexible travellers who can take advantage of the very cheapest seats.

In this area, as in many other industries, we imagine that we may see a more pronounced polarisation of the offer, from the very cheapest 'no-frills' basic service provision to a more sophisticated selection process. Thus enabling consumers to take better-informed decisions at a price that takes account of the value of the service and information element. The trade-off between consumers' time – in seeking out offers and conducting negotiations – and money, in the form of the potential discounts obtainable, will nowhere be more transparent.

Business Travellers on the Web

Corporate business travellers, whose itineraries are at the same time more complex and less flexible than those of leisure travellers, are less likely to switch wholesale to Internet searches on a regular basis, despite the potential savings. Toyota's travel purchasing manager, for example, has gone the direct route of negotiating discounts at source with the airlines, on the basis of an understanding of the company's travel patterns and needs, rather than seeking to save a few dollars here and there on each flight by dint of diligent *ad hoc* surfing.

Business and Leisure Travel and 'Remote' Technology

We have seen that the advent of vidioconferencing and other related technologies has not at a stroke decimated business travel – instead, they have farced a reappraisal of the reasons *why* we should travel instead of doing business remotely. E-mail and videoconferencing allow us to avoid some of the time – consuming trips we used to undertake in the past, while thrusting a greater resonance onto those trips we do continue to take. The advent of cheap webcams – now included free in some home PC packages – will allow us to see our, friends and family *via* the Internet in real time for the cost of a local telephone call. At the same time we know that more and more travellers are taking trips abroad with the purpose of visiting friends and family, and we find it hard to imagine that these might be diminished by the technical capacity to see small, jerky images on a screen.

Just as the telephone failed to sound the death knell for the travel industry, but instead spurred an increase in travel by fostering personal and commercial networks, we feel that fears voiced about the possible adverse impact of new technology will prove to be largely unfounded. Indeed, increased 'remote' contact may well inspire more face-to-face trips. Casa Rovira, a small family-run hotel in Tarragona, Spain, reports an interesting mixture of the effects of demographic change and the consumer technology revolution. An Internet listing enables potential visitors from around the world to consider a visit to Casa Rovira as a possibility when planning and booking forthcoming visits to Europe using the Internet. Many of these travellers were older than the usual customer base – but stayed longer, spent more and tended to arrive when the weather was milder, leading to a welcome extension of the normal working season by a month at each end.

Changes in Working Patterns

Self-employment and Small Firms

The proportion of people working as self-employed is set to increase over the next few years, with a forecast 4.25 million in the UK by 2005. Recent research conducted by the Future Foundation suggests that this might be a conservative estimate. Substantial proportions of younger consumers say they would like to become self-employed or run their own business in the future, and of these nearly half say that they intend to do so within the next five years. In parallel, the growth of the smallest firms has increased at the expense of medium-sized firms.

The self-employed, or those running small businesses, will have different travel requirements to those travellers working for a multinational. Their trips to gain new business will be speculative and therefore largely self-funded. The prestige conferred by high-grade travel when one is within a large organisation and hierarchical niceties prevail will be undermined by the principle of having to justify costs from a personal budget. Few small businesses will be able to resist shifting a meeting by a few hours to qualify for a £ 100 saving for each of the staff members involved. The sharing of information with the customer empowers them to exploit systems that were previously concealed. Every business travel provider – whether offering rail, car rental or accommodation – ignores that at their peril.

Self-employment offers the flexibility to take time away from work – in theory, at least, though we know that many of those in the first phase of establishing a business work longer hours. Once the business is established and has a management structure in place, there is no obstacle to taking extended periods of leave, or to combining work travel with a leisure element. The distinction between home and work is becoming increasingly blurred by taking work home and having access to the office *via* e-mail and the internet, not to mention the mobile phone, 24 hours a day. We know that some 15% of consumers frequently work from home, accessing work systems *via* a modem, with over 50% agreeing that they sometimes work from home. In the same way, we think the distinction between work time and holiday time will increasingly become eroded.

Women Workers

The proportion of women in the labour force has reached 48%, largely due to more women returning to work sooner after childbirth – if indeed they have children. This is a huge change in social terms, but only a limited number of hotel and travel companies have accounted for women's differential requirements when travelling abroad for business. We forecast a more widespread broadening of the offer, with specialised women's rooms *without* trouser presses, but with more appropriate facilities.

Time Pressure

The Desire to be Transported

For many consumer groups – particularly working women – there is an acute sense of time pressure. The importance of 'time off' to individuals whose daily lives are full of routine, stress and obligation is easy to underestimate – and yet for many the process of booking and planning for a holiday is daunting and exhausting in itself.

We see an opportunity for travel service providers to offer a seamless, stress-free service, the objective of which is a totally relaxing experience. All potentially vexing decisions, such as destination, are taken out of the hands of the travellers, leaving them to concentrate instead on choosing their holiday reading list. While this may sound routine for the excessively wealthy and pampered, we feel that if such a service were offered at a price comparable to that of an activity holiday, there would be enthusiastic take-up.

Changing Modes of Consumption in the Travel and Hospitality Industry

Further Destinations, Greater Expectations, More Specialisation

We are travelling more often – and further afield, according to reviews of travel patterns. In recent years we have witnessed the 'democratisation' of many increasingly exotic destinations, whose price once rendered them out of reach of the mass market; this in turn has widened the gap between the experience of the independent traveller and the more 'passive' mainstream travel consumer. We expect to see this pattern deepening, with those determined to plough their own furrow turning to ever more exotic locations and ever more specialised pastimes in order to have an out-of-the-ordinary experience.

Specialisation is the new watchword across the industry, too, with companies offering activities and accommodation to suit any demographic segment, pocket or inclination. There is a move towards holidays with an educational element – learning to cook in an Irish manor house, for instance, or in a Tuscan villa, improving one's creative writing on a Greek island. Motels for singles, for women travellers and for the older traveller are already commonplace, and we imagine that as ever more defined niche segments are able to identify kindred spirits *via* the Internet, then this in turn will create demand in the travel and hospitality sector.

Polarisation of Prices

As consumer affluence increases, we are seeing an interesting paradox emerging: that of the polarisation of the offer between the most basic provision and the most extravagant. This is plainest in the hotel sector, as well as in the emerging war between low-cost airlines and their standard rivals. In late 1999, as British Airways conceded the damage done to its profits by Go, its low-cost subsidiary, and KLM recognised its inability to beat the low cost offers to Amsterdam and so decided it might as well join them, it was clear that the story was only just beginning. It is worth noting that while only 5% of passenger journeys are accounted for by low cost airlines in Europe in the United States, where the phenomenon is more established, this figure is as high as 25%.

We have mentioned that the self-employed and those travelling under their own steam, for whom cost is an issue, have embraced the new offers with gratitude. But there are other motivations: consumers feel disgruntled at the prospect of full-price fares now that they have seen that it is possible for airlines to operate cheaply and well on much lower tariffs.

At the same time, airlines are struggling to justify their top fares with ever more luxurious and personal services to their highest-paying customers. When an economy class fare to Los Angeles from London Heathrow can cost as little as £ 200, the normal business class fare is twenty-five times that. Virgin Atlantic prides itself on its personal attention and indulgent services that it claims make their Upper Class travellers feel that the difference is worth it.

In the hotel sector, too, we have seen the same divergence: the Travelodge chain has burgeoned in the UK, with their no-frills, no extras policy. The Formula 1, Première Classe and Bonsai chains in France are a further example of this. With credit-card check-in, no mini bar or room telephone, and plain, decent, basic rooms, these hotels are finding a wide clientele among travellers who want a bed for the night but little more.

The paradoxical counterpoint to this is the boom in the luxury end of the market. Designer hotels, such as St. Martin's in London and boutique hotels such as the Malmaison family in the north of the UK, flaunt their award – winning restaurants and seem set up to cater for the technological needs of any business traveller.

Conclusion

Consumers' expectations are increasingly soaring – and they often bring points of reference from other sectors, particularly in the area of information provision. For this reason it is vital to understand their choice mechanisms, as well as their behaviour in other areas of consumption - how responsive are they to direct communications? How strongly do they respond to brands in the travel and hospitality industry? Is there a concept of loyalty? What is, the trade-off between time and money in their buying decisions?

It is worth bearing in mind, of course, that competition for consumers, travel spend will not come from within the travel and tourism industry alone. Potential travellers may defer a customary big annual holiday in order to pay off a chunk of their mortgage, assist their children through university or upgrade their home computer, for example. In years to come, the proportion of wages to be assigned to future pension and personal welfare provision might well be much greater or we might be obliged to remain in the workforce for very many more years, given the forecasts for greater longevity we have mentioned earlier. We will have longer lives to fill and fund, and a lengthening of the customary working life may well prove to be the solution. Both these changes would have a profound impact on the travel industry, as we know it.

Keeping changing consumer lives under constant review will be the key to understanding changing patterns fo consumption in the travel industry in years to come – and to offering ever-more relevant and appetizing travel and hospitality propositions.

8

Environment for Travel and Tourism

An organisation's external environment comprises two strata – the macroenvironment and the microenvironment. In this chapter we discuss to an analysis of the microenvironment.

The microenvironment comprises those influences that the organisation experiences frequently. For most businesses, it concerns the industries in which they operate. Within this arena, business may compete with each other or, in some circumstances, collaboration may be more appropriate. We discuss two models for industry analysis in this chapter. Then we discuss the scope of collaborative behaviour, before considering the way in which competitors in an industry fall into strategic groups.

After studying this chapter, students should be able to:

- explain the importance of industry and market analysis;
- describe the construction and application of Porter's five forces framework;
- explain the limitations of Porter's five forces framework;
- describe how competitive analysis can be used for a nation or region;
- define and distinguish between competitive and collaborative behaviour in industries;
- describe and explain the limitations of the resource-based model of industry analysis;

- define strategic groups and describe their usefulness in competitive analysis.

Industries and Markets

The Importance of Industry and Market Identification

Some strategic management texts wrongly use the terms *industry* and *market* inter – changeably. Kay (1995) pointed out that to confuse the two concepts can result in a flawed analysis of the competitive environment and, hence, in flawed strategy. Modern organisations such as vertically integrated travel companies may operate in more than one industry (or industrial sector) and in more than one market. My Travel plc (formerly Airtours), for example, is a vertically integrated UK based travel group that operates in the airline, travel intermediary (tour operator and travel distribution), accommodation and cruising sectors of the travel industry. It also has major markets in Scandinavia, continental Europe, the UK and North America. Each industry (or industrial sector) and market has its own distinctive structure and characteristics which have particular implications for the formulation of strategy. Industries are centred on the supply of a product while markets are concerned with demand. It is important, therefore, to understand and analyse both industries and markets to assist in the process of strategy selection.

The most commonly used frameworks for analysing the external business environment distinguish between two levels or strata of environmental influence:

- The *micro- (or near) environment* is that which immediately surrounds a business, the parts of which the business interacts with frequently and over which, it may have some influence. For most purposes, we can identify competitors, suppliers and customers as comprising the main constituents of this stratum of the environment.
- The *macro – (or far) environment* comprises those influences that can affect the whole industry in which a business operates. The macro environment comprises influence arising from political, economic, sociodemographic and technological factors. The nature of these factors normally means that individual businesses

are unable to influence them – strategies must usually be formulated to cope with changes in the macroenvironment.

It is sometimes, difficult to define a particular industry precisely. Porter (1980) defined an industry as a group of businesses whose prodcuts are close substitutes, but this definition can be inadequate because some organisations and industries produce a range of products for different markets.

While an industry is centred upon producers of a product, a market is centred on customers and their requirements (needs and wants), A particular market consists of a group of customers with a specific set of requirements which may be satisfied by one or more products. Analysis of a market will therefore involve gaining understanding of customers, their requirements, the products which satisfy those requirements, the organisations producing the products and the means by which customers obtain those products (distribution channels).

As well as selling their products in markets, businesses also obtain their resources (labour, materials, machinery, etc.) in markets – referred to as resource markets. Additionally, most businesses are interested in markets for substitute products and they will also be keen to investigate new markets for their products.

Ways of Defining and Understanding Markets, Industries and Strategic Groups in Strategy

Kay (1995) considered the differences between markets, industries and strategic groups. A core competence (or distinctive capability) becomes a competitive advantage only when it is applied in a market, an industry or a strategic group. Competitive advantage is a relative term in that an organisation can enjoy a competitive advantage by reference to other suppliers to the same market, other organisations in the same industry, or other competitors in the same strategic group. Demand factors determine the market, while supply factors determine the industry. By way of example Kay cited Eurotunnel and P&O Ferries. Both serve the same market as they represent alternative options customers might choose in order to cross the English Channel. However, they are in very different industries in that one is a shipping company whilst the other is the manager of a large infrastructure project. The strategic group is viewed as the competitive battleground and is determined by classifying companies with similar strategies. Thus Lufthansa and

British Airways are part of the same strategic group, Southwest Airlines, a low cost airline operating only domestic services in the USA, would be in a different strategic group.

It is important for organisations to identify the relevant market, industry and strategic group and to understand that they are not the same. In attempting to reposition-the company through the purchase of a tour operator, the company failed to successfully distinguish between an industry and a market. A later attempt at repositioning its core business has been more fundamental and ultimately more successful. The company's core business is now firmly in the branded hotel sector and the company, now renamed SixContinents plc, owns a number of brands including: Holiday Inn, Intercontinental Hotels and Crowne Plaza.

Source: Adapted from Kay (1995).

Industry and Market

- Industries *produce* goods and services – the supply side of the economic system.
- Markets *consume* goods an services that have been produced by industries – the demand side of the economic system.

The Relationship Between a Business Organisation, its Industry and Markets

Analysis of its industry and markets allows an organisation to:

- identify other industries where it may be able to deploy its core competencies;
- understand the nature of its customers and their needs;
- identify new markets where its core competences may be exploited;
- identify threats from existing and potential competitors in its own and other industries;
- understand markets from which it obtains its resources.

Analysis of the competitive environment (industry and market) is important to the development of an organisation's future strategy; as is analysis of the macroenvironment and internal analysis. The industry and market context will play an important role in shaping an organisation's competences and core competences. The core competences of a business must continually be reviewed in relation to changing customer needs, competitors' competences, and other market opportunities.

Competitive Analysis

What is Competitive Analysis?

Competitive analysis aims to establish the nature of the competition in the industry and the competitive position of the business in relation to its product and resource markets. Industry dynamics, in turn, are affected by changes in the microenvironment. For example, ageing populations in many developed countries have significantly affected the demand for tourism products, with the growth in cruising and long-stay holidays being but two industry responses to the trend. There is a danger that competitive analysis can be seen as a 'one off' activity, but like all components of the strategic process, it should be undertaken on an ongoing basis. The competitive analysis framework developed by Porter (1980) is the most widely used and is explained in this section.

Porter's Five Forces Framework of Competitive Analysis

Porter (1980) developed a framework for analysing the nature and extent of competition within an industry. He argued that there are five competitive forces, which determine the degree of competition within an industry. Understanding the nature and strength of each of the five forces within an industry assists managers in developing the competitive strategy of their organisations. The five forces are:

- The threat of new entrance to the industry.
- The threat of substitute products.
- The power of buyers or customers.
- The power of suppliers (to businesses in the industry).
- Rivalry among businesses in the industry.

By determining the relative 'power' of each of these forces, an organisation can identify how to position itself to take advantage of opportunities and overcome or circumvent threats. The strategy of an organisation may then be designed to exploit the competitive forces at work within an industry.

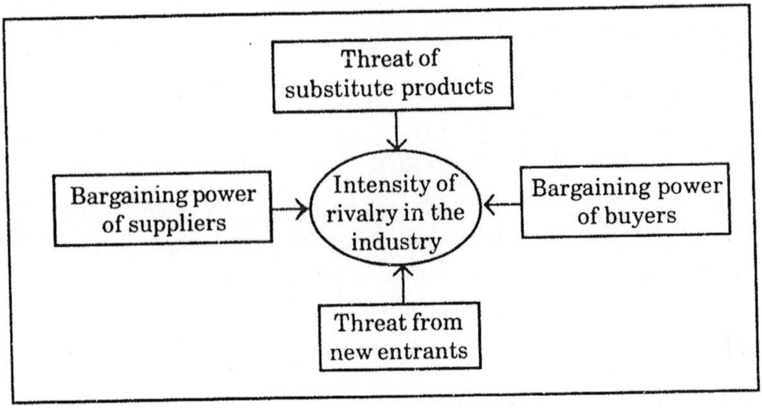

Fig. 8.1 : Poster's five forces framework (adapted from Porter, 1980).

Before considering the detailed aspects of the five forces framework, a number of points should be noted:

1. Although originally developed with commercial businesses in mind, the framework can, provide valuable insights for most organisations, destinations or attractions.
2. When using Porter's framework it is important to identify which of the five forces are the key forces at work in an industry. In many cases, it transpires that one or more of the five forces prove to be 'key forces' and the strategic analysis must focus on these if it is to use the framework fruitfully.
3. The dynamic nature of the competitive environment (meaning that it is constantly changing) means that the relative strength of the forces in a particular industry will change over time. It is therefore important that the five forces analysis is repeated on regular basis so as to detect such changes before competitors and allow an early adjustment of strategy.
4. Before any conclusions can be drawn about the nature of competition within an industry each of the five forces must be analysed in detail.

5. The framework should be based at the level of the *strategic business unit* (SBU) rather than at the level of the entire organisation. That is to say, when considering the five competitive forces facing an organisation it is not the entire organisation that should be considered (except where the organisation is simple and consists of one SBU only) but the forces should be considered in relation to constituent SBUs. This is because, individual organisations may be diverse in their markets and operations. A vertically integrated travel company such as Thomson, for example (a UK subsidiary of Tui, a German company) operates tour operations, travel agents and an airline. In each of these sectors the company faces different sets of competitors, suppliers and substitutes and also faces varying regulatory processes. As Johnson and Scholes (2002) pointed out, an airline might compete simultaneously in several different arenas such as long haul, domestic and European. In each of these the airline might target different target groups, such as leisure, business and freight, and the competitive forces are different in each of these.
6. The five forces are not independent of each other, with pressures from one competitive force having the potential to trigger off changes in the other forces. For example, potential new entrants to a market finding their route to be blocked may find new routes to the market by bypassing traditional distribution channels using agents or intermediaries and sell directly to consumers. Thus easyJet, the UK-based low cost airline, rejected distribution through travel agents or did not feature prominently on GDS systems. Instead tickets were sold directly to consumers (at first through a telephone call centre and more recently through the Internet), thereby cutting out the travel agents and the commission, which would ordinarily have been paid to them. Thus the bargaining power of one set of buyers (the travel

agents) was reduced by the introduction of a new market entrant whilst the bargaining power of another set (consumers) was increased as a result of increased competition provided by the new entrant. EasyJet now sell over 90% of their flights over the Internet.

We will now discuss each of the five forces in turn in the context of various forms of travel and tourism organisation.

Force 1: The Threat of New Entrants to the Industry

The threat of entry to an industry by new competitors depends upon the 'height' of a number of entry barriers. Barriers to entry can take a number of forms.

The Capital Costs of Entry

The size of the investment required by a business wishing to enter the industry (or industry sector) will be an important determinant of the extent of the threat of new entrants. The higher the investment required, the less will be the threat from new entrants. The lower the required investment, the greater the threat. In some areas of tourism such as the, building of a hotel, or a visitor attraction, starting a cruise line or launching an airline, the capital costs are dearly quite high. However, in some cases it might be possible to avoid or defer some capital costs by separating ownership from the management of the assets or by leasing. Separating ownership and management is common in the hotel sector where a property company may own the physical assets but a hotel operator manages the hotel. Leasing aircraft and ships is common in the airline and cruising sectors and allows high up-front costs to be spread out over a period of time. In other areas of travel and tourism such as starting up a tour operator or travel agency, the capital costs might be relatively low since neither require the purchase of expensive assets.

Brand Loyalty and Customer Switching Costs

If the companies in an industry produce differentiated products and customers are brand loyal, then potential new entrants will encounter resistance in trying to enter the industry. Brand loyalty will also be an important factor in increasing the costs for customers of switching to the products of new competitors. In some instances, tourism destination products are able to differentiate their products fully. There is only one Louvre art gallery in Paris where the Mona Lisa can be viewed, and the Emperor penguin can only be viewed in extreme southern latitudes. Thus customers cannot switch to new entrants if they want to experience these attractions. However, in many cases tourism consumers are driven by price and exhibit little brand loyalty. Thus consumers may switch from existing tour operators, travel agents, hotel groups, and airlines to new entrants on the basis of a more competitive offering. In some cases, however, switching costs are imposed through customer loyalty schemes such as the 'Frequent Flyer' programmes operated by the airlines.

Economics of Scale or Scope Available to Existing Competitors

If existing competitors are already obtaining substantial economics of scale it will give them an advantage over new competitors who will not be able to match their lower unit costs of production. A new entrant offering package holidays to Spain from the major European markets (Germany, the UK and Scandinavia) would face strong competition from large entrenched operators such as TUI, First Choice and Thomas Cook. These operators often have long-standing arrangements with accommodation suppliers in Spain and, given their ability to contract bed spaces in bulk, are able to negotiate highly favourable terms which may not be available to a smaller new entrant.

Access of Input and Distribution Channels

New competitors may find it difficult to gain access to channels of distribution, which will make it difficult to provide their products to customers or obtain the inputs required. In the case of the tour operator cited previously, such is the shortage of some categories of accommodation, in Spain that existing operators have often contracted all the available capacity, thereby excluding new entrants to access to the necessary inputs. Furthermore, the existing large tour operators have established distribution channels (such as travel agents, call centres and the Internet) in their major markets which they have developed over the years in order to provide the most cost-efficient means of distribution. A new entrant would require heavy investment in order to secure such access.

The Resistance Offered by Existing Businesses

If existing competitors choose to resist strongly it will make it difficult for new organisations to enter the industry. For example, if existing businesses are obtaining economies of scale it will not be possible for new entrants to undercut prices. In some cases, existing competitors may make price cuts or increase marketing expenditure in order to deter new entrants. It has sometimes been claimed that such 'predatory' pricing behaviour has sometimes been undertaken by the large airlines in order to deter new lowcost carriers.

If barriers to entry make it difficult for new competitors to enter the industry then this will limit the amount of competition within it. As a result, competitors within the industry will attempt to seek to strengthen the barriers to entry by cultivating brand loyalty, increasing the costs of entry and 'trying up' input and distribution channels as far as is possible. Potential new entrants will lobby for the removal or reduction of such barriers in order to allow them to enter the industry and compete for business. In other words, they will try to make the industry 'contestable'.

Force 2: The Threat of Substitute Products

A substitute can be regarded as something which meets the same needs as the product of the industry. For example, an individual wishing to cross the English Channel can choose to travel by cross channel ferry, by hovercraft or by the train service through the Channel Tunnel. These products all provide the benefit to the customer of crossing to France, despite the fact the ferry and rail services are provided by different industries. The extent of the threat from a particular substitute will depend upon two factors.

The Extent to which the Price and Performance of the Substitute can Match the Industry's Product

Close substitutes whose performance is comparable to the industry's product and whose price is similar will be a serious threat to an industry. The more indirect or materially different the substitute, the less likely the price and performance will be comparable. Since most travel products are of high cost and the expenditure is usually seen as a luxury rather than a necessity, the products compete for disposable income with other high cost items such as cars and 'white goods' (refrigerators and washing machines).

The Willingness of Buyers to Switch to the Substitute

Buyers will be more willing to change suppliers if switching costs are low or if competitor products offer lower price or improved performance. This is also closely tied in with the extent to which customers are brand loyal. The more loyal customers are to one supplier's products (for whatever reason), then the threat from substitutes will be accordingly reduced.

Kay Concept : Switching Costs

One of the key strategic manoeuvres in maintaining customer loyalty is to increase the cost – to the customer – of changing to a new supplier. If switching costs arc high, then customers will have an economic disincentive to switch and hence will tend to stay with the existing supplier.

Competitors in an industry will attempt to reduce the threat from substitute products by improving the performance of their products, by reducing costs and prices, and by differentiation.

Force 3: The Bargaining Power of Buyers

The extent to which the buyers (customers) of a product exert power over a supplying organisation depends upon a number of factors. Broadly speaking, the more power that buyers exert, the lower will be the transaction price. This has obvious implications for the profitability of the producer.

The Number of Customers and the Volume of Their Purchases

The fewer the buyers and the greater the volume of their purchases the greater will be their bargaining power. A large number of buyers each acting largely independently of each other and buying only small quantities of a product will be comparatively weak. Thus the major cruise lines operating in the Caribbean (of which there are relatively few) have power over the many competing small Caribbean island destinations when deciding on their cruise schedules and negotiating port charges, but individual travel agency customers have limited bargaining power when dealing with large travel agency chains which have multiple branches.

The Number of Businesses Supplying the Product and Their Size

If the suppliers of a product are large in comparison to the buyers, then buying power will tend to be reduced. The number of suppliers also has an effect – fewer suppliers will tend to reduce the bargaining power of buyers as choice and the ability to 'shop around' is reduced. Thus individual airlines wanting to serve London are faced with a situation where they have to deal with a situation where the three largest airports (Heathrow, Gatwick and Stansted) are owned and operated by a single company, BAA plc.

Switching Costs and the Availability of Substitutes

If the costs of switching to substitute products are low (because the substitutes are close in terms of functionality and price), then customers will accordingly be more powerful. Customers will not be financially penalised for moving their business from one Spanish resort to another.

We should bear in mind that buyers are not necessarily those at the end of the supply chain. At each stage of a supply chain, the bargaining power of buyers will have a strong influence upon the prices charged and the industry structure.

In the supply chain for hotel rooms at destination, for example, the buyers include consumers, tour operators, airlines and other transportation groups, and event promoters. The amount of power which each buyer exerts can differ substantially. Tour operators might be able to exert far greater pressure on hotels than can individual consumers.

Force 4: The Bargaining Power of Suppliers

Organisations must obtain the resources that they need to carry out their activities from resource suppliers. These resources fall into the five categories we have previously encountered: human, financial, operational, physical and intellectual.

Resources are obtained in resource markets where prices are determined by the interaction between the organisations supplying a resource (suppliers) and the organisations from each of the industries using the particular resource in question. It is important to note that many resources are used by more than one industry. As a result, the bargaining power of suppliers will not be determined solely by their relationship with one industry but by their relationships with all of the industries that they serve.

The major factors determining the strength of suppliers are discussed below.

The Uniqueness and Scarcity of the Resource that Suppliers Provide

If the resources provided to the industry are essential to it and have no close substitutes then suppliers are likely to command significant power over the industry. If the resource, can be easily substituted by other resources, then its suppliers will have little power. It is for this reason, for example, that people with rare or exceptional skills can command higher salaries than lesser skilled people. Similarly, the limited number of aerospace suppliers gives them considerable power. The worldwide suppliers of large jet aircraft are limited to two (Boeing of the USA and Airbus, a collaboration between France, Germany, the UK and Spain) whilst the large scale suppliers of jet aircraft engines are limited to four (General Electric and Pratt and Whitney of the USA, Rolls-Royce of the UK and SNECMA of France).

How many other Industries have a Requirement for the Resource

If suppliers provide a particular resource to several industries then they are less likely to be dependent upon one single industry. Thus, the more industries to which they supply a resource, the greater will be their bargaining power. Thus in some developed markets such as London and New York, hotels often find it difficult to recruit an adequate supply of staff as they have to compete for labour with many other industries.

Switching costs between Suppliers

In some cases switching between suppliers may be difficult and costly. Close working relationships may have been built up over a protracted period of time so that any new supplier would not have the necessary knowledge or experience required or systems and services may have been tailored towards the requirements of a particular supplier. Thus an airline which operated an all-Boeing fleet of aircraft would find it difficult to switch quickly to supply from Airbus since pilots would have been trained for Boeing aircraft, capacity would have been calculated using Boeing seat configurations, engineers would have been trained to maintain Boeing aircraft and parts would have been stored only for the Boeing aircraft.

The Number and Size of the Resource Suppliers

If the number of organisations supplying a resource is small and the number of buyers is large, then the greater will be the power of the suppliers over the organisations in any industry. If the suppliers are small and there are a large number of them, they will be comparatively weak, particularly if they are small in comparison to the organisations buying the resource from them. For example, most of the suppliers of food and services to an international hotel group such as Sheraton are weak because they are small in comparison to the hotel company. Shemton has a number of suppliers at its various locations and is able to switch suppliers if necessary to gain lower input costs or higher quality.

In summary, therefore, suppliers to an industry will be most powerful when:

- the resource that they supply is scarce;
- there are few substitutes for it;
- switching costs are high;
- they supply the resource to several industries;
- the suppliers themselves are large;
- the organisations in the industry buying the resource are small.

When the opposite conditions apply then suppliers will be relatively weak.

Force 5: The Intensity of Rivalry among Competitors in the Industry

Businesses within an industry will compete with each other in a number of ways. Broadly speaking, competition can take place on either a price or a non-price basis.

Price competition involves businesses trying to undercut each other's prices, which will, in turn, or dependent upon their ability to reduce costs of production. Non-price competition will take the form of branding, advertising promotion, additional services to customers, and product innovation. In some sectors of travel and tourism competitive rivalry is fierce, while in others it is less intense or even non-existent since concentrated oligopolies or monopolies are formed. The competition amongst upscale hotels in many parts of Southeast Asia, for example, has been intense over recent years. A building boom during the 1980s and 1990s was followed by economic slowdown after 1997 which severely affected occupancy rates and led to heavy discounting of room rates. This can be contrasted with rail services in many countries such as France, Italy and Germany where state controlled enterprises hold monopoly positions.

In highly competitive markets, companies engage in regular and extensive monitoring of key competitors. Lynch (2000) cited four examples:

- examining price changes and matching any significant move immediately;
- examining any rival product change in great detail and regularly attempting new initiatives in one's own organisation;
- watching investment in new competing operations;
- attempting to poach key employees.

In Figure 8.1 it can be seen that the other four forces point inwards towards this fifth force. This representation is intentionally to remind us that the strength of this force is largely dependent upon the contribution of the other four that 'feed' it. However, there are also some conditions within the industry itself that may lead specifically to a higher degree of competitive rivalry. These specific factors include the following.

The Relative Size of Competitors

When competitors in a sector are of roughly equal size, rivalry will tend to be increased as the competing companies try to gain a greater degree of market dominance but profits will usually fall as a result of this increased rivalry. The UK outbound tour operating industry might be such a sector. Four large tour operators (Thomson, MyTravel, First Choice and Thomas Cook) have, for a number of years, jostled each other in the fight for market share and profits in the industry have proved to be somewhat volatile. Where there is a dominant organisation, there may be less rivalry (and consequently higher level of profitability) because the larger organisation is often able to stop or curtail moves by smaller competitors. Air fares between Britain and South Africa, for example, have traditionally been very high as long established airlines (British Airways and South African Airways) have, with the support of national governments, kept most competition away from these particular routes, thus making them highly profitable.

The Nature of Costs in Industry Sectors

If sectors of an industry have high fixed costs in that they are capital intensive, rivalry amongst competitors may become more intense as price-cutting becomes a way of filling capacity and thus helping to dilute the high fixed costs. Thus, in the cruise sector and amongst hotels and airlines, discounting during the period close to departure or when the accommodation is required is commonplace. This is as a result of the inherent perishability of the product and the high level of fixed costs.

The Maturity of the Markets Served

If the market is mature and thus only growing slowly, competition is likely to be more intense than a market that is still growing vigorously. This is because, in a mature market, the only way for an organisation to achieve higher sales is by taking market share from competitors. This, in turn, intensifies rivalry in the industry. In markets which are still growing vigorously, however, new opportunities open up for organisations and thus sales can be increased without taking market share from competitors.

The Degree of Brand Loyalty of Customers

If customers are loyal to brands then there is likely to be less competition and what competition there is will be non-price. If there is little brand loyalty then competition will be more intense. Cruise passengers, for instance, have traditionally been very loyal to a particular cruise line and even to their preferred ship whereas North European package tourists taking Mediterranean holidays have shown themselves to be willing to switch brands freely, lured by a high level of price competition. Such brand loyalty is closely linked to a further factor – that of differentiation.

The Degree of Differentiation

Where products can be easily differentiated, rivalry is likely to be less intense, whereas where differentiation is difficult to achieve, rivalry is likely to be more intense. Continuing, the example from above, it is relatively easy to differentiate a cruising product through the type, size, quality and crew of a ship, whereas in a package holiday to the Mediterranean, tour operators may use similar types of aircraft, accommodation, ground handling agents and distribution channels, and offer the same destination choice and consequently the opportunities to differentiate their product offerings are more limited.

Government Regulation

The degree of government regulation will have an influence over the extent of competitive rivalry in a sector. The international airline industry has traditionally been heavily regulated, with governments taking direct roles in setting inter governmental agreements in order to exert control. Accordingly, international air travel between many countries is regulated through a complex web of bilateral treaties negotiated between the governments at either end of air routes. Similarly in the UK, the government acting through the Civil Aviation Authority's Air Travel Organisers' Licence (ATOL) system seeks to control the capacity of air inclusive tour operators. In both these cases rivalry might be more intense if government regulation ceased to exist. By contrast, government controls over the international hotel sector are rare other than through normal planning restrictions.

The Height of Exit Barriers

The height of exit barriers (the ease with which organisations can leave an industry) will have an impact upon competitive rivalry. Where high capital costs have been incurred by the purchase of high value fixed assets such as aircraft, cruise liners or the construction of hotels or visitor attractions, it may be difficult to exit from these sectors as such assets cannot easily be put to other uses and may be difficult to sell, particularly in times of economic downturn. Consequently, overcapacity may persist in such sectors for a period of time, leading to increased rivalry between competitors. For example, overcapacity in some Asian hotel markets, such as Kuala Lumpur, Singapore and Bangkok, resulted in heavy discounting in the late 1990s and this, in turn, reduced profit margins and returns on investment.

A high degree of rivalry will usually reduce the potential profitability of an industry and may lead to innovations that serve to stimulate consumer demand for the travel and tourism products. In recent years, many sectors of the travel and tourism industry have become more competitive as the result of the influence of several factors, including technology advances, government deregulation (and in some cases privatisation) and limits on supply. Thus the competition amongst European tour operators to secure hotel rooms and self catering accommodation rooms at prime Spanish resorts, the competition between European cities as short break destinations and the increased competition in the European and North American air travel markets are all examples of increasingly competitive sectors of travel and tourism.

The Five Forces Framework and Profitability – A Summary

As has been discussed, a relationship can be established between an industry's or company's position in respect to the five forces and its potential profitability. Table 8.1 shows a summary of how the five forces can help to determine company and industry profitability.

Table 8.1
Porter's Five Forces and Profitability – A Summary

Force	*Profitability is likely to be higher if there is/are:*	*Profitability is likely to be lower if there is/are:*
Bargaining power of suppliers	weak suppliers	strong suppliers
Bargaining power of buyers	weak buyers	strong buyers
Threat of new entrants	high entry barriers	low entry barriers
Threats from substitute products	few possible substitutes	many possible substitutes
Competitive rivalry	little rivalry	intense rivalry

Limitations of the Five forces Framework

Porter's a five forces framework represents a good starting point for the understanding of competitive forces and has obvious value as a tool for managers seeking a better understanding of such forces. However, the framework has been subject to several important limitations. The major limitations of the framework are as follows.

It Implies that Suppliers, Buyers and Competitors are Threats

The framework is built on the premise that suppliers, buyers and competitors represent threats that need to be tackled. However, some organisations have built successful strategies on the basis of building close working relationships with suppliers, buyers and competitors. *Collaborative strategy* or *partnering* has become an important part of the overall travel and tourism competitive landscape and is discussed by a number of authors, including Bennett (1997), Donne (2000), Oum and Park (1997), Rhoades and Lush (1997), and Evans (2001a) in relation to airlines; Evans (2001b) in relation to travel businesses; Dev and Klein (1993), Olsen (1993) and Go and Pine (1995) in relation to hotels; and, Buhalis and Cooper (1998) and Go and Appelman (2001) in relation destination enterprises.

It Claims to Assess Industry Profitability

Porter (1980) argues that the framework makes it possible to assess the potential profitability of a particular industry. While there is some evidence to support this claim, there is also strong evidence to suggest that company-specific factors are more important to the profitability of individual businesses rather than industry factors (Rumelt, 1991).

It Implies that the Five Forces Apply Equally to All Competitors in An Industry

In reality, the strength of the forces may differ from business to business. The framework implies that if, for example, supplier power is strong then this will apply to all the businesses in the industry. In fact, supplier power may differ from business to business in the industry. Larger businesses will face less of a threat from suppliers than will smaller ones. Similarly, businesses with strong brand names will be less susceptible to, buyer power and substitutes than those with weaker brands.

The European Airline Industry – Forces Driving Competition

New Entrants

- Relatively high entry barriers

- High capital costs for start-ups
- Well-established brands
- Some examples of tacit government support for 'flag carriers'
- Shortages of airport take-off and landing slots
- Corporate jets, low cost carriers, and regional airlines challenging larger more established airlines.

Buyers

- Decreasing customer loyalty
- Airline frequent flyer programmes
- Greater choice on some routes
- Complicated and confusing fare structures
- Competition from charter carriers on some routes
- Consolidation amongst travel intermediaries.

Substitutes

- Development of high speed trains, particularly in France, Italy, Germany and Spain
- Extensive motorway network for car usage
- New telecommunication technologies, such as teleconferencing

Suppliers

- Oligopoly of aircraft and aircraft engine suppliers
- Oligopoly of aircraft leasing companies
- Local monopolies of infrastructure providers (airports and surface transport)
- National monopolies and undercapacity of air traffic control providers.

Rivalry Among Competitors

- Varies on different routes but increasing generally
- Increasing price competition and continuing quality and service competition
- Extensive use of GDS systems and increasing use of Internet distribution
- Sophisticated yield management systems in widespread use enabling *price discrimination* to take place
- Collaboration through strategic alliances and code sharing

- Charter, regional and new low cost entrants providing increased competition for established carriers
- Established carriers adding to service quality or dropping service features to compete with new entrants.
- Market liberalisation during the 1990s and continuing privatisation of state owned airlines.
- Failure of some established airlines (Swissair and Sabena) in late 2001.

In discussing the increasing rivalry amongst Europe's competing airlines, Holloway (1998) noted that the nature of competition is changing as market liberalisation has enabled access for new entrants to the market. Now operational practices, lower service levels, Internet distribution and operation of a single aircraft type keep costs at low levels in a manner pioneered by Southwest Airlines in the USA. New entrants to the European airline market such as Ryanair and easyJet operate highly profitable networks (Donne, 2000) and have induced now demand for air travel among the population, intense competition among airlines has also been triggered by overcapacity resulting from over-ordering aircraft in the mid-1990s and expansion policies pursued by several major airlines. An environment of deregulation and privatisation has resulted in a somewhat more open market but, congestion at several major airports, air traffic control limitations, and strong entrenched airlines have limited competition on some routes. The turbulent environment has placed a high degree of pressure on airlines to adapt in order to survive. As a sign of adaptation the formation of strategic alliances has become a defining characteristic of the global air transport sector.

The Competitive Analysis of Nations or Regions

Porter's 'Diamond'

Porter's five force analysis was developed during the 1980s and has proved to be highly influential in providing a framework for the analysis of a wide variety of organisations including those in the public and not for profit sectors. In a later work, Porter (1991) developed his ideas relating to competition and related them to countries in trying to explain why some nations are more competitive than others and some regions within countries are also more competitive than others. For a full discussion of the contribution of this framework to strategic thinking, see Stonehouse *et al.* (2000). Tourism greatly contributes to wealth creation, as it did to Spain in the 1960s and 1970s, to Greece since the early 1970s and to Turkey since the mid-1980s (Wahab and Cooper, 2001). Porter developed his 'diamond' analysis to assess, the competitive advantage of nations. The diamond represents a framework consisting of four factors which individually and through the linkages between them can be used to assess the degree to which a country or region enjoys a relative competitive advantage. The four factors are:

- Factor conditions (physical resources, human resources, capital resources, infrastructure and knowledge resources).
- Market structures, organisation and strategies.
- Demand conditions.
- Related and supporting industries.

In addition, Porter identified two further factors: government (which can influence any of the four factors) and chance events (which can shift competitive advantage in unpredictable ways).

In Porter's analysis each of these factors should be analysed and the relative strengths or weaknesses evaluated. An important aspect of Porter's work relates to the importance of *clusters*. Clusters are geographic concentrations of interconnected companies and institutions in a particular field. They encompass an array of linked industries and other entities which are important to competition. Thus where such clusters can be identified, a mutually supportive set of enterprises exists that compete and collaborate in such a way that may give rise to competitive advantage being established.

The Porter diamond is shown in Fig. 8.2

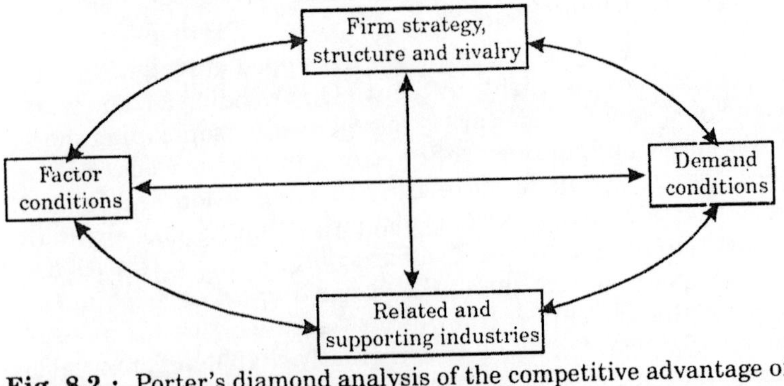

Fig. 8.2 : Porter's diamond analysis of the competitive advantage of nations (adapted from Porter, 1990).

In their paper, which is based on an earlier work (ECES, 1998), Wahab and Cooper (2001) discussed Porter's diamond in a tourism context and applied the analysis to Egypt. The authors concluded that whilst Egypt clearly has great potential as a tourist destination, some of the potential has yet to be realised and, consequently, the country has not yet reached a position of comparative advantage.

Improving the Competitiveness of a Tourist Destination

A list of guidelines for improving the competitiveness of a tourist destination were produced by Smeral (19%) building on the work of Porter (1990) and reported by Wahab and Cooper (2001). The guidelines set out below include factor conditions (which are background considerations), but of specific importance to the tourism sector are market structures, organisation and strategies, demand conditions and government.

1. *Market structures, organisation and strategies:*
   - Image building within the context of global competition.
   - Aggressive and innovative marketing to foster growth and expansion of tourism's value-added through special interest motivations.
   - Information coordination and intensification of knowledge pertaining to a destination's strengths and weaknesses within a competitive environment at the international, national and regional levels.
2. *Demand conditions*
   - Expanding the destination's share of quality tourism movement from primary, secondary and opportunity markets, offering them quality facilities and services.
   - Reducing demand seasonality through strategies aiming at guaranteeing a steady flow of tourist traffic from various markets.
   - Enhancing tourist receipts by concentrating mostly on higher spending tourist arrivals.
   - Encouraging repeat visitors through offering them diversified attractions separately presented or in combined forms.
   - Holistically oriented local, regional and national policy.

3. *Government*
   - Encouragement of systematic and continuous research into tourism market trends, demand changes and innovations in leisure and tourism activities.
   - Serious and systematic control of and guidance to the travel and tourism industries to keep total quality at its most appropriate to face global competition.
   - Improving academic and professional education and intensifying quality training in tourism to meet industry requirements.
   - Eliminating 'red tape' and avoiding all administrative hurdles including any conflict or overlapping of jurisdictions.
   - Ameliorating environmental quality.
   - Proactive management of change and better usage of state commitments under the Free Trade in Services Agreement.

An Alternative Approach to Competitive and Collaborative Analysis

Competitive and Collaborative Arenas

It is not always the case that businesses in an industry compete with each other – they might time-to-time, have reasons to collaborate with each other. Accordingly, in some 'arenas', businesses compete whilst in others, they may work together.

At the root of this understanding is the fact that organisations and industries are open systems – they interact with many environments. The 'arenas' in which the organisation operates are described below.

- *The industry* – the industry within which the organisation currently deploys its resources and competences in producing products.
- *Resource markets* – the markets from which the organisation, its competitors and other industries obtain their resources.
- *Product markets* – markets where the organisation sells its products. These can be subdivided into markets for the organisation's products, markets for substitute products, and new markets to which the organisation may be considering entry.

- *Other industries* – where businesses possess similar competences to those of the organisation. Such industries are important for two reasons. The first is that the business may be considering entry to them. The second is that the organisations in these industries are potential competitors who may enter the business's industry and markets.

Each of these arenas must be analysed as they directly affect an organisation's competitive positioning and hence its chances of outperforming competitors.

The competitive and collaborative arena framework builds upon Porter's 'five forces framework but explicitly recognises that the competitive environment is divided into four separate but interrelated arenas.

A Resource-based Approach to Environmental Analysis

Limitations of Existing Frameworks of Analysis

This chapter has so far concentrated on explaining the traditional strategic management frameworks employed in the analysis of the competitive environment. The resource based approach to strategic management, which emphasises the importance of core competence in achieving competitive advantage, employs a different approach to analysis of the competitive environment. There are several limitations to existing (traditional) frameworks:

- they do not sufficiently integrate external and internal analysis;
- they presuppose that businesses are naturally competitive and not collaborative in their behaviour;
- they tend to emphasise product and service markets rather than those where organisations obtain their resources;
- they do not adequately recognise the fact that organisations themselves may alter their own competitive environments by their competence leveraging and building activities;
- they do not adequately recognise the fact that organisations currently outside a company's industry and market may pose a significant competitive threat if they

possess similar core competences and distinctive capabilities;

- similarly, they do not recognise that the leveraging of existing competences and the building of new ones may enable businesses to compete outside their current competitive arenas.

The Resource-based Framework

A resource based framework for analysis of the business and its competitive environment is shown in Figure 8.3. Analysis is divided into five interrelated areas:

- the organisation;
- its industry;
- product markets (existing markets, markets for substitutes, potential new markets);
- resource markets;
- other industries.

The significance of each area is considered below.

The Organisation

'The organisation,' concerns the configuration of the internal value chain, its competences, resources and core competences.

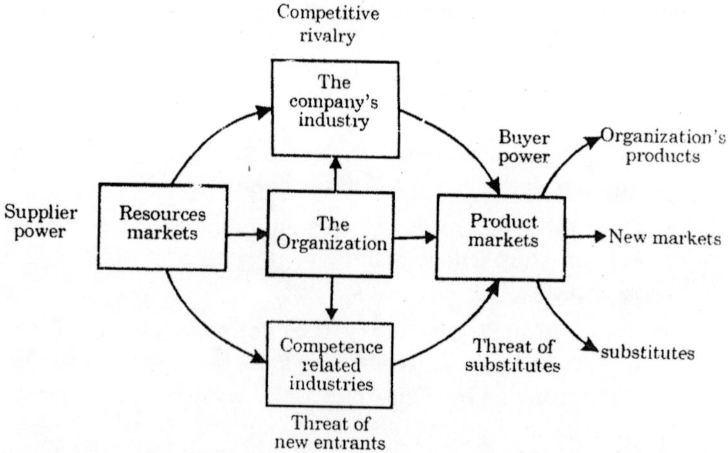

Fig. 8.3 : The resource based model of strategy. (Note: competence related industries are those where businesses possess similar competences to those of competitors).

The Organisation's Industry

The organisation's industry consists of the business and a group of companies producing similar products, employing similar capabilities and technology.

Analysis of the industry therefore examines over time (for each player in the industry):

- the skills and competences of the competitors;
- the configuration of value adding activities;
- the technologies employed;
- the number and relative size of competitors in the industry;
- the performance of competitors (particularly in financial terms);
- ease of entry to and exit from the industry;
- strategic groupings.

This analysis will assist the organisation in gaining greater understanding of its core competences, its major competitors and their core competences, and competitive and collaborative opportunities and threats.

Product Markets

Product markets are those where businesses deploy their competences and sell their products and services. A business may operate in one or more product markets. In addition, a business will be interested in understanding markets to which it is considering entry on the basis of its core competences and also markets for substitute products. Each of these markets will have its own characteristics and each market can be analysed in terms of:

- customer needs and motivations;
- unmet customer needs;
- market segments and their profitability;
- the number of competitors to the market and their relative market shares;
- the number of customers and their relative purchasing power;

- access to distribution channels;
- potential for collaboration with customers;
- ease of entry;
- potential for competence leveraging;
- need for new competence building.

Unless an organisation's products and services are sold at a profit, the business will ultimately fail. Market driven businesses, which set out to meet existing customer needs, anticipate their currently unmet needs and actually seek to shape the needs of their customers are likely to be the most successful.

Market Leading Products – the Ease of Center Parcs

Center Parcs (originally a Dutch company), in developing a new holiday and short break concept for northern European climates, was able to take advantage of the shift away from coastal holidays, the trend towards more activity based holidays and the commercial requirement to lengthen the season. In responding to these factors Center Parcs developed large inland sites with a variety of activities from aromatherapy to orinteering. The activities include swimming in a large enclosed sub-tropical swimming complex and indoor sports such as badminton and squash. The activities can be undertaken in all weather conditions thereby making the destination resort into an all year round attraction. The product proved innovative and attracted both high occupancy rates throughout the season and a number of imitators, such as Oasis (in the UK) which was developed by the Rank Organisation as a me to product and was subsequently taken over by Center Parcs. The high quality and diversity of the facilities and the siting in scenic rural retreats away from the perceived tackiness of the seaside allowed the company to attract largely high spending middle class customers. Such customers are often taking a second holiday in traditionally non-peak periods of the year for northern European climates.

Market Subgroups

An important part of understanding the market is identifying subgroups within the market that share common needs. Such shared characteristics will cause specific customer groups to have different needs and to act and behave differently to other customer groups (or *segments*). Fundamentally, segmentation means subdividing the total market into customer subgroupings, each with their own distinctive attributes and needs. Customer groups are commonly segmented according to demographic variables (or 'people dividers'), like age, sex, occupation, socio-economic grouping, race, life-style, buying habits, geography (i.e. where they live). When customers are other businesses, they can be grouped by the nature of the business, organisation type and by their size. Each segment is then analysed for its size and potential profitability, for customer needs and for potential demand, based on ability and willingness to buy. Segmentation analysis assists in the formulation of strategy by identifying particular segments and consumer characteristics, which can be targeted.

Customer Motivations

Once market segments have been identified, they must be analysed to reveal the factors that influence customers to buy or not buy products. It is particularly important to understand factors affecting customer motivations such as:

- sensitivity to price;
- sensitivity to quality;
- the extent of brand loyalty.

Differences in customer motivations between market segments can be illustrated by reference to the market for air travel. The market can be segmented into business and leisure travel. Customers in each group have very different characteristics and needs. Business travellers are not particularly price-sensitive but are sensitive to standards of service, to scheduling, and to availability of connections. Leisure travellers on the other hand are generally much more price rather than service conscious and are less sensitive to scheduling and connections. Market research has an important role to play in building understanding of customer needs so that they can be targeted by appropriate product or service features.

Potential new markets are those where the product or service bought by custumers is based upon similar competences to those of the organisation or where customer needs are similar to those of customers in the business's market. If conditions are favourable the organisation may consider using its current competences to enter new markets. Of course it may also have to build new competences in order to be able to meet new customer needs.

Resource Markets

Resource markets are those where organisations obtain finance, human resources, materials, equipment, services, etc. It is evident that businesses will normally operate in several such markets, each with its own characteristics, depending upon the company specific resources that are required. Resource markets can be analysed in terms of:

- resource requirements;
- number of actual and potential resource suppliers;
- size of suppliers;
- supplier capabilities and competences;
- potential for collaboration with resource suppliers;
- access by competitors to suppliers;
- the natrue of the resource and the availability of substitutes.

By analysing each of its resource markets, the managers of a business can identify the extent of competition that they face from suppliers of resources, the competition that they face from other competitors using the same resources, and the potential for collaboration with suppliers (if appropriate).

Competence Related Industries

Other industries comprising businesses possessing similar competences and which often produce products which are substitutes for those of the business in question must also be analysed. This analysis is necessary for three reasons. First, the organisation may face a threat from other competitors possessing similar competences, which may seek to enter its industry and markets. Second, the organisation may be able to enter industries where competences are similar to those which it already possesses. Third, the organisation may be able to enter the markets currently served by competitors in the competence related industry.

Competence related industries can be analysed for:

- key competences of the businesses in the industry;
- the number and size of the businesses in the industry;
- the threat from competitors in such industries who may leverage their competences to enter the markets of the business;
- opportunities for the business to leverage its existing competences and build new ones in order to enter competence related industries and their markets;
- substitutability of the products of the industry for those of the business, how close the substitute product is to satisfying the same consumer demands as the business's product or service.

A Summary of the Resource-based Model

The competence/resource-based model is more complex than the five forces framework but offers a more comprehensive analytical framework. It enables an organisation to establish the extent of competition within its own industry and market. It also enables the organisation to asses the threat of competition from competitors in industries where similar competences to their own are employed. Equally, based on this model, the organisation is able to identify other markets, which it may be able to enter by leveraging its existing competences and by adding new ones.

Once adapted the framework enables managers to:

- understand the nature of competition within the industry and markets (both product and resource) in which they operate;
- understand the threat from competitors in other industries;
- understand potential opportunities in new industries and markets.

Strategic Group Analysis

What are Strategic Groups?

A business can rarely confine its analysis to the level of the industry and markets in which it operates. It must also pay particular attention to its closest competitors who are known as its 'strategic group' (Porter, 1980). Strategic groups cannot be precisely defined but they consist of organisations possessing similar competences, serving customer needs in the same market segment and producing products or services of similar quality. Such analysis allows the managers of a business to compare its performance to that of its closed competitors in terms of profitability, market share, products, brands, customer loyalty, prices and so on. In this way managers are able to *benchmark* the performance of their organisation against closest rivals.

In the accommodation industry for example, we can observe a number of important strategic groupings. Although the London Ritz Hotel and a small Blackpool guesthouse both provide the same service (providing accommodation and meals for guests – and hence are technically competitors – they operate in quite different strategic groups. They are unlikely to appeal to the same customers and their products, distribution channels, identities and prices are quite different. The Ritz strategic group will include other luxury hotels in London and key world capitals, whereas the Blackpool guesthouse strategic group will include other Blackpool guesthouses and those at competing resorts.

Strategic group analysis (sometimes called competitive group analysis) is an interesting way of analysing the competitive structure in an industry and assessing the positioning of key competitors. By plotting how the major organisations in an industry (or a sub-sector within it) compete along two competitive dimensions, managers start to understand the relative position of their company and its products or services relative to major competitors.

There are three steps involved in the analysis and graphical representation of strategic groups.

1. Identify the important competitive dimensions in an industry, taking into account the information available. Competitive dimensions are the specific factors the firms are using to compete within the industry. The competitive dimension; might include factors such as quality (perceived or actual), price, geographical scope or typical customer types.
2. Construct two-dimensional plots of the competitive dimensions.

3. Analyse the firm's position relative to competitors.

Competitor Profiling

Strategic group analysis enables an organisation to identify its key competitors. A useful further step is to profile these key competitors in order to gain a more detailed insight as to how and where the competitors might pose a threat or under what circumstances might collaboration be sought. Such an analysis might be carried out using the following headings:

- Overview
- Objectives
- Resources
- Past record of performance
- Current products and services
- Present strategies.

Competitor Profiling – Whitbread plc

A hotel operator seeking to expand in the UK hotel industry would need to profile existing key competitors. One of these would certainly be Whitbread plc which holds the master franchise for Marriott hotels in the UK and has developed the leading brand of 'Lodge' hotels which offer 'value for money' accommodation with few 'add-ons.

Overview – The UK Company Whitbread plc was a major brewer founded in the middle of the nineteenth century. The end of the twentieth century and the start of the twenty-first marked a watershed in the company's history, as Whitbread sold its breweries and then exited its pubs and bars business. After several decades of diversification, during which the beer and pubs giant branched out into new markets, Whitbread re-focused its business on the growth areas of hotels, restaurants and health and fitness clubs. The reinvention of Whitbread as a leading UK leisure business naturally coincided with the end of the brewing and pub-owning tradition which Samuel Whitbread had begun so many decades before.

Objectives – The priorities, on behalf of shareholders, are to grow the business and to achieve annual improvements in the return on their capital. The business is focused on growth sectors of the UK leisure market–lodging, eating out and active leisure.

Resources – The company has a turnover of some £ 3.5 billion a year with profits standing at over £ 300 million. Approximately 60000 people are employed by the company, of which about 20000 are employed by the hotel businesses.

Past record of performance – The company has consistently recorded adequate levels of profitability but in recent years some variability in profits has been apparent. The repositioning of the company to move away from brewing and bars to focus on three core areas in which it possesses strong brands has started to show results. Between 1993 and 2001 Whitbread was Britain's fastest growing hotel company, developing more hotels and more rooms than any other operator and the Whitbread Hotel Company accounts for approximately 59 per cent of the group's profits.

Current products – In the hotel sector the company has a two-pronged assault, based on consistent value for money budget hotels and internationally branded four-star hotels in the fast growing UK hotel market.

Present strategies – The company is trying to achieve its stated objectives through:

- Growing the profitability, scale and market share of the company's leading brands
- Seeking new brands that have the potential to reach significant scale.
- Managing the business so that economic value is added by each of the activities.
- Ensuring that each of the brands is a leader in its field for customer service.
- Becoming the employer of choice in the UK leisure industry.
- Working to meet responsibilities to the wider stakeholders in the business, including commercial partners and the communities in which the company's brands operate.

Adapted from: www.whitbread.co.uk

9

SWOT Analysis

Introduction

SWOT analysis (sometimes referred to as TOWS analysis, particularly in the USA), is an acronym where the letters stand for Strengths, Weaknesses, Opportunities and Threats. The analysis has become a major analytical tool and has become firmly established in the literature. Although it is the most widely used technique for summarising the results of the various types of analysis described in the previous chapter, it nevertheless can be undertaken in various ways. Consequently, different approaches are advocated in the many texts which cover this analytical technique, but here a structured and logical approach is suggested. The chapter first covers the general principles of SWOT analysis before going on to consider how the analysis should be carried out.

After studying this chapter, students should be able to:

- explain what is meant by SWOT analysis;
- understand the relationship between the SWOT presentation and detailed internal and external analyses;
- describe how a SWOT should be constructed;
- consider the way in which points can be presented in a SWOT;
- apply the SWOT analysis principles to travel and tourism organisations;

- understand the relationship between the SWOT analysis and strategic formulation.

General Principles

Some Basics

The strengths and weaknesses are based on the internal analysis of an organisation and the opportunities and threats are based on analysis of the environment that is external to the organisation. The key distinguishing characteristic between the strengths and weaknesses on the one hand and the opportunities and threats on the other is the degree of control that managers may have. With the internal strengths and weaknesses managers can exert control whereas with regard to the opportunities and threats, managers may not be able to control such factors. If, for instance, the organisation has a strong balance sheet (a strength) this will have resulted from managerial decisions. If, instead, the organisation is seen as being overstaffed (a weakness), managers can address the issue through reducing staff numbers. However, by way of example, changing government policies, product changes by competitors or a war breaking out (all of which might produce opportunities or threats to an individual organisation depending on the circumstances are beyond the control of managers.

SWOT

SWOT is the key technique for presenting the results of strategic analysis, which provides a platform for going on to formulate the strategy for the future. The strengths and weaknesses should be based upon the internal analysis of the organisation whilst the opportunities and threats should be based upon an analysis of the organisation's external environment.

Although it is very common in practice to begin the process of formulating strategy by asking the participants in a rather informal way to draw up a SWOT for their organisation, such a process represents a limited use of the technique. It is, however, useful for getting the participants to become quickly and fully engaged in the process of strategy formulation (Finlay, 2000). It can also help identify the wide range of factors that might warrant further more detailed investigation. The final SWOT presented should however be based on a thorough, wide-ranging and detailed audit and assessment of an organisation and its environment so that points presented fire evidence based and thus can be fully justified. Thus the SWOT should be seen primarily as representing the end point of the analysis (rather than the starting point) in which findings can be presented in a clear, concise manner.

The SWOT represents a *position statement,* stating where the organisation is at the time of the analysis in relation to its environment. It is not the strategy itself and should not involve making statements about what should be done next. Instead it provides a firm platform for planning for the future of the organisation, i.e. formulating the strategy which is the next stage in the strategic process.

SWOT implementation

	Factors which help the organisation achieve its objectives	Factors which prevent the organisation achieving its objectives
Internal factors under the control of managers	Strength	Weakness
External factors outside the control of managers	Opportunity	Threat

Fig. 9.1 : The logic of SWOT analysis (adapted from Wickham, 2000).

How it is Constructed

The SWOT is often presented in a Table. Fig. 9.1 shows a SWOT and its underlying logic.

The SWOT should have a strategic focus in that it concentrates on those factors which have:

- A major impact on past performance.
- A major impact on future performance.
- Distinguish the organisation from its competitors.

In presenting the SWOT table, a number of rules should be followed.

- Too much detail should be avoided so that the key points can be clearly seen. Each point should be kept short and to the point, so that an overview can quickly be gained. The detailed justifications for the points presented in the table should be presented separately.
- Many of the points presented in the SWOT may be relative rather than absolute and consequently a matter of some judgement. Thus it is difficult to say at exactly what level a high level of financial gearing becomes a weakness or a share of a particular market becomes a strength.
- The SWOT should not concentrate solely on 'hard' facts (such as financial measures or market growth statistics) that can be measured or proved. Softer factors such as organisational culture or the leadership skills exhibited by managers may be more difficult to measure but they are nevertheless important for organisational performance.
- The analysis should prioritise and combine points. The most important points should be shown first and points that are not key or strategic in nature should be excluded. In some cases it may be necessary to combine smaller points to make one large overarching point. For example, if a SWOT is partly based on a financial analysis of an organisation which indicates a strong financial position, the SWOT should not have individual points on high level of profitability, low gearing, adequate liquidity, etc. for to do so would confuse the presentation. The point presented

in the SWOT should be that the organisation has a strong financial position. The justification for making such a point would be provided by the assessments relating to profitability, gearing liquidity and so on.

- The presentation should be specific avoiding blandness and be realistic in its assessment.

Typical Contents

In his analysis of the problems of presenting a valid SWOT, Lynch (2000) stated that 'probably the biggest mistake that is commonly made in SWOT analysis is to assume the analysis is bound to be "correct" if it contains every conceivable issue and is truly comprehensive'. This is not the case: 'it merely demonstrates a paucity of real thought and a lack of strategic judgement about what, is really important for the organisation' have been employed in its preparation.

'Another common error is to provide a long list of points but little logic; argument and evidence. A short list with each point

Internal

Strengths	*Weaknesses*
• Market dominance • Core strengths • Economies of scale • Low-cost position • Leadership and management skills • Financial and cash resources • Operational ability find age of equipment • Innovation processes and results • Organisational structure • Reputation • Differentiated products • Good balance of products • Product or service quality	• Share weakness • Few core strengths and low on key skills • Old oquipment with higher costs than competition • Weak finances and poor cash flow • Management skills and leadership lacking • Poor organisational structure • Low quality and reputation • Products not differentiated • Dependent on few products • Products concentrated in mature or declining PLC Stages • Low market share

External	
Opportunities	*Threats*
• New markets and segments	• New market entrants
• New products	• Increased competition
• Diversification opportunities	• Increased pressure from customers, and suppliers
• Market growth	• Substitutes
• Competitor weaknesses	• Low market growth
• Strategic space	• Economic cycle downturn
• Demographic and social change	• Technological threat
• Change in political and economic environment	• Change in political or economic environment
• New take-over or partrnership opportunities	• Demographic change
• Economic upturm	• New international barriers to trade
• International growth	• Environmental impacts of activity
	• New destinations

Fig. 9.2: Some possible factors in a SWOT analysis (adapted from Lunch, 2000).

Internal	
Strengths	*Weaknesses*
• Airports used are more convenient than those used by other no-frills airlines	• Airports used have poorer facilities and are less convenient than those used by big carriers
• Management flexibllity	• Poor reputation for punctuality
• Lower costs than established airlines	• Cash flows
• Ease of booking flights	• No long-term safety record
• Recognised logo and corporate image	• Poorer than avarage customor service
• Use of IT facilities	
• Better than average employee relations	

External	
Opportunities	*Threats*
• Strong business demand for cheap air fares • Strong leisure demand for cheap air fares • Increasing use of the Internet • Many secondary airports underused	• The further entry of subsidiaries of the big carriers • Existing carriers changing to 'no-frills' mode of operations • Higher airport charges • Increasing competition from charter carriers

well argued is more likely to be convincing (Lynch, 2000). In order to keep the SWOT focused it is suggested that a maximum of seven points should be presented under each of the SWOT headings. However, it might be the case that in some circumstances the overriding importance of certain points mean that far fewer than six points are presented.

In Figure 9.2 a number of issues are presented for possible inclusion in a SWOT presentation. It should be noted that this list is indicative since the issues will vary enormously depending upon individual circumstances.

In presenting an example of implementing a SWOT, Finlay (2000) applied the concept to a fictitious 'no frills' airline, which has newly entered the airline market. The example is shown in Figure 9.3.

Conclusion

Although it has been supplemented by more recent techniques, SWOT is a tool that is widely used and understood by students and managers. It should represent a solid foundation for moving on to strategic formulation but care has to be taken in implementing the SWOT so as to ensure it is not bland, and is fully supported by the evidence that is available. Crucially, as Haberberg and Rieple (2001) point out in their comprehensive treatment of the subject area, the SWOT analysis should not be viewed as the start of the analysis. Instead, 'in order to arrive at a proper SWOT appraisal, other analyses need to be carried out first'.

10

Strategy and Direction for Travel and Tourism

This chapter is concerned with two aspects of strategic formulation:

- The bases of competition – *competitive strategy*
- The direction of development – *strategic direction.*

An important point is that the focus of strategy at this level not upon the entire organisation (as in corporate level strategy) but upon breaking the entire organisation down into its constituent parts, i.e. its strategic business units (SBUs). The concerns at this level of strategy include:

- How can advantage over competitors be achieved?
- Which products or services should be developed in which markets?

The study of strategic management offers several explanations of how competitive advantage can be achieved and sustained. This chapter focuses on two of the major explanations of competitive advantage: competitive positioning and core competence.

The *competitive positioning* approach is based largely upon Porter's generic strategy framework (Porter, 1980, 1985). The *core competence* or *resource-based* approach explains competitive advantage in terms of the (development and exploitation of an organisation's core competences. These two approaches can be seen as complementary and mutually enriching rather than mutually exclusive. The two frameworks are first explored separately and then the linkages between them are developed.

The chapter ends with a discussion of the general mechanisms that organisations employ to grow and develop in order to sustain and develop their competitive advantage strategic directions. We use the Ansoff matrix as a starting point for this discussion:

After studying this chapter, students should be able to:

- explain the concept of competitive advantage;
- describe and evaluate Porter's generic strategy framework;
- describe and evaluate the strategy clock and Poon's tourism competitive strategy concepts;
- explain the concept of hybrid strategy;
- explain the role of core competences and distinctive capabilities in building competitive advantage;
- explain the role of the value chain in linking core competences and generic strategies.
- identify the strategic direction available to organisations;
- identify where core competences and strategies can be exploited;
- provide illustrative examples from travel and tourism of competitive strategy and strategic directions.

Competitive Strategy

Competitive strategy is concerned with the bases on which a strategic business unit might achieve competitive advantage in its chosen market or markets. For public service or publicly funded organisations such as tourist offices, museums and art galleries or historic monuments, the concern is with an equivalent issue. Here the concern can be expressed in terms of the bases on which the organisation chooses to sustain the quality of its services within agreed budgets or, as it is often expressed; how it provides 'best value.'

Michael Porter's Generic Strategies

Introduction

Perhaps the oldest and best-known explanation of competitive advantage is given by Porter in his *generic strategy* framework. Although this framework has been increasingly called into question in recent years, it still provides useful insight into competitive behaviour. The framework and its limitations are considered in this section. Perhaps its main use is that it provides a framework that forces managers to think about the underlying basis upon which they are attempting to compete.

According to Porter (1985), competitive advantage arises from selection of the generic strategy which best fits the organisation's competitive environment and then organising value adding activities to support the chosen strategy. There are three main alternatives.

- *differentiation* – creating a customer perception that a product is superior to those of competitors so that a premium price can be charged;
- *cost leadership* – being the lowest cost producer of a product so that above-average profits are earned even though the price charged is not above average.
- *focus* – utilising either a differentiation or cost leadership strategy in a narrow profile of market segments (possibly just one segment).

Any organisation that fail to make a strategic decision to opt for one of these strategic stances is in danger of being 'stuck in the middle' (to use Porter's terminology). In other words, the organisation in failing to decide, tries both to be the cost leader and the differentiator and achieves neither, and in the process confuses consumers.

Porter's Generic Strategy Framework

Porter argues that an organisation must make two key decisions on its strategy:

- Should the strategy be one of differentiation or cost leadership?
- Should the scope of the strategy be broad or narrow?

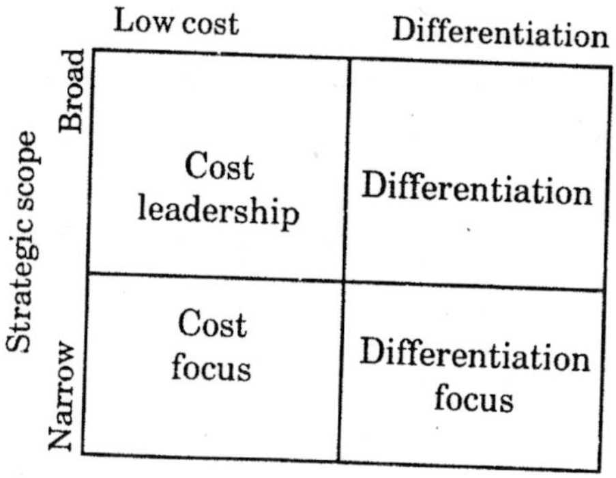

Fig. 10.1 : The generic strategy framework (adapted from Porter, 1985).

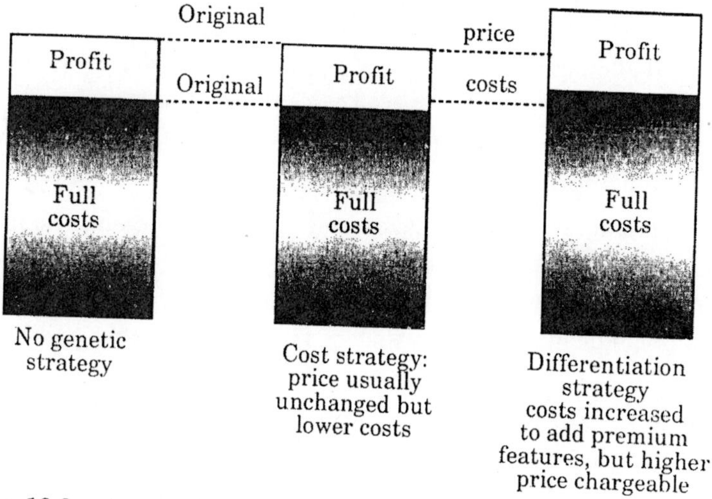

Fig. 10.2 : A simplified understanding of cost and differentiation strategies. (Note that price = full costs plus profits).

In other words, the organisation must decide whether to try to differentiate its products and sell them at a premium price or whether to gain competitive advantage by producing at a lower cost than its competitors. Higher profits can be made by adopting either approach. Second, it must decide whether to target the whole market with its chosen strategy or whether to target a specific segment or niche of the market.

Cost Leadership Strategy

A cost leadership strategy is based upon a business, organising and managing its value adding activities so as to be the lowest cost producer of a product (a good or service) within an industry.

There are several potential benefits of a cost leadership strategy:

- The business can earn higher profits by charging a price equal to, or even below that of competitors because its costs are lower.
- It allows the business the possibility to increase both sales and market share by reducing price below that charged by competitors (assuming that the product's demand is price elastic in nature).
- It allows the business the possibility to enter a new market by charging a lower price than competitors.
- It can be particularly valuable in a market where consumers are price sensitive.
- It creates an additional barrier to entry for organisations wishing to enter the industry.

Value chain analysis is central to identifying where cost savings can be made at various stages in the value chain and its internal and external linkages.

A successful cost leadership strategy is likely to rest upon a number of organisational features. Attainment of a position of cost leadership depends upon the arrangement of value chain activities. Examples of how costs savings might be achieved include the following.

- Reducing costs by copying rather than originating product design features. For example, a tour operator might copy the design and functions of an existing web site developed by a competitor.
- Using less expensive resource inputs. For example, easyJet, the 'no frills' airline, lowers costs by substituting operational resources in the form of computer technology

for more expensive labour inputs by using the Internet as its primary source of bookings.

- Producing products with 'no frills', thus reducing labour costs and increasing labour productivity. For example the low cost so-called no frills airlines such as Southwest Airlines in the United States and Ryanair, easyJet, Go and Buzz in the UK have removed additional product features thus leading to reduced staffing and other costs.
- Achieving economies of scale by high volume sales perhaps based on advertising and promotion, allowing high fixed costs of investment in modern technology to be spread over a high volume of output. For example, LastMinute.com promoted their late booking website heavily in the early stages, allowing it to raise investment capital and achieve market leadership in its area of operations which has allowed the company to invest heavily on developing its Internet technology.
- Using high volume purchasing to obtain discounts for bulk buying of resource inputs such as accommodation or transportation requirements. For example Tui has grown to a pre-eminent position in European tour operations allowing it to demand lower prices for resource inputs than might be available to smaller competitors.
- Locating activities in areas where costs are low or government help, such as grant support, is available. For example, British Airways has located call centres at peripheral locations in the UK such as Newcastle and Glasgow where abundant fairly cheap labour is available and where government aid in the form of tax savings is available for incoming investors.
- Obtaining 'experience curve' economies. For example, the operator of an established theme park may be able to operate the park with lower costs than a new entrant since they might have experience of staff scheduling, minimising power costs, purchasing new rides, waste disposal, etc.

- Standardising products or resource inputs. For example, Holiday Inn is able to franchise its concept internationally to franchisers because it is fairly standardised throughout the world. Southwest Airlines is able to achieve economies in maintenance, purchasing and crew training because it operates only one aircraft type (albeit in various versions), the Boeing 737.

Cost Leadership at Southwest Airlines and EasyJet

(A) The Southwest Airlines low cost, no frills model of cost leadership

Product Features	
Fares	Low Simple, unrestricted Point-to-point services No interlining
Distribution	Direct sales and travel agents Ticketless
In-flight	Single class, high density No set assignment No meals Snacks and light beverages only
Frequency	High
Punctuality	Very good
Opetating features	
Aircraft	Single type (Boeing 737), four variants High utilisation (over 11 hours/day)
Sectors	Short to aveage – below 800km (500 miles)
Airports	Secondary or uncongested 15 – 20 minute turnarounds
Growth	Target 10% per annum Maximum 15% per annum
Staff	Competitive wages Profit-sharing since 1973 High productivity

Sources : Adapted from Doganis (2001)

(B) Cost comparison of low cost easyJet and conventional short haul airline British Midland in 1998.

Cost category	*easyJet (pence per seat-km)*	*bmi British Midland (pence per seat-km)*
Direct opeating costs		
Cabin/flight crew salaries	0.43	0.92
Fuel	0.35	0.55
Airport charges	0.55	1.20
Maintenance	0.39	0.41
Depreciation	0.58	0.75
En-route	0.02	0.26
Aircraft rentals	0.80	1.23
Insurance		0.02
TOTAL DIRECT	3.14	5.34
Indirect operating costs		
Station costs	0.01	1.86
Handling	0.31	0.40
Passenger services	0.04	0.63
Sales reservations	0.18	0.47
Commission	0.01	0.78
Advertising promotion	0.27	0.31
General and administration	0.17	0.44]
Other	0.06	0.14
Total Indirect	1.05	4.52
Total Operating Costs	4.19	9.86
Other operating comparisons	easyJet	British Midland
Average aircraft size	122 seats	148 seats
Passenger load factor	76.1%	69.2%
Fleet comparison	4 Airbus 321 7 Boing 737–300 5 Boing 737–400 12 Boing 737–500 6 Fokker 100 3 Fokker 70	9 Boeing 737-300

Source: Adapted from Doganis (2001) based on Civil Aviation Authority data and company annual reports.

A cost leadership strategy coupled to low price is best employed in a market or segment where demand is price elastic.

Under such circumstances sales and market share are likely to increase significantly thus increasing economies of scale, reducing unit costs further, so generating above average profits.

Price Elasticity of Demand

Economists use the term *price elasticity* to describe the extent to which the volume of demand for a product is dependent upon its price. The coefficient to elasticity is expressed in a simple equation.

$$\text{Ep} = \frac{\text{Percentage change in quantity}}{\text{Percentage change in price}}$$

The value of Ep (price elasticity) tells us the price responsiveness of the product's demand. If, for any given price change, Ep is more than –1, it means that the change in price has brought about a higher proportionate change in volume sold. This relationship between price change and quantity is referred to as price elastic demand.

Demand is said to be price inelastic if the quantity change is proportionately smaller than the change in price (resulting in an Ep of less than –1). The larger the value of Ep, the more price elastic the demand and conversely, the nearer Ep is to 0, the more price inelastic the demand.

The price elasticity of demand (the value of Ep) is dependent upon the nature of the market's perception of a product. Products tend to be price elastic if the market sees a product as unnecessary but desirable. Products will have price inelastic demand if the customer perceives a *need* for a product rather than a *want* (such as the demand for most medicines, tobacco, etc.)

Alternatively, if a price similar to that of competitors is charged accompanied by advertising to boost sales, similar results will be obtained.

Differentiation Strategy

A differentiation strategy is based upon persuading customers that a product is superior in some way to that offered by competitors. Differentiation can be based on premium product features or simply upon creating consumer perceptions that a product is superior. The major benefits to a business of a successful differentiation strategy are:

- Its products will command a premium price.
- Demand for its product will be less price elastic than demand for competitors' products.
- Above average profits can be earned.
- It creats an additional barrier to entry to new businesses wishing to enter the industry.

A business seeking to differentiate itself will organise its value chain activities to help create differentiated products and to create a perception among customers that these offering are worth a higher price.

Differentiation can be achieved in several ways:

- by creating products that are superior to competitors' by virtue of design, technology, performance etc. For example, only two airlines, Air France and British Airways, are able to offer flights which cross the Atlantic in under four hours since they are the only airlines featuring Concorde supersonic aircraft in their fleets,
- by offering a superior level of service. For example, an upscale hotel chain such as Mandarin – Oriental (which operates largely in Southweast Asia) differentiates by offering a very high level of service, which is achieved by having a high ration of staff to guests,
- by having access to superior distribution channels. For example, a multiple chain of travel agents which has been established for some time may have been able to develop network of branches in prime retail locations (especially important in the retail sector) which it would take a newcomer some time and expense to accumulate,
- by creating a strong brand name through design, innovation, advertising, frequent flyer programmes and so on. For example, the development by American Airlines of the world's largest frequent flyer programme (American Advantage) creates a loyalty for its brand among passengers.
- by distinctive or superior product promotion. For example, the 'I ♥ New York', 'Glasgow's Miles Better' and British Airways' 'The Worlds Favourite Airline' were successful examples of promotion which highlighted the distinctive

features of the respective products or destinations concerned.

A differentiation strategy is likely to necessitate emphasis on innovation, design, research and development, awareness of particular customer needs and marketing. To say that differentiation is in the eyes of the customer is no exaggeration. It could be argued that it is often brand name or logo which distinguishes a product rather than real product superiority. For example, prices of holidays at fashionable St Tropez in the south of France, or Marbella on Spain's Costa del Sol command prices well above those of similar local resorts because their 'brand' status is superior.

A differentiation strategy is employed in order to reduce price elasticity of demand for the product so that its price can be raised above that of competitors without reducing sales volume, so generating above-average profits.

Differentiation at Hyatt Regency Hotels

Hyatt Corporation, based in Chicago, opened its first hotel in 1957. The hotel management company now manages over 200 hotels in the USA and in many other countries. The company's core brand, Hyatt Regency, operates in the crowded deluxe category of international hotels vying for custom with others in this category such as Ritz-Carlton, Shangri-La and Regent International Hotels. It was in 1967 that Hyatt first received significant international attention when it opened the world's first 'atrium' hotel. The Hyatt Regency in Atlanta featured a 21-storey atrium lobby tower, which was a significant and dramatic departure from traditional hotel architecture. The challenge for hotel architects was no longer to eliminate extra space but instead to create grand, wide-open public spaces. The atrium idea (which has often been copied subsequently) has been taken on by other Hyatt Regency Hotels ranging from Kota Kinabalu (Sabalh, Malaysia) to Chicago O'Hare Airport and San Francisco. Although not all Hyatt Regency hotels now feature atriums in their design, the hotel chain retains a reputation for creative and innovative architectural design. Thus in this case design acts as a means of differentiating the product from those of competing product offerings in a crowded sector of the market.

Source: Adapted from www.Hyatt.com

Focus Strategy

A focus strategy is aimed at segment of the market for a product rather than at the whole market. A particular group of customers is identified on the basis of age, income, lifestyle, sex, geography, other distinguishing demographic characteristics or on the benefits sought from travel and tourism products. Within the segment a business employs either a cost leadership or a differentiation strategy.

The major benefits of a focus strategy are:

- It requires a lower investment in resources compared to a strategy aimed at an entire market.
- It allows specialisation and greater knowledge of the segment being served.
- It makes entry to a new market less costly and simpler.

A focus strategy will require :

- identification of a suitable target customer group which forms a distinct market segment;
- identification of the specific needs of that group;
- establishing that the segment is sufficiently large to sustain the business;
- establishing the extent of competition within the segment;
- production of products to meet the specific needs of that group;
- deciding whether to operate a differentiation or cost leadership strategy within the market segment.

Focus strategies can be developed in travel and tourism in a range of different circumstances by:

- focusing on a particular group of buyers. Contiki, for example, markets its coatch-based holidays to customers in many parts of the world. The company founded by a New Zealander as a safe and secure means for Australians and New Zealanders to see Europe now offers tours (which combine activities and sightseeing) in North America, Australia, New Zealand and Europe targeted at the 18 – 35 age groups,
- specialising in particular geographic destinations. For example, Sunvil Holidays, a small specialist. UK-based tour operator, was founded, and is still owned by an entrepreneur from a Greek Cypriot background. Although

it has now diversified into other areas, the company is able to compete with larger rivals in the market for holidays to Cyprus by utilising in-depth knowledge of the destination and a network of contacts,

- catering for the benefits sought by a particular group of buyers. For example, PGI Adventure Holidays in the UK provide holidays for children offering a large range of organised activities at an all-inclusive price.
- resort destinations targeting particular market segments. La Manga in Spain has, for example, successfully targeted sports enthusiasts particularly golfers.

Many organisations use a focus strategy to enter a market before broadening their activities into other related segments.

Table 10.1 provides a summary of the key features of generic competitive strategies.

Criticisms of Porter's Generic Strategy Framework

A Critical Evaluation of the Framework

In recent years Porter's generic strategy framework has been the target of increasing criticism (see for example Cronshaw *et al., 1990;* Mintzberg, 1991; Baden-Fuller and Stopford, 1992; Miller, 1992; Johnson and Scholes, 2002; and in a travel and tourism context, Poon, 1993). At least six objections to Porter's model have been advanced.

A Business can Apparently Employ a Successful 'Hybrid' Strategy Without Being 'Stuck in the Middle'

Porter argued that a business must choose between a differentiation and cost leadership strategy. To be 'struck in the middle' between the two, he argued, will result in sub-optimal performance. There is evidence to suggest, however, that some companies with lower than industry-average costs can nevertheless sell their products on the basis of differentiation. That is, they employ a combined or 'hybrid' strategy. The effects of innovations or economies of scale may allow a successful hybrid strategy to be employed. An airline flying a new fuel-efficient aircraft type for example may achieve the benefits of cost leadership and differeatiation simultaneously. A successful hybrid strategy will be based upon a conscious decision by senior mangers to combine differentiation with price and cost control. Under such circumstances a business can be successful. When a business slips into the situation unconsicously it can still be regarded as being 'stuck in the middle' but is less likely to be successful.

Are Low Cost Airlines Really Pursuing Cost Leadership Competitive Strategies?

It could be argued that none of Porter's categories should be regarded as alternatives and that in reality to categorise competitive strategy in this way is simplistic and possibly misleading.

In the case of the low cost European airlines, for example, they clearly need to control their costs strictly and be *cost leaders* (in order to offer the lowest priced products). However, they also choose to *focus* on highly price sensitive customer groups whilst *differentiating* their products by providing a limited range of added service benefits. Additional cost savings are becoming more difficult to achieve. As easyJet chairman Stelios Haji-loannou has stated 'there are only so many frills you can cut' (Doran, 2002). The airline is now considering the purchase Airbus aircraft alongside its existing Boeing fleet. The easyJet chairman remarks that 'it is time we look at contestable markets to reduce our costs. This has never been done [by a low cost carrier] with the purchase of aircraft' (Doran, 2000).

Cost Leadership does not, in and of itself, Sell Products

Buying decisions are made upon the basis of desirable product features or upon the price, not on the basis of the unit cost itself, which may not be known by consumers.

Differentiation, Strategies can be Used to Increase Sales Volumes Rather than to Charge a Premium Price

Porter's work does not consider the possibility that a business employing a differentiation strategy might choose not to charge a premium price, but rather to increase sales and market share by foregoing the premium price for an introductory period. This criticism, however, does not fundamentally undermine Porter's thinking.

Price can Sometimes be Used to Differentiate

Porter does not consider the possibility that price may be used to differentiate a product. Mintzberg (1991) argues that price, alongwith image, support, quality and design, can be used as the basis of differentiation.

Table 10.1
Key Features of Generic Competitive Stragegies

	Differentiation	*Cost leadership*	*Focus*
Aim	Ability to charge a premium price	To be lowest cost supplier	Either to charge a premium price or to be lowest cost supplier in particular segments of the market
How?	Superior product/service Advertising and promotion Branding Distribution channels Different locations Customer care Technology Licences/regulation	High volume sales Economies of scale New technology High productivity Low cost inputs Low distribution costs Low location costs	As for differentiation or cost leadership applied to particular segments
Strategy entails	Changed perception Higher price than rivals Quality Innovation	Price equal to or below rivals Acceptable quality Advertising to sell high volume	Identifying market segments and consumer needs Choose differentiation or cost leadership strategy for a segment or niche
When to use	Price insensitive Established position in the market	Price sensitive market Market entry	For firms not large enough to target whole market Firms possessing specialist skills

A 'Generic' Strategy cannot give Competitive Advantage

It is evident that in order to outperform competitors a business must do things better than and differently to them. The word 'generic' could be construed to imply that Porter is arguing that there are general recipes by which competitive advantage can be achieved. This, however, is not the case. Porter's framework is merely a framework by which competitive strategies can be grouped to assist in understanding and analysis.

The Resource/Competence Based Strategy has Arguably Superseded the Generic Strategy Framework

The resource based approach argues that it is the core competences of the individual business which give it competitive advantage and not generic strategies. In fact the two approaches do not preclude each other. The relationships between the two approaches are discussed in a later section of this chapter.

Despite these criticisms, Porter's work can, in modified form, constitute the basis of a useful framework for categorising and understanding sources of competitive advantage. On such approach is the 'strategy clock' framework developed by Bowman in 1995 and reported by Haberberg and Rieple (2001), and Johnson and Scholes (2002).

Other Competitive Strategy Frameworks

The Strategy Clock Framework

The strategy clock framework develops and adds to Porter's original model, and consequently some aspects are open to similar criticisms. However, it is a more sophisticated approach, which recognises and deals with some of the criticisms of Porter and in particular recognises that in certain circumstances a 'hybrid' combined strategy can be successful. The model is shown in Figure 10.3, with brief explanations of the categories used.

In concluding this section, it is possible to say that the extent of differentiation, price and cost control will depend upon the nature of the market in which the business is operating. In markets where consumers show a preference for quality then the emphasis be less on price and costs whilst in markets where demand is price sensitive the emphasis will be on keeping both price and costs as low as possible. Of course, organisations may also seek to shape customer attitudes by advertising and

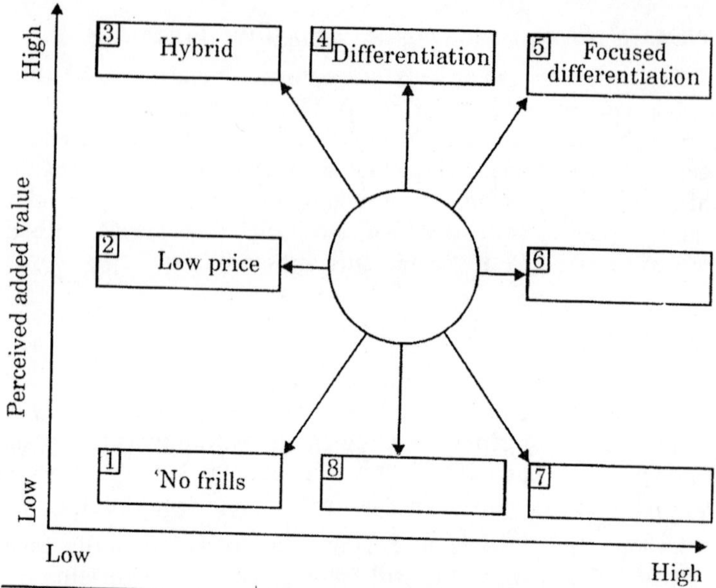

Segment	Needs/risks
1. No frills	Likely to be segment specific
2. Low price	Risk for price war and low margins; need to be cost leader
3. Hybrid	Low cost base and reinvestment in low price and differentiation
4. Differentiation	
(a) Without price primium	Perceived added value by user, yielding market share benefits
(b) With price primium	Perceived added value sufficient to bear price premium
5. Focused differentiation	Perceived added value to particular segment, warranting price premium
6. Increased price/ standard value	Higher margins if competitors do not follow; risk of losing market share
7. Increased price/low value	Only feasible in monopoly position
8. Low value/standard price	Loss of market share

Note: Strategies 6, 7 and 8 are strategies doestined for ultimate failure.

Source: Adapted from Faulkner and Bowman, 1995.

Fig. 10.3 : The strategy clock.

promotion so as to modify market conditions.

Competitive Strategies for Travel and Tourism – Poon's Framework

The approaches to competitive strategy outlined in this charter up to this point have not been developed in a travel and tourism context specifically, although the approaches can be applied to the industry. Poon (1993), conscious of the limitations and criticisms levelled at the approach of Porter, developed a rather different approach, which, she argued, takes into account the realities of the industry. The key realities identified by Poon were:

1. The service orientation of the industry and its need to focus on the quality of service delivery which in turn is inextricably linked with the development of human resources.
2. The increasing sophistication of travel and leisure consumers.
3. The industry-wide diffusion of informalion technology.
4. The radical transformation of the industry, which requires continuous innovation to ensure competitive success, is achieved.

In order successfully to respond to these industry realities Poon postulates that travel and tourism organisations need to apply four principles in developing their competitive strategies:

- Put customers first.
- Be a leader in quality.
- Develop radical innovations.
- Strengthen the organisation's strategic position within the industry's value chain.

The principles of competitive success in travel and tourism (according to Poon) are outlined in Fig. 10.4

Competence Based Competitive Advantage

The generic strategy model is not the only one that seeks to provide an explanation of the sources of competitive advantage. The *competence* or *resource based model* emphasises that

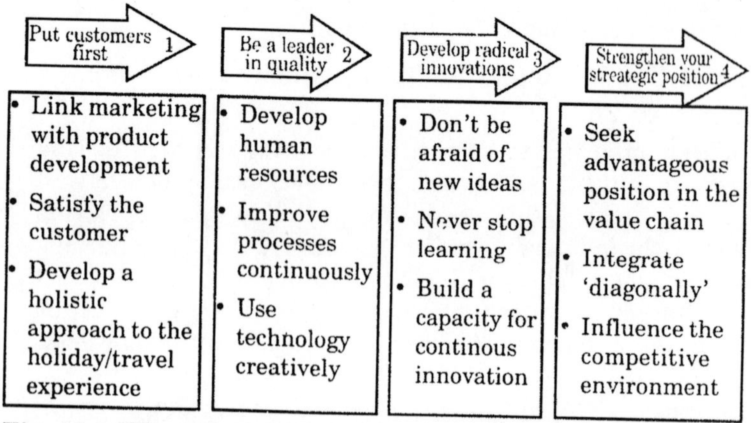

Fig. 10.4 : The principles of competitive success in travel and tourism. *Note*: Diagonal integration – a process whereby firms use information technologies logically to combine services for bst productivity (adapted from Poon, 1993).

competitive edge stems from attributes of an organisation known as *competent* or *capabilities,* which distinguishes it from its competitors allowing it to outperform them.

Core Competence and Distinctive Capabilities

This chapter builds upon the analysis to explore the ways in which existing competences can be extended and new ones cultivated. It goes on to examine how and where these core competences can be exploited so as to acquire and prolong competitive advantage. Much of the recent attention to the concept of core competence is based upon the work of Prahalad and Hamel (1990), Stalk, Evans and Shulmann (1992), who advocated the idea of competing on the basis of capabilities, and Kay (1993), who advances the idea that competitive advantage is based upon distinctive capability.

Core Competences

Perhaps the best known explanation of core competence is that provided by Prahalad and Hamel (1990):

> Core competences are the collective learning of the organisation, especially how to co-ordinate diverse production skills and integrate multiple streams of technologies.

Prahalad and Hamel specified three tests to be applied in the identification and development of core competence. A core competence should:

- equip a business with the ability to enter and successfully compete in several markets;
- add greater perceived customer value to the business's products and services than that perceived in competitor's products;
- be difficult for competitors to imitate.

According to Prahalad and Hamel (1990), there are many examples of core competence, resulting in competitive advantage. They argued that competitive advantage is likely in practice to be based upon no more than five or six competences. These competences will allow management to produce new and manticipated products, and to be responsive to changing opportunities because of operational skills and the harnessing of technology. Given the turbulent business environment in many sectors of travel and tourism, such adaptability is essential if competitive advantage is to be built and sustained.

Application of Core Competences at Novotel

Founded by two French entrepreneurs in 1967 the, Novotel chain of hotels (now a part of Accor, one of the world's leading hospitality groups) expanded steadily during the 1960s and 1970s. The expansion first in France, then in the rest of Europe followed by other parts of the world owed much to the exploitation of a core competence in reliability. The company developed a standard format for hotel room designs, for furnishing and for standards of service allowing a uniform standard of service to be delivered (particularly to business customers) throughout the group. The reliability core competence was underpinned by a competence in control that enabled the company to ensure that standards were maintained.

In 1987 Novotel went a step further in developing a rigid set of rules and procedures, the '95 Bolts' that specified every aspect of the operation of the hotels in minute detail. Even the personal greeting to guests was standardised. The strategy was not a success as the new systems made it difficult for staff to show personal warmth or to act spontaneously in meeting customer requirements and managers were unable to vary prices in order to match those of local competitors. The core competence (control) had been turned into a core rigidity and in 1992 a new strategy was developed. The new strategy gave hotel general managers greater autonomy whilst supporting them through new systems which enabled them to learn from one another and to share best practices.

Source : Adapted from Haberberg and Rieple (2001)

Distinctive Capabilities

Kay (1993) took the concept of capability, initially identified by Stalk, Evans and Shulmann (1992), to develop a framework which explains competitive advantage in terms of what he defines as *distinctive capability*. This idea of distinctive capability has much in common with that of core competence in that it views competitive advantage as being dependent upon unique attributes of a particular business and its products.

According to Kay (1993), distinctive capability results from one or more of the following sources.

- *Architecture* – the unique network of internal and external relationships of an organisation which produces superior performance. These can be unique relationships with suppliers, distributors or customers which competitors do not possess. Equally, the unique relationships may be internal to the business and based upon the way that it organises its activities in the value chain.
- *Reputation* – this stems from several sources including superior product quality, characteristics, design, service and so on.
- *Innovation* – the ability of the business to get ahead and stay ahead of competitors depends upon its success in researching, designing, developing and marketing new products. Equally it depends upon the ability of the business to improve the design and organisation of its value adding activities.
- *Strategic assets* – businesses can also obtain competitive advantage from assets like natural monopoly, patents and copyrights which restrict competition.

Core Competence, Distinctive Capability and Competitive Advantage

So what do the concepts of core competence and distinctive capability add to our understanding of competitive advantage?

1. They provide us with insight into how an organisation can build attributes which can deliver superior performance.
2. They inform the process of determining where such competence and capabilities can be exploited.
3. A core competence becomes competitive advantage when it is applied in a particular market or markets.

The process of building new core competences or extending existing ones must take into account the following considerations:

- *Customer perceptions* – competences, capabilities and products must be pereceived by customers as being better value for money that those of competitors. The organisation's reputation (although difficult to measure) can be particularly important in this regard.
- *Uniquences* – core competences must be unique to the organisation and must be difficult for competitors to emulate. Similarly there must be no close substitutes for these competences.
- *Continuous improvement* – core competences, products and services must be continuously upgraded to stay ahead of competitors. Product and process innovation are particularly important.
- *Collaboration* – competitive advantage can result from the organisation's unique network of relationships with suppliers, distributors, customers and even competitors. There is the potential for 'multiplier effects' resulting from separate organisations' complementary core competences being combined together.
- *Organisational knowledge* – competences must be based upon organisational knowledge and learning. Managers must improve the processes by which the organisation learns, builds and manages its knowledge. Knowledge is, today, potentially the greatest source of added value.

Sustainable Competitive Advantage

It is a worthy cause for travel and tourism organisations to strive to achieve a competitive advantage. However, if the position cannot be maintained over a period of time then it may not be worth the effort and investment that are necessary to achieve such a position in the first place. Sustainable competitive advantage will have been achieved 'when an organisation receives a return on investment that is greater than the norm for its competitors, and when this enhanced return persists for a period long enough to alter the relative standing of the organisation among its rivals' (Finlay, 2000). Sustainability in this sense depends on three factors.

1. *Durability* – no advantage is sustainable for ever, as competitors will seek to mutate it. Reputation has the potential, however, for providing long-lasting advantage as the standing of well known long-lasting market leaders such as British Airways, Thomson and American Express testifies.

2. *Transparency* – the harder it is for outsiders to understand how an organisation does what it does the harder it will be for imitators. Disney has long been admired for the way in which it successfully manages and operates its theme parks, and competitors have found it difficult to exactly replicate the successful formula.

3. *Reputability*—once a rival has understood the competences needed to copy a rival, they will need to obtain the resources necessary to replicate the rival's product. If the resources are freely available in markets then this might not pose a problem but in some circumstances they may be limited. Thus airport take off and landing slots, hotel rooms in popular resorts, specialist staff such as pilots, access to airline routes and access to distribution channels are all examples of resources which might be restricted for some reason.

Core Competence, Generic Strategy and the Value Chain – A Synthesis

How the Different Approaches 'Agree'

It has been, argued (see for example Heene and Sanchez, 1997) that the resource or competence-based approach is largely incompatible with the competitive positioning or generic strategy approach advocated by Porter (1980, 1985). Mintzberg, Quinn, and Ghoshal (1995), however, make the case that the two approaches are in many respects complementary rather than mutually contradictory. Perhaps the best way of illustrating the linkages between the approaches is through the value chain of the organisation.

As competitive advantage is based upon the unique approach of the individual organisation to its environment, it is not possible to identify a one-for-all prescription, which will guarantee superior performance in all situations. Both the competitive positioning and the resource based approach, however, provide frameworks which allow broad sources of competitive advantage to be categorised for the purposes of analysis and development of future strategy.

A differentiation strategy, for example, will be likely to be dependent upon core competences in areas of the value chain like design, marketing and service. Similarly a cost or price based strategy may well require core competences in value chain activities like operations, procurement and perhaps in marketing. It is much less likely that a cost leader will have core competences based on design and service. Possible relationships between core competences, generic strategies and the value chain are shown in Table 10.2.

Where to Exploit Core Competences and Strategies

As core competences and business strategies are developed, it is necessary to decide where they can be exploited. Core competences and strategies can be targeted on existing customers in existing markets or it may be possible to target new customers in existing markets. Alternatively it may be possible to target new customers in new markets. These markets may be related to markets currently served by the organisation or they may be unrelated markets. The organisation may also consider employing its competences in a new industry.

These decisions, on where to deploy core competences, are concerned with determining the *'strategic direction'* of the organisation. Once this decision has been made then decisions must be made on the *methods* to be employed in following the chosen strategic direction.

The process of exploiting existing core competences in new markets is known as competence leveraging. In order to enter new markets it is often necessary for the organisation to build new core competences, alongside the existing core competences,

Table 10.2

Possible Relationships between Genetic Strategic and Core Competences in Relaiton, to the Value Chain

Value chain activity	*Areas of competence associated with differentiation*	*Areas of competence associated with cost/price based strategies*
Primary activities		
Inbound logistics	Control of quality of inputs	Strict control of the cost of inputs. Tendency to buy larger volumes of standard inputs
Operations	Control of quality of output, raising standards	Lowering operational costs and achieving high volume operations
Marketing and sales	Sales (and customer relations) on the basis of quality technology, performance, reputation, outlets etc.	Achieving high volume sales through advertising and promotion
Outbound logistics	Ensuring efficient distribution	Maintaining low distribution costs
Service	Adding to product value by high quality and differentiated service	Minimal service to keep costs low
Support activities		
The bussiness's infrastructure	Emphasis on quality	Emphasis on efficiency and cost reduction
Human resource developmont	Training to create a culture and skills which emphasise quality, customer service, product development	Training to reduce costs
Techoology development	Developing new products, improving product quality, improving product performance, improving customer service	Reducing production costs and increasing efficiency
Procurement	Obtaining high quality resources and materials	Obtaining low cost resources and materials

which are being leveraged, so as to satisfy new customer needs. Identification of customer needs to be served by core competences is based upon analysis of the organisation's competitive environment using the resource based framework. The remainder of this chapter considers the alternative strategic directions an organisation can pursue.

Strategic Directions

Introduction

Just as every product or business unit must determine an appropriate competitive strategy in order to achieve an enhanced competitive position relative to rivals so every organisation must also decide upon its attitude towards growth or alternative *directions* of strategic development. That is, should the direction taken be to expand, cut back or continue operations unchanged?

As with the other key business level decisions (relating to the competitive stance and strategic methods) decisions related to strategic direction are usually taken at the strategic business unit or product level since conditions in one part of the organisation may be different from those in another part. A vertically integrated travel company might want to expand its airline activities whilst at the same time reducing the size of its tour operations because of the market conditions pertaining to these two parts of the business. In this case there might be over-capacity in tour operating but under-capacity in airline capacity.

At the overall organisational (or 'corporate') level however, managers must be mindful of the overall *balance* between the directions taken by individual business units since available resources will be finite. Necessary resources may not be available to invest in all aspects of the organisation simultaneously so that resources may be taken from one area to invest in another area in order to allow it to develop and grow. These principles of selective investment and growth are consistent with the thinking embodied in the product life cycle and portfolio models (such as the Boston Constancy Group matrix).

In general terms, three orientations are possible with regard to directional strategy:

- Growth strategies – expanding the activities of the SBU.

- Stability strategies – maintain the activities of the SBU.
- Retrenchment strategies – reduce the activities of the SBU.

Having chosen the general orientation (such as growth), the management of an organisation can then choose more specific strategies. Growth for example can be broken down according to Ansoff (1987) into four district categories. We will now turn to book briefly at three strategic directions of growth, stability and retrenchment.

Growth – Igor Ansoff's Product-market Framework

The most commonly used model for analysing the possible strategic *growth* directions which an organisation can follow is the Ansoff matrix, shown in Fig. 10.5. This matrix which has two variables (products and markets), shows potential areas where core competences and generic strategies can be deployed. There are four broad alternatives:

- *market penetration* – increasing market share in existing markets utilising existing products.
- product development – entering new markets and segments using existing products;
- *market development* – developing new products to serve existing markets;
- *Diversification* – developing new products to serve new markets.

It should be emphasised that the matrix is related to the level of risk that managers are prepared to accept. Entering new markets or producing new products present areas of risk since many new products fail and managers will not have precise knowledge of market conditions when they enter new markets. Thus the lowest risk option is market penetration, with diversification representing the highest risk category.

Market Penetration

The main aim of a market penetration strategy is to increase market share using existing products within existing markets. This may involve taking steps to enhance existing core competences or building new ones. Such competence building may be intended to improve service or quality so as to enhance

Markets \ Products	Existing	New
Existing	Market penetration (increase market share)	Product development (new or improved products)
New	Market development (new customers, new market segments or new countries for existing products)	Diversification (new products into new markets)

Fig. 10.5 : The Ansoff matrix (growth vector components) (adapted from Ansoff, 1987)

the reputation of the organisation and differentiate it from its competitors. Equally, competence development may be centred on improving efficiency se as to reduce costs below those of competitors.

Mature or declining markets are more difficult to penetrate than these which are still in the growth phase, which provide more opportunities. In the case of a declining market, the organisation may also consider the possibility of retrenchment or withdrawal so as to re-deploy resources to more lucrative markets.

Market penetration is likely to be appropriate when:

- The existing market has growth potential.
- Other competitors are leaving the market.
- The organisation can take advantage of its acquired experience and knowledge in the market.
- The organisation is unable for some reason (such as lack of resources or regulatory restrictions) to enter new markets.

When a business's current market shows signs of saturation then it may wish to consider alternative directions for development.

Market Penetration at Travelodge

The concept of 'lodge' hotels has taken root in the UK over the past ten to fifteen years. The hotels, often located at convenient roadside locations, offer good quality standardised rooms capable of accommodating a family at a reasonable price. The growth of these hotels has placed pressure on older 'three and four star' properties and on the traditional bed and breakfast establishments. The Travelodge chain (which was developed by the Forte Group before its acquisition by Granada plc in the mid 1990s) was bought by the Compass Group of companies in 2000.

Travelodge, which was overtaken by the Travel Inn brand (owned by Whitbread pic) in the late 1990s as the largest UK lodge brand, announced ambitious growth plans in late 2001. The chain, which has 213 hotels and over 12000 rooms in the UK, intends to add a further 5000 rooms to its portfolio over five years and aims to have a presence at every major travel hub in the UK. Part of the growth will be achieved through deploying the strategic method of franchising after a deal was signed with Jarvis Hotels plc. The Travelodge managing director commented that franchising 'fits perfectly with our business as it will enable us to extend the portfolic while still protecting our brand standards'.

Market Development

Market development is based upon entry to new markets, employing essentially unchanged products (although they may be modified in detail). The new markets may be new geographical areas or new segments of existing markets. In either case the strategic option attempts to attack new customers for the existing range of products. The key to success in market development is the transferability of the product as it is *repositioned* in new markets. McDonald's fast food restaurants, for instance, have advanced inexorably from country to country with only minor amendments to the overall product concept in order to take into account national cultural differences and purchasing habits. Entering new markets is likely to be based upon leveraging existing competences but may also require the development of new competences. Entering new segments of existing markets may require the development of new competences, which serve the particular need of customers in these segments.

Internationalisation and globalisation are commonly used examples of market development. It is likely that an organisation will need to build new competences when entering international markets to deal with linguistic, cultural, logistical and other potential problems.

Marker development is likely to be appropriate when:

- the existing market has little or no growth potential;
- regulatory or other restrictions prevent an increase in an organisation's market share in its current market;
- other geographic markets or market segments offer good growth potential;
- existing products are easily transferable.

The major risk associated with market development is that it centres on entry to markets of which the organisation's managers may have only limited experience and consequently costly mistakes may be made.

Market Development at Holidaybreak plc

Holidaybreak plc was founded in 1973 as Eurocamp Travel Limited – a family run business, based in Cheshire, UK offering camping holidays in Brittany. From modest beginnings the business grew steadily, benefiting from the growing interest in France as a holiday destination. In the early 1980s mobile homes and destinations outside France were added to the product range. The 1980s were years of innovation and growth as the UK market to France expanded rapidly and the company's Eurocamp brand took over leadership of the camping sector.

In 1984 the core Eurocamp brand was launched on the Dutch market followed by Germany in 1988. Since the floatation of the company on the London Stock Exchange in 1991 the business has continued to develop and the corporate name was changed from Eurocamp to Holidaybreak plc to reflect the diversity of the company's expanding activities. In recent years the marketing reach of the Eurocamp brand has been extended into several new territories, notably Switzerland, Belgium, Denmark and most recently Poland, whilst customers have increasingly opted for mobile home rather than tent accommodation.

Product Development

Product development centres on the development of new products for existing markets. As with the previous two growth directions, the intention is to attract new customers, retain existing ones and to increase market share. Providing new products will be based upon exploiting existing competences but may also require that new competences are' built (such as in product research and development).

Product development offers the advantage to a business of dealing with customer needs of which it has some experience because they are within its existing market. In a world of shortening product life cycles, product development has become an essential form of strategic development for many organisations.

Product development is likely to be appropriate when:

- an organisation already holds a high share of the market and could strengthen its position by the launch of new products;
- the existing market has good potential for growth providing opportunities of good economic returns for new product launches;
- customer preferences are changing and they are receptive to new product ideas or new destinations;
- competitors have already launched their own new products.

Although when mentioning product development 'new' products are considered, it is possible to consider new products in several different ways. There are very few products that are totally new. Holidays to the moon might be such as example. Many new products are variations on existing products or products that are new to a particular organisation. Thus new products might be:

- completely new to a particular organisation as for example when a tour operator launches an airline;
- developments of additional lines of existing products, as for example when tour operators launch new destinations;
- creations of differing quality versions of the same product, as for example when British Airways added an additional airline class in 2000 for those paying 'full economy' (as opposed to discounted fares).

Introducing new products is, however, highly risky because many new products fail. Johnson and Scholes (2002) cited four factors, which could reduce the risks of failure. New products should :

- have a market focus;
- build on existing core competences;
- involve cross-disciplinary teams in their development;
- involve good internal communications so that all within the organisation are kept informed.

Product Development at Club Med

In the 1990s, after two decades of spreading the gospel for all-inclusive resort vacations and their easy lifestyle, Club Med took its formula to sea in the world's largest sailing ships that have all the facilities of a cruise ship. Stretching the length of two football fields and rigged with five 164-foot masts and seven computer-monitored sails, the two Club Med ships marry twentieth-century technology with the romance of large ocean-going sailing ships. They sail with little in the way of listing while the officers are on the bridge watching their computers.

Club Med cruises are basically a product of French culture and traditions, with the same informal, carefree ambience that Club Med has developed at its resort villages which are situated around the world.

Diversification

Diversification is growth achieved through new products and new markets. Diversification can be achieved by developing in a number of directions and by utilising a number of different methods. Figure 10.6 summarizes the directions and methods of diversification available to managers.

It is an appropriate strategic option when :

- Current products and markets no longer provide an acceptable financial return.
- The organisation has underutilised resources and competences.
- The organisation wishes to broaden its portfolio of business interests across more than one product/market segment.
- The organisation wishes to make greater use of any existing distribution systems in place, thus diluting fixed costs and increasing returns.

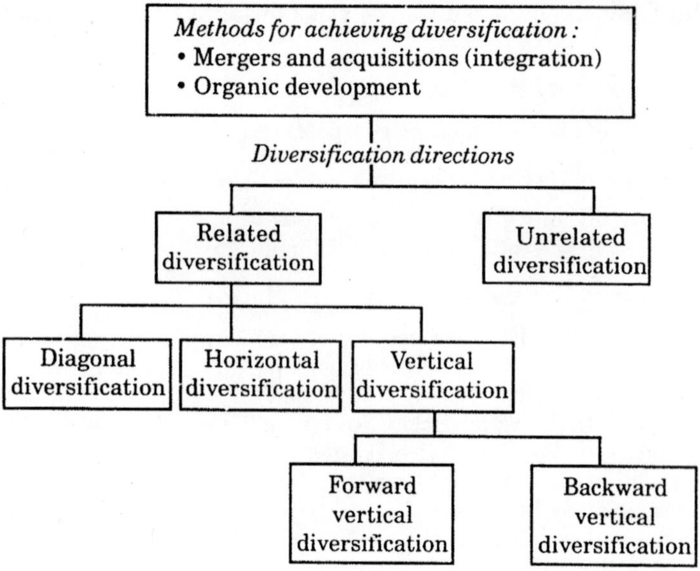

Fig. 10.6 : Directions and methods of diversification.

- The organisation wants to spread risks.
- There is a need to even out the cyclical effects in a given sector.

Related diversification is said to have occurred when the products and/or markets share some degree of commonality with existing ones. This 'closeness' can reduce the inherent risks (since managers are dealing with both new markets and new products) associated with diversification. In practice, related diversification usually means growth, into similar industry sectors or *forward* or *backward* in an organisation's existing supply chain.

Unrelated diversification is growth into product and market areas that are completely new and with which the organisation shares no commonality at all.

Related diversification (sometimes termed *concentric* diversification) can follow four main patterns, as shown in Figure. 10.7.

Vertical backward diversification occurs when an organisation seeks to operate in markets from which it currently obtains its resources (i.e. extending the value chain in an *upstream* direction). A tour operator developing a hotel chain or an airline would be an example of this. Upstream diversification provides greater control over supplies of resources. The benefits of vertical backward diversification are that :

- supplies are guaranteed;
- the costs of supplies are internalised, i.e. brought within the organisation's control;
- supplies may be denied to competitors or made more expensive to acquire;
- the portfolio of activities is broadened giving protection against risk;
- potential problem areas with regard to supplies are identified and dealt with quickly.

Vertical forward diversification describes the situation in which an organisation seeks to operate in markets currently

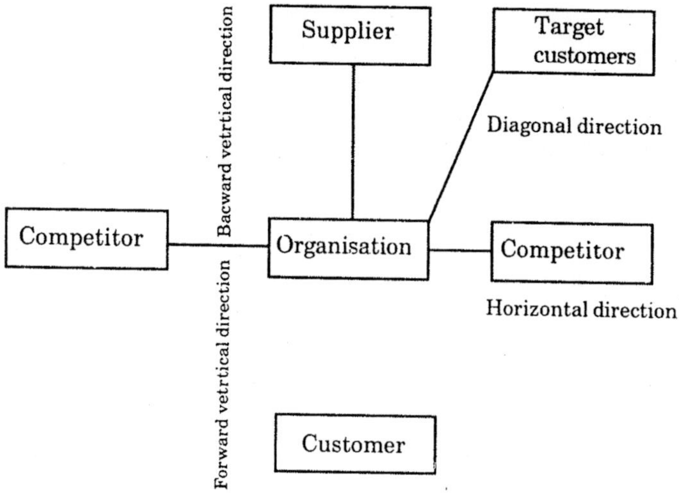

Fig. 10.7 : Patterns of related diversification.

served by its customers or distributors (i.e. extending the value chain in a *downstream* direction). In this case an example would be a tour operator developing a distribution network such as a chain of travel agents and/or call centre. This form of diversification gives an organisation closer contact with customers and can give significant marketing advantages in that it gives an organisation market intelligence that might not be forthcoming when dealing through an intermediary such as an independently owned chain of travel agents. The benefits of vertical backward diversification are that:

- guaranteed outlets are provided for products to be distributed;
- the costs of distribution are internalised;
- distribution outlets are denied to competitors;
- information is gathered regarding consumer purchasing behaviour both for one's own products and for competing products;
- the portfolio of activities is broadened giving protection against risk.

Vertical diversification should not be confused with *vertical integration,* which concerns mergers or takeovers in order to integrate existing organisations. That is a further decision regarding the *method* of diversification to be employed. Rather than purchase an existing travel agency chain, for example, a tour operator might choose to develop such a chain from scratch.

Horizontal diversification involves an organisation entering complementary or competing markets. An example of this would be a tour operator working with or taking over another tour operating organisation or an airline strategic alliance when two or more airlines work in a complementary manner to achieve common objectives. This should not be confused with *horizontal integration,* which is the acquisition of a competitor. Diversification may be achieved by integrating a competitor that had been acquired but it might also be achieved through joint developments (such as alliance), or by developing internally. The benefits of horizontal diversification are that :

- market share is increased;
- greater purchasing power leads more favourable rates being negotiated with suppliers and distributions;
- economies of scale are derived from the enlarged organisation;

- opportunities to increase market share are denied to competitors;
- competitors may be come collaborators.

Related diversification has the benefit of leveraging existing competences as well as requiring the building of some new competences. In other words, it draws upon existing organisational knowledge as well as requiring the building of some new skills and knowledge.

Related Diversification at First Choice plc

First Choice is a leading European leisure travel company comprising mainstream and specialist tour operations, travel retail and aviation businesses. First Choice employs over 14000 people, operating from 13 countries worldwide. The business was formed in 1973 and for many years traded as Owners Abroad plc. In 1994 the company was restructured and rebranded as First Choice Holidays plc.

In recent years the group has diversified both horizontally and vertically, largely through acquisitions. The UK travel industry rapidly began to consolidate in the late 1990s and First Choice played an active role, acquiring in June 1998 two key UK tour operators – the United Travel Group and Hayes & Jarvis. In the same year, other acquisitions included the retail agencies Bakers Dolphin and intatravel to complement the opening of new travel shops under the name of Travel Choice and an initial stake (25%) in Holiday Hypermarket (out-of-town travel superstores). UK acquisitions in 1999 were of premium niche market operators: Meon (Meon Villas and Longshot Golf Holidays). Flexigroup (ski holidays and conferences) and Sunsail international (leading yacht charter and water-sports club operator). Within retail, Ferrychoice, a small regional agency chain, and a number of small Irish agents were also acquired. In May 2000 the remaining outstanding interest in Holiday Hypermarket was acquired.

The year 2000 saw the commencement of the anticipated consolidation within the European tour operating industry. In particular there was a convergence of a small number of European participants principally in the UK and Germany, the two most dominant markets in Europe. First Choice did not participate in this mass market consolidation; instead it chose clearly to set out a strategy to differentiate itself from the traditional main competitors, acquiring smaller more specialised companies than its competitors. In 2000 two key acquisitions marked the start of First Choice's expansion into European markets: the European tour operating businesses of the Ten Tour Group, which provided an immediate presence in six important markets in mainland Europe, and Barceló Travel of Spain, which involved the purchase of three principal businesses – tour operations, retail travel and destination management services. In particular the Barceló Travel acquisition also contained the ability to create a hotel joint venture with its former parent company Barceló Travel Group.

Through these and further acquisitions during 2001 within Continental Europe, First Choice now has a presence in France, Spain, Italy, Portugal, Germany, Belgium. The Netherlands, Austria and Switzerland. A strategic alliance with Royal Caribbean Cruise Lines initiated in 2000 strengthened the group's position in the growing cruise sector whilst providing an investment of £ 200 million in First Choice by the cruise line.

11

The Demand for Tourist Travel

Introduction

Leisure travel has become a key feature of the leisure society which now characterises many developed countries. One corollary of this is that tourist travel has become a global activity and it is assuming a much greater role in the leisure habits of developed societies now that holidays and overseas travel have become more accessible to all sections of the population. This growth in travel also poses many challenges for the transport industry since understanding the demand for tourist transport is a critical part of the strategic planning process for transport operators and organisations associated with the management and marketing of transport services for tourists. At government level, accurate information on the use of tourist transport infrastructure is critical when formulating transport policies and particularly in assessing the future demand. At the level of individual transport operators, it is necessary to have a clear understanding of the existing and likely patterns of demand for tourist transport, to ensure that they are able to meet the requirements of tourists. This means that for transport providers, high quality market intelligence and statistical information are vital in the strategic planning process and day-to-day management of transport, so that the services offered are responsive and carefully targeted at demand, cost-effective and efficient. Ultimately, transport companies seek to operate services on a commercial basis so that supply matches demand as closely as possible but there are also situations in which such services are subsidised to meet social objectives not related to tourism. In such situations, tourism is really an added bonus for subsidised services.

The types of information required by decision-makers associated with tourist transport provision are usually gathered through the marketing research process and are likely to include the following:

- the geographical origin and spatial distribution of demand in the generating region ;
- the demographic and socioeconomic characteristics of tourist travel demand (e.g. age, sex, family, status, social class, income and expenditure);
- the geographical preferences, consumer behaviour and images of tourists for holiday destinations and tourist travel habits, including the duration of visit;
- when it is likely to occur (e.g. temporal and seasonal distributions of use);
- who is likely to organise the holiday (e.g. independently or as part of a package);
- the choice of transport likely to be used in the tourist transport system;
- future patterns of demand (e.g. short- and long-term forecasts of tourist travel);
- government policy towards tourist transport operations;
- the implications of tourist travel demand for infrastructure provision and investment in tourist modes of transport (e.g. aircraft, airports, passenger liners, ferries and ports).

The purpose of this chapter is to examine a range of the main types of data sources available to assess the demand for tourist transport at different spatial scales, from the world scale down to individual countries. International and domestic sources of data are introduced, with the emphasis on the relative merits and weaknesses of each source. As most tourism textbooks tend to focus on definitions of tourism, tourists and ways of measuring tourism *per se*, rather than on the implications of tourism statistics for assessing the demand for tourist transport, the discussion here is more focused on transporting the tourist. A case study of international outbound tourist travel from Japan shows how a government's tourist travel policy can be used to encourage a growth in demand for outbound travel, and the consequences fcr tourist transport provision. The implications for managing international and tourist transport systems are emphasised. Lastly, the role of forecasting the demand for tourist transport is discussed in relation to the assessment of future growth scenarios for tourist travel. This is important because it enables travel organisations (e.g. tour operators) and transport providers to plan ahead to remain competitive and anticipate tourist travel requirements.

The International Demand for Tourist Travel

Ryan (1991) discusses the economic determinants of tourism demand which are associated with the purchase of an intangible service, usually a holiday or transport service, which comprises an experience for the tourist. The consumption of tourist transport services as part of a package holiday, or as a separate service to meet a specific need (e.g. a business trip or a visit to see friends and relatives), has manifested itself at a global scale in terms of the worldwide growth in international tourist travel. Among the economic determinants of the growth in international tourist are rising disposable incomes and increased holiday entitlement in developed countries. Transport operators have stimulated demand by more competitive pricing of air travel and other forms of travel for international tourists. This has been accompanied by the 'internationalisation' of tourism as a business activity (see Witt *et al.* 1991), as global tourism operators emerge through mergers, takeovers, strategic alliances (e.g. airlines cooperating and code sharing on homes), investment in overseas destinations and diversification into other tourism services. One consequence is that tourist transport operators view the determinants of tourist travel as crucial to their short- and long-term plans to service provision.

Aside from the economic determinants of the demand for travel, Ryan (1991) emphasises the significance of psychological dererminants of demand in explaining some of the reasons why tourists travel. Although there is no theory of tourist travel, a range of tourist motivators exists (Pearce 1992; Ross 1994). Ryan's (1991 : 25 - 29) analysis of tourist travel motivators (excluding business travel) identifies reasons commonly cited to explain why people travel to tourist destinations for holidays. These include:

- a desire to escape from a mundane environment;
- the pursuit of relaxation and recuperation functions;
- an opportunity for play;
- the strengthening of family bonds;
- prestige, since different destinations can enable one to gain social enhancement among peers;
- social interaction;
- educational opportunities;
- wish fulfilment;
- shopping.

Although it is possible to identify a range of motivators, it is possible to classify tourists according to the type of holiday they are seeking and the travel experience they desire. For example, Cohen (1972) distinguished between four types of tourist travellers:

- *the organised mass tourist* on a package holiday; they are highly organised and their contact with the host community in a destination is minimal;
- *the individual mass tourist,* who uses similar facilities to the organised mass tourist but also desires to visit other sights not covered on organised tours in the destination;
- *the explorers,* who arrange their travel independently and who wish to experience the social and cultural lifestyle of the destination;
- *the drifter,* who does not seek any contact with other tourists or their accommodation, seeking to live with the host community (see Smith 1992).

Clearly, such a classification is fraught with problems, since it does not take into account the increasing diversity of holidays undertaken and inconsistencies in tourist behaviour (Pearce 1982). Other researchers suggest that one way of overcoming this difficulty is to consider the different destinations tourists choose to visit, and then establish a sliding scale similar to

Cohen's (1972) typology, but which does not have such an absolute classification. Pearce (1992) produces a convincing argument which highlights the importance of considering the tourists' destination choice. By establishing a blueprint for tourist motivation, Pearce (1992) argues that –

> Tourism demand should not be equated with tourism motivation. Tourism demand is the outcome of tourists' motivation as well as marketing, destination features and contingency factors such as money, health and time relating to the travellers' choice behaviour. . . . Tourism demand can be expressed as the sum of realistic behavioural intentions to visit a specific location. . . . [which is] . . . reduced, to existing travel statistics and forecasts of future traveller numbers. Tourist motivation is then a part rather than the equivalent of tourism demand. (Pearce 1192 : 113)

In other words, transport providers need to recognise the Travellers' choice, behaviour and travel intentions at destinations to understand fully the wider transport requirements beyond simple aggregate patterns of travel statistics.

The implication of research on motivation and demand is that governments and transport operators need to recognise what economic, social and psychological factors are stimulating tourist travel. This may help in establishing the different types of travellers and their preferences for various destinations and specific activity patterns on holiday. Tour operators selling holidays need to recognise the complexity of tourist motivation to travel and airlines need to understand the precise effect on the availability of aircraft. In particular, they must be able to rotate and interchange different aircraft in a fleet to meet daily and seasonal travel requirements through complex logistical exercises. For airports, the expected number of passengers, use of airspace and runways need to be planned in advance and they need to take account of where there is going to be a long-term growth in demand. This also means that infrastructure such as airports has to consider future investment and development plans. More specifically, transport operators will need to understand the range of motives and expectations of certain types of traveller since the level of service they provide will need to match the market and the requirements of travellers. Operators need to understand not only the dimensions of demand; but the market segments and the behaviour and expectations of consumers which they will need to accommodate in providing a high quality tourist experience.

Throughout much of the chapter, the emphasis is on establishing patterns of tourism demand. Yet one should not forget the significance of domestic tourism which Pearce (1995a) argues is ten times greater than international tourism in numerical terms. However, all too often data sources on domestic tourism are poorly documented and irregular in terms of survey timing. Therefore prior to discussing international tourism, one example of domestic tourism in China is used to illustrate the type of patterns of tourist activity that developed in spite of a limited transport system.

Domestic Tourism Patterns in China: Development Amid Infrastructure Constraints

There is a growing research literature on tourism in China (e.g. Lew and Yu 1995; C.M. Hall 1997) and a wide range of articles have been published in academic journals, particularly those with an Asia-Pacific focus (e.g. *Pacific Tourism Review).* Much of the interest in China has been focused on its post – 1979 opening up to international tourism and the effect on the demand and supply for tourism infrastructure (e.g. transport). As reviews of tourism research in China show (e.g. C.M. Hall 1997), much of the effort has been expended on the urban and coastal areas where rapid tourism development has occurred and on the implications for the management of ancient heritage sites. Only recently has a new genre of studies emerged that begins to deal with more diverse aspects of tourism such as rural tourism (e.g. Getz and Page 1997) and domestic tourism (Zhang 1997).

In terms of the growth of domestic tourism in China and the history of travel, recent reviews (Sofield and Li 1997) highlight the significance of ideological traits in shaping tourism in post-revolutionary China. Prior to the 1970s, the large proportion of domestic travel was business-oriented, VFR (visiting friends and relatives) or health-related (i.e. to visit a spa). Zhang (1997) highlights the problem of documenting the volume, patterns and activities of domestic tourism prior to 1970 since 'there are no statistics on tourism during this period' (Zhang 1997: 565). Low living standards and shortages of accommodation and transport acted as constraints to domestic travel. Economic reform in China stimulated the growth of inbound tourism to help raise much-needed foreign revenue and yet as Zhang (1997: 566) argues not much attention was given to the development of domestic tourism [for Chinese]. The improvement of facilities and supplies appropriate for domestic tourists was ignored. As the lack of adequate passenger transportation was the 'bottleneck' in the development of the national economy, demands were far from satisfied, consequently curbing the growth of domestic tourism.

One of the principal drivers of domestic tourism demand in China in the late 1980s was rising living standards, which saw the national average per capita income rise by 3.44 times that of 1979 or RMB 1189 (RMB = renminbi yuan). However, in the coastal areas and large cities, rates of income were higher (e.g. Shanghai RMB 4501; Beijing RMB 3035). Using statistics from China's National Tourism Administration, Zhang (1997) documents the post-1985 growth in arrivals and receipts from domestic tourism. As Table 11.1 shows, the 1990s experienced a significant growth in arrivals. Zhang (1997) explains this growth in terms of both the spillover effects of developing international

Table11.1
Growth in Domestic Tourism in China

Year	*Domestic tourist arrivals (millions)*
1986	270
1987	290
1988	300
1989	240
1990	280
1991	290
1992	330
1993	410
1994	520
1995	630
1996	640

Source: Modified from Zhang (1997).

tourism and expanding the opportunities for growth. In addition, the private sector began to recognise the market opportunities for domestic tourism as government policies progressively moved to the simultaneous promotion of international and domestic tourism. This was also facilitated by economic growth which enabled greater investment in domestic tourism infrastructure. The development of a socialist market economy system after 1992 has generated economic growth of 9 per cent in China's GNP per annum. Patterns of consumption by China's population have risen in parallel with this and domestic tourism has been a major beneficiary. For example, between 1990 and 1995, domestic arrivals grew by 17.62 per cent while average receipts increased by nearly 52 per cent. Domestic tourism arrivals reached 640 million in 1996, an increase of 2.286 times the arrivals in 1990. Zhang (1997) points to the China Domestic Tourism Sample Survey which documents the growth in domestic package holidays from 8.2 million in 1993 34.65 million in 1995.

To explain such a growth in domestic travel, one needs to examine a greater coordinated level of development among the constituent parts of the tourism industry (especially in transport). For example, by 1995 China had 1.35 billion m^2 of road in its urban areas, a 500 million m^2 increase in 1990. Other major infrastructure projects such as the Beijing–Jiujiang–Jiulongand Nanning–Kumming railway projects plus other infrastructure projects such as the Beijing-Shijiazhuang and Shanghai–Hangzhou expressway proejcts have assisted in intercity tourist travel. Greater mobility resulting from the growth in other forms of urban transport has favoured domestic travel. Yet as Hilling (1996: 225) explains 'the relatively flat terrain of a number of the larger cities (Beijing, Shanghai, Tianjin) undoubtedly favours cycling, as does the serious inadequacy of public transport in the face of rapidly rising demand and urban roads which cannot easily accommodate larger vehicles – in Beijing an estimated 12 per cent of the urban road network cannot take buses'. This is supported by Zhang (1997 : 568) who argues that 'the transportation capacity is still not satisfactory, and the basic infrastructure needs further improvement'. Against these constraints, one also has to recognise that in the early 1990s the Chinese 'government began to introduce a national holiday system allowing employees 7 – 15 days' annual leave based on

Table 11.2
Expenditure (RMB) on Domestic Tourism in China

Category	*1993*	*%*	*1995*	*%*
Transport	125.50	28.2	157.46	26.6
Accommodation	81.30	18.3	104.82	17.7
Food & beverage	81.60	18.3	109.09	18.4
Urban transport	—	—	19.63	3.3
Communication	4.00	0.9	3.94	0.7
Sightseeing	23.10	5.2	34.76	5.9
Entertainment	9.70	2.2	16.59	2.8
Shopping	86.20	19.4	102.94	17.4
Other caregories	33.80	7.6	42.86	7.2

Source : Modified from Zhang (1997).

length of service. This combined with the gradual introduction of a five-day week to generate opportunities for long distance domestic travel.

In terms of tourist travel in China, Table 11.2 illustrates the proportion of expenditure on various aspects of domestic tourism. Transport remains the dominant element of expenditure and it increased in 1996 when the use of urban transport was included. If one also adds the use of transport at destinations for sightseeing, then transport accounts for a significant element of tourism expenditure. Therefore, the 1990s can be characterised as the decade in which domestic travel for pleasure began to develop. As Zhang (1997) explains, travel is associated with the acquisition of new knowledge and understanding in Chinese society, but he also adds that most Chinese people are not affluent enough to travel extensively. Yet even though the cost of domestic travel by rail and coach increased twice in 1996, and again in early 1997 and despite the fact that 60 million Chinese are estimated to live in poverty, Zhang (1997) argues that 1 billion people are able to meet their basic needs and the market for domestic travel is around 300 million trips per annum. Much of the demand is urban-based and Zhang believes it could exceed 400 million trips per annum by the year 2000.

Table 11.3
Air travel in China 1990 – 2015

Year	*Revenue passenger kilometres (billions)*
1990	11.6
1995	32.8
2000	71.6
2005	124.6
2010	193.4
2015	291.9

Source: Boeing Commercial Airplane Group (1996).

Constraints on further tourism growth are related to shortage of supply of budget hotels aimed at the domestic market. But 'passenger transportation is the bottleneck of development' (Zhang 1997: 571) and could act as a major constraint on the country's ability to meet the growing demand for domestic travel. According to Ballantyne (1996), air travel in China is characrerised by infrastructure problems and a poor image of safety. This is compounded by the scale and demand for domestic, and to a lesser degree, international air travel in China. The Boeing Commercial Airplane Group (1996) assessed the existing and expected growth in air travel in China as indicated in Table 11.3. Such growth rates highlight the importance of demand management (Taplin 1993) to accommodate the volumes involved. While China has a five-year plan to upgrade 40 airports, Beijing, Shanghai and Guangzhou currently handle 42 per cent of the country's total air passenger volume. To address such shortcomings, the Chinese government invested US$ 1.42 billion in aviation infrastructure in 1996, a 30 per cent increase on 1995 levels of investment. China's airport authorities are seeking overseas capital to assist in the investment programme, and Ballantyne (1996: 20) summarizes the situation for domestic air travel since 'China's airlines have become vibrant and yet while the scale of tourism demand in China is of a scale many people find hard to recognise and comprehend', much of the data is dependent upon state statistical sources which have not been extensively used by researchers. The example of domestic tourism demand in China also raises a further debate: whether tourism demand can be stimulated by infrastructure in developing countries. Hilling (1996) outlines two schools of thought which are pertinent here.

Firstly, the supply-led school of thought has traditionally viewed demand as following the provision of infrastructure (White and Senior 1983). A more recent explanation and now widely used model used in transport provision is that it should be a response to demand. Hilling (1996) explains that in supply-led models, development would occur where a latent demand existed. In the demand-led model now coming increasingly into vogue due to the enormous cost of transport infrastructures investment, such as in China, tourism use of infrastructure is seen as a new market to support the demand for infrastructure investment. But it is not the case that infrastructure is being provided in advance of demand. In China, a demand-led model probably characterises the situation affecting the domestic tourism market, with economic cost-benefit criteria assuming a higher priority in infrastructure development decisions, given the scarcity of resources to meet all transport needs.

For the remainder of this chapter the emphasis is on the dimensions of international tourism demand, due to its global significance. A focus on international tourism will illustrate the interrelationship between government policy and tourism demand as well as the implications for developing transport systems which both domestic and international travellers can use. However, the 'analysis [of international tourism] is complicated by the paucity of appropriate data. (Pearce 1987: 35). So, what sources of data are available to assess the demand and use of different modes of tourist transport?

Data Sources on International Tourist Travel

The analysis of tourism, tourists and their propensity to travel and previous travel patterns is a complex process . . . involving not only the visitor and his movements but also the destination and host community' (Latham 1989: 55). Tourist transport providers will often have statistical information relating to their own organisation's services and tourist use. But how can a new entrant into the tourist transport business examine the feasibility of providing a transport service? What statistical information on tourist transport is available? How is it gathered? And who publishes it?

At a global scale, Hilling (1996 : 1) acknowledges that 'there are vast differences in the availability of transport, indeed there is a stark contrast between a relatively immobile Third. World and the highly mobile advanced economies . . . much of the infrastructure is poorly maintained and in disrepair and is inadequate for present needs without the . . . complication of growth of demand in the future'. The global discrepancies which exist in transport provision obviously have a major impact on the tourism–generating potential and patterns of demand which result. As Table 11.4 shows, the developed regions of North America, Europe and Oceania comprise 26 per cent of the earth's land area, 15 per cent of the population and contain 26 per cent of the world's commercial vehicles. Africa is notable for its under–provision and Japan is responsible for 64 and 67 per cent respectively of Asia's commercial and passenger vehicles. While newly industrialised countries (NICs) such as Thailand, South Korea and Brazil have experienced increased mobility, the gap between developing and developed countries is certainly great and reflected in terms of patterns of international tourism demand.

One immediate problem which confronts the researcher interested in tourist transport is the absence of international statistics which monitor every mode of tourist travel. For example,

Table 11.4
World Transport Provision in 1990

	percentage of world total			
	Area	*Population.*	*Commercial vehicles*	*Passenger vehicles*
North America	16.1	5.2	40.1	35.2
Europe	3.6	9.4	18.2	37.4
Oceania	6.3	0.5	1.9	2.0
Former USSR	16.4	5.7	0.2	4.8
Central & South America	15.1	8.5	8.7	6.7
Africa	22.2	12.1	3.5	2.0
Asia	20.2	58.8	27.4	11.7
(excluding Japan)			(9.7)	(3.8)

Source : Modified from Hilling (1996 :2) based on the *United Nations Statistical Yearbook.*

organisations such as the International Civil Aviation Organisation (ICAO) publish annual statistics on international air travel for their members, airline operations. Table 11.5 provides a very general indication of the scale of passenger activity at the world's major airports (based on ICAO data). The data is unable to identify tourist and leisure trips, being a broad measure of terminal passengers and international travel. Such data is dependent upon the willingness of airports to report statistical information on passenger flows and sometimes ICAO estimates the flows on the basis of part-year data. In this respect, Table 11.5 only indicative of the scale of travel at an aggregate level. Not surprisingly, the data in Table 11.5 confirms Hillings' (1996) identification of a world transport gap. Table 11.5 is dominated by North America and Europe, and in the case of Singapore, Japan, Thailand and Hong Kong it represents the rapid expansion in air travel in Asia-Pacific. In contrast, aviation statistics collected by national aviation organisations such as the UK's *Civil Aviation Authority. UK Airports* outline the origin and destination of all terminal passengers. This data relates to air transport movements at UK airports and is based on operators' requirement to report each service they operate, passengers uplifted and discharged. Only data on direct flights is recorded. Table 11.6 is only an indication of the relative importance of passenger flows between the UK and other countries. Like Table 11.5, it is not possible to distinguish between arrivals and departures or the regional breakdown of flights. However, Table 11.6 does highlight the dominance of Western European travel flows, which comprised nearly two thirds of the total passenger movements to and from the UK in 1996. This was followed by the USA and a range of other destinations throughout the rest of the world. Such industry-specific studies do provide an indication of the volume of travel. For example, in the case of cruising, the following case study outlines the sources, patterns of demand and significance of single industry-based studies.

Table 11.5
Traffic Movements and Passenger Folws at World Airports in 1995

Country	*Location*	*Name*	*Terminal passengers (millions)*	*International terminal passengers (millions)*	*Commercial air transport movements (thousands)*	*International commercial air transport movements (thousands)*
(1)	(2)	(3)	(4)	(5)	(6)	(7)
USA	Chicago	O'Hare	67	7	828	N/A
USA	Atlanta	Hartsfield	57	3	578	N/A
USA	Dallas	Fort Worth	56	3	864	N/A
UK	London	Heathrow	54	47	421	348
USA	Los Angeles	International	54	13	703	N/A
Germany	Frankfurt	Frankfurt-Main	37	30	366	287
USA	San Francisco	International	36	6	396	N/A
USA	Miami	International	33	14	499	163
Rep. Korea	Seoul	Kimpo International	31	13	197	81
USA	New York	John F. Kennedy	30	17	324	97
USA	Detroit	Metropolitan	28	3	432	N/A
France	Paris	Charles de Gaulle	28	26	325	286
Hong Kong	Hong Kong	International	27	27	150	150
USA	New York	New York	27	4	400	N/A
France	Paris	Orly	27	11	233	92

Table 11.5 : *(Contd.)*

(1)	(2)	(3)	(4)	(5)	(6)	(7)
Netherlands	Amsterdam	Schiphol	25	25	291	280
USA	Houston	Houston International	25	3	354	N/A
USA	Boston	Logan	24	3	442	N/A
USA	Orlando	Orlando International	22	3	300	N/A
UK	London	Gatwick	22	21	193	159
USA	Honolulu	International	22	6	250	N/A
Singapore	Singapore	Changi	22	22	156	156
Japan	Tokyo	New Tokyo International	22	21	120	116
Thailand	Bangkok	Bangkok International	21	15	149	107
Italy	Rome	Fiumicino	21	12	209	111

1. All commercial movements including positioning and local movements.

Source: HMSO (1997 : 135) based on ICAO (1995) *Civil Aviation Statistics of the World.*

Table 11.6
United Kingdom International Passenger Movements by Air: Arrivals Plus Departures by Country of Embarkation or Landing 1986-96

	1986	*1988*	*1990*	*1992*	*1994*	*1995*	*1996*
European Union[1]							
Austria	381	707	904	966	1,143	1,173	1,161
Belgium	986	1,229	1,406	1,528	1,880	1,865	1,925
Denmark	622	696	862	1,047	1,283	1,390	1,598
France	3,667	4,882	6,202	6,566	7,260	6,567	6,399
Finland	206	306	377	321	415	493	618
Germany	3,820	4,492	5,572	5,537	6,190	6,539	6,939
Greece	3,349	3,796	3,556	4,470	4,963	4,578	3,589
Irish Republic	2,107	3,521	4,429	4,323	5,126	6,017	6,938
Italy	2,714	3,095	3,392	3,586	4,188	4,693	4,941
Luxembourg	106	136	144	160	160	161	161
Netherlands	2,312	2,896	3,251	3,536	4,013	4,285	4,941
Portugal and Madeira[2]	2,044	2,157	2,247	2,559	2,692	2,761	2,674
Spain and Canary Islands	12,678	14,865	11,782	13,076	17,645	18,267	17,789
Sweden	566	762	947	956	1,122	1,213	1,306
Total EU	35,558	43,541	45,072	48,641	58,080	160,003	160,979
Other Western Europe							
Norway	706	824	858	916	1,074	1,166	1,283
Switzerland	2,112	2,489	2,730	2,595	2,647	2,717	2,870
Yugoslavia[3]	899	1,047	1,066	68	93	132	173
Gibraltar	174	315	290	208	147	167	158
Cyprus	617	812	1,325	2,151	1,940	1,834	1,521
Turkey	257	913	669	885	1,613	2,166	2,368
Malta	746	1,062	1,014	1,181	1,186	1,063	948
Other[4]	72	85	89	99	112	128	161
Total Other Western Europe	5,583	7,544	8,040	8,102	8,812	9,372	9,481
Total Western Europe	41,142	51.084	53,112	56,744	66,892	69,375	70,460
Rest of world							
USSR[3]	168	250	288	297	384	397	399

	1986	*1988*	*1990*	*1992*	*1994*	*1995*	*1996*
Rest of Eastern Europe	375	501	687	915	1,207	1,365	1,565
North Africa	734	932	845	988	1,079	1,149	1,148
South Africa[5]	395	493	613	654	772	942	1,043
Rest of Africa	859	757	843	913	962	899	969
Israel	445	492	464	537	762	862	885
Persian Gulf States	314	290	295	337	329	359	363
Saudi Arabia	296	262	255	300	338	337	357
UAE	190	261	301	420	557	644	698
Rest of Near East & Middle East	364	317	332	442	493	564	605
USA	6,335	8,574	10,143	11,430	12,173	13,249	14,402
Canada	1,501	1,877	2,057	1,979	2,096	2,292	2,543
South America	106	151	250	321	391	409	466
Central America	0	31	64	29	237	306	471
Caribbean	419	611	645	717	933	1,003	1,116
Australia	409	476	522	661	714	834	714
New Zealand	85	107	121	123	153	135	158
India	312	426	561	520	751	855	970
Pakistan	211	248	261	235	280	309	340
Rest of Indian sub-continent[6]	196	223	294	314	394	424	449
Japan	357	552	838	1,035	1,186	1,241	1,348
Hong Kong	516	644	731	809	947	939	1,023
Singapore	429	452	538	515	585	604	765
Thailand	144	223	306	316	350	380	441
Rest of Asia	252	305	405	589	824	1,031	1,162
Total Rest of world	15,411	19,454	22,661	25,397	28,899	31,528	34,400
ALL AIR PASSENGER movements	56,554	70,540	75,772	82,141	95,790	100,902	104,861

1 Austria, Finland and Sweden joined the EU in 1995, but are included in the EU section for all years to show the time series on a consistent basis.

2 Includes Azores and Cape Verde Islands.

3 Or former constituent states.

4 Includes Iceland and the Faroe Islands.

5 Includes Botswana, Zimbabwe and the Republic of South Africa.

6 Includes Indian Ocean Islands.

Source: HMSO (1997) *Transport Statistics,* based on the Civil Aviation Authority's *United Kingdom Airports.*

Case Study : The Demand for Specific Forms of Tourist Transport–cruising

There has been a growing academic interest in cruising and research studies have considered its historical development (Douglas and Douglas 1996) and its impact on Pacific island destinations (Table 11.7). More social psychologically based studies (e.g. Morrison *et al.* 1996; Moscardo *et al.* 1996) and a range of research concerned with the economics of cruising (Bull 1996) and the economic impacts of cruise tourism (Dwyer and Forsyth 1996) provide an up-to-date series of reviews of cruising and tourism. More specific industry-derived, studies and commentaries (Cockerell 1997; Burt 1998; Dickinson and Vladmir 1997) indicate the scale and volume of growth in individual contexts. These complement the studies by industry analysts such as Peisley (1995) which outline the prospects for the cruise ship industry.

There is a growing recognition that crusing has been capacity-led over the last two decades. As Burt (1998: 4) argues 'capacity is filled whenever new ships are brought into service' and the state subsidies used in France, Finland, Italy and Asia to maintain their shipbuilding industry (often up to 30 per cent of production costs) have made cruise ships a competitive capital purchase. This is fuelled by what Burt (1998) indicates is an average of 9 per cent growth per annum in passenger demand, a figure confirmed by Peisley's (1995) analysis of data from the industry body – the Cruise Lines International Association (CLIA). For example, in the USA, the demand increased from 3.3 million passengers in 1989 to 4.6 million in 1994. Morrison *et al.* (1996) argue that cruising has outperformed any other vacation category in the USA over the last 25 years. North America accounts for 80 per cent of the world cruising market, much of which has focused on the Caribbean. In 1994, CLIA examined the demographic profile of cruise ship passengers, which can be summarized thus:

Table 11.7
Cruise Ship Passenger for Selected Pacific Island Ports as a Percentage of Total Tourist Arrivals, 1989 – 93

Destination	*1988*	*%*	*1989*	*%*	*1990*	*%*	*1991*	*%*	*1992*	*%*	*1993*	*%*
Fiji	19,991	9	30,392	11	27,874	9	27,332	10	29,835	10	7,933	3
New Caledonia	42,762	41	33,169	29	42,158	33	35,330	30	49,802	38	38,742	31
Solomon Islands	4,547	30	2,981	23	2,616	23	2,649	19	4,886	28	2,656	19
Tonga	7,536	25	7,120	23	5,789	20	5,760	19	7,338	22	4,442	13
Vanuatu	50,932	74	41,311	63	41.867	54	37,023	48	59,346	58	43,059	49

Source: Modified from Douglas and Douglas (1996) and World Tourism Organisation Compendium of Tourism Statistics 1988 – 93.

- A quarter of passengers were under 40 years of age, with a third over 60 years of age.
- Less than two-thirds of clients earn less than US$ 60,000 per annum.
- A quarter of passengers still have children at home.

As a result, CLIA identified the profile of existing and the 'hot prospect' market segments (Table 11.8) where the future

Table 11.8
Profile of Existing and Future North American Cruise Ship Passengers, 1994

	Curise passenger of 1990s (%)	*Future projections (%)*
Male	54	53
Female	46	47
Age profile		
25 – 39	29	50
40 – 59	36	39
60 or over	35	11
Average	50	42
Income profile (US$)		
20,000 – 39,999	31	36
40,000 – 59,999	30	40
60,000 – 99,999	28	20
100,000 and over	114	—
Marital status		
Married	76	70
Single	24	30
Household structure		
Children in the household	27	46
Vacation with chidren	15	29
Vacation without children	12	17
No children in the household	72	54

Source: Modified from Peisley (1995) based on Cruise Lines International Associatin Survey.

cruise ship passengers are likely to seek shorter and cheaper products. In fact, Peisley (1995: 8) argues that 'a younger lower income clientele with more family commitments would certainly suit the mass or middle market lines which believe that the mega-ships with all the entertainment facilities . . . . [may have] the capacity to keep prices down' Table 11.9 outlines the ranking of' cruise ship companies in terms of capacity, highlighting the market dominance by the Carnival Corporation, Royal Caribbean and P

Table 11.9
Cruise Ship Companies and Capacity 1995 and 1998

	Number of berths		*Rank*	
Company	*1995*	*1998*	*1995*	*1998*
Carnival Corporation	36,649	56,512	1	1
Royal Caribbean Cruise Line	16,530	28,969	2	2
P and O Cruises Division	14,531	22,306	3	3
Kloster Cruise	11,253	11,731	4	4
Cunard	7,983	6,127	5	8
Costa Crociere	7,565	9,765	6	6
Chandris	6,434	11,684	7	5
Regency Cruises	5,008	6,408	8	7

Source: Modified form Peisley (1995).

and O Cruises Division. The destinations in which the North American Cruise Ship industry piled its trade in 1994 were:

- the Caribbean (52 per cent)
- the Mediterranean (9.2 per cent)
- Alaska (7.8 per cent)
- Trans-Panama Canal (5.9 per cent)
- Mexicana Riveria (5.3 per cent}
- Northern Europe (3.8 per cent)
- Bermuda (3 per cent)
- the South Pacific
- other regions (10.8 per cent)

Source: Peisley (1995).

Peisley (1995) documents the problems which various cruise ship lines have faced in terms of market segmentation and tailed attempts to position certain products in niche markets. However, critics believe the cruise ship industry is not sufficiently mature to support niche marketing, though Carnival carried 90,000 child passengers in 1994, which is a new development to attract families. Peisley (1995) also documents regional initiatives in Far East Asia and Oceania to develop the cruise passenger market with its sought-after tourist spending. The main markets appear to be firmly developed in North America, the UK, Europe and Asia and it is predicted that the passenger business will grow to reach 8 million a year by the new millennium.

At a smaller scale, Cockerell (1997) discussed the development of river cruising in Europe. In the UK, the Passenger Shipping Association (PSA) collates data on river cruises. In 1990 Germany dominated both ocean and river cruises with 184,000 ocean cruise sales in the UK compared to 218,000 in Germany. By 1996, however, the figures were 416,000 in the UK compared to 255,000 ocean cruise sales in Germany. Table 11.10 outlines the popular destinations, assisted by the UK tour operator Thomson Holidays becoming a member of the PSA, thereby providing data on volume and destinations chosen. While the Nile was a major growth

Table 11.10
River Cruise Passengers Booked in the UK

Cruise Location	*1992 (000s)*	*1996 (000s)*
Nile	15.0	70.0
Rhine and tributaries	20.0	27.0
Neva/Volga	—	15.0
Danube	1.0	10.0
Yangtse	0.1	5.0
Rhone	1.0	5.0
Elbe	0.6	4.0
Mississippi	0.5	2.0
Other rivers (e.g. Amazon, Irrawaddy and Po)	5.0	4.0
Total	43.2	142.0

Source : Passenger Shipping Association and Cockerell (1997).

market in 1996, the terrorist attack in Egypt in 1957 may well have severely affected this market. New river cruise destinations, facilitated by the opening up of the former Eastern Europe, have meant the Neva-Volga cruise is one of the fastest-growing segments of the UK cruise market which travels between Moscow and St Petersburg. Although the Rhine retains a prominent position, new options such as cruises on the Elbe now compete with those on the Rhine. Likewise, the new canal between the Rhine and the Danube has also led to a major growth in Danube cruises. The construction of a new dam on the Yangtse river in China also prompted a major growth in cruises prior to the flooding of the scenic Three Gurges region in 1997. Therefore this case study illustrates how a range of cruise industry data sources can be combined to analyse the demand for tourist activities based on the marine environment (Orams 1998). However, it also illustrates how dependent the researcher is upon the industry sources to generate reliable, consistent and regular data which documents tourist use of such transport. For this reason, one is forced to refer to international tourism statistics as they are more consistent and comprehensive in their treatment of tourist travel, particularly in relation to transport issues.

Tourism Statistics

Within an international context, tourism statistics provide an invaluable insight into:

- tourist arrivals in different regions of the world and for specific countries;
- the volume of tourist trips;
- types of tourism (e.g. holidaymaking, visiting friends and relatives and business travel);
- the number of nights spent in different countries by tourists;
- tourist expenditure on transport-related services.

Such information may indicate the order of magnitude of tourist use of transport systems and their significance in different locations. In this context, Latham's (1989) seminal study on tourism statistics is essential reading, since it provides a useful insight into the complex process of assessing the demand for international tourist transport. Studies by Latham (1989), Jefferson and Lickorish (1991) and Veal (1992) document the procedures associated with the generation of tourism statistics, which often use social survey techniques such as questionnaire-based interviews with tourists at departure and arrival points.

Unlike respondents in other forms of social survey work, tourists are a transient and mobile population. This raises problems related to which social survey method and sampling technique one should use to generate reliable and accurate statistical information that is representative of the real world. Due to the cost involved in undertaking social surveys, it is impossible and impractical to interview all tourists travelling on a specific mode of transport. A sampling framework is normally used to select a range of respondents who are representative of the population being examined. While there are a number of good sources which deal with this technical issue (see S.L.J. Smith 1989 and Veal 1992), it is clear that no one survey technique and sampling framework is going to provide all the information necessary to enable decision-makers to make strategic planning decisions. It is possible to discern three common types of tourism survey:

- pre-travel studies of tourists' intended travel habits and likely use of tourist transport;
- studies of tourists in transit or at their destination, to provide information on their actual behaviour and plans for the remainder of their holiday or journey;
- post-travel studies of tourists once they have returned to their place of residence.

Clearly there are advantages and disadvantages with each approach. For example, pre-travel studies may indicate the potential destinations which tourists would like to visit on their next holiday but it is difficult to assess the extent to which holiday intentions are converted to actual travel. In contrast, surveys of tourists in transit or at a destination can only provide a snapshot of their experiences to date rather than a broader evaluation of their holiday experience. One interesting survey instrument which, in part, addresses the potential weaknesses associated with surveys of holiday experience would seek to assess the tourists' previous travel behaviour and their changing travel behaviour through time. Where retrospective post-travel studies are used, they often incur the problem of actually locating and eliciting responses from tourists which accurately record a previous event of experience. Each approach has a valuable role and generally individual transport operators and tourism organisations use the approach appropriate to their information needs.

The most comprehensive and widely used sources of tourism statistics that directly and indirectly examine international tourist travel are produced by the World Tourism Organisations (WTO) and OECD (Pearce 1987, 1995a), National governments also compile statistics on international tourism for their own country (inbound travel) and the destinations chosen by outbound travellers. These are normally commissioned by national tourism organisations as a specialist research function, though it depends upon each country and how the management public sector tourism is organised. WTO publishes a number of annual publications which include the following: the *Yearbook of Tourism Statistics* (published since 1947 as *International Travel Statistics*, then as *World Travel Statistics,* and now as *World Travel and Tourism Statistics).* This has a summary of tourism statistics for almost 150 countries and areas, with key data on tourist transport, and includes statistical information in the following order:

- world summary of international tourism statistics;
- tourist arrivals;
- accommodation capacity by regions;
- trends in world international tourism arrivals, receipts and exports;
- arrivals of cruise passengers;
- domestic tourism;
- tourism payments (including international tourism receipts by countries calculated in US$ millions, excluding international fare receipts);
- tourism motivations (arrivals from abroad and purpose of visit);
- tourism accommodation;

- county studies which examine the detailed breakdown of tourism statistics collected for each area, including tourism seasonality.

In addition to WTO, OECD produces *Tourism Policy and International Tourism in OECD Member Countries.* Although the data collected is restricted to 27 countries (BaRon 1997), it deals with other issues such as government policy and barriers to international tourism.

International Tourist Travel: Trends and Patterns

Both WTO and OECD statistics are compiled by each agency from returns and data which national governments supply according to the criteria laid down by each organisation. International tourist arrivals have risen from 25 million in 1950 to 593 million in 1996. Figure 11.1 illustrates the growth in arrivals by WTO region since 1986; it shows there was a 75 per

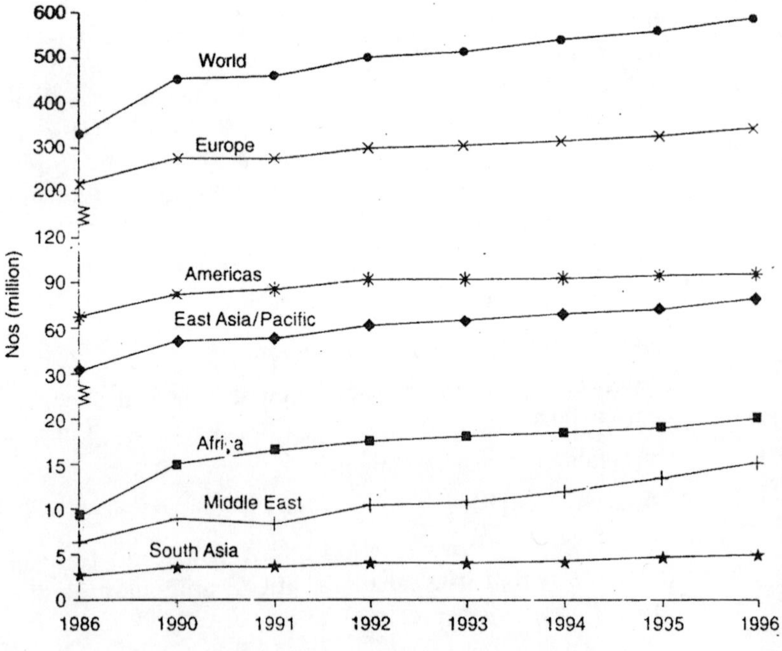

Fig. 11.1 : International tourism arrivals by region 1986 – 96 (*Source*: World Tourism Organisation).

pent growth in total arrivals between 1986 and 1996. This is a good rate of growth given the prevailing global economic conditions which had a bearing on different tourism regions.

The key feature of Figure 11.1 is the continued dominance of Europe, with, 352 million arrivals in 1996, although the relative position of Europe in world arrivals has declined from a 64 per cent market share in 1986 to 59 per cent in 1996. Europe recorded one of the lowest regional growth rates for the period 1986 – 96, with an average of 5 per cent per annum. However, Latham (1992) argues that Europe's continued dominance as an origin and destination area for tourism is due to the fact that its population contains segments with a high disposable income and a highly developed tourism infrastructure. The Americas received nearly 115 million arrivals in 1996, which represents a 19 per cent market share of world arrivals. The Americas recorded a decline in their market share from 21 pet cent in 1986.

The East Asian Pacific region experienced a 47 per cent growth in arrivals between 1986 and 1996, with 87 million arrivals. This comprised 15 per cent of world arrivals in 1996, a significant growth from the 10 per cent share in 1986. Africa (excluding Egypt and Libya) received 20.6 million arrivals in 1996, which comprised 3.5 per cent of the world share of arrivals; that increased by an average of 8.3 per cent per annum in the decade 1986 – 96. South Asia, however, received 4.5 million arrivals which represented 0.8 per cent of world arrivals and the Middle East received 153 million arrivals in 1996, which comprised 2.6 per cent share of world arrivals.

As arrivals have grown, tourist receipts increased from $ 352 billion in 1994 to $ 423 billion in 1996. Tourist arrivals are not distributed evenly in each region, with some countries and their destinations performing better than others. In terms of the specific countries and their position in world arrivals, Table 11.11 provides a detailed breakdown by each WTO region (see BaRon 1997 for more detail). What Table 11.11 highlights is the significance of global tourism flows in contributing to such trends. Both Hoivik and Heiberg (1980) argue that up to four-fifths of all international flows were between Europe, North America and Japan, and one-twentieth between other countries in the world. Pearce (1995a) has examined these flows in more detail and Rowe (1994) lists the country-to-country flows in order of magnitude:

Table 11.11
World Tourism Arrivals and Key Destinations

1996 ranking	*WTO region main destination*	*Tourist arrivals*	
		1996 (000s)[1]	*% of world total*
(1)	(2)	(3)	(4)
	World	**593,638**	**100.0**
	Top Ten	289,535	48.8
	Africa (CAF)	20,562	3.5
39	Morocco	2,693	0.5
27	South Africa	4,944	0.8
31	Tunisia	3,885	0.7
	Other Africa	9,040	1.5
	Americas (CAM)	**114,706**	**19.3**
	Northm America	83,605	14.1
10	Canada	17,386	2.9
7	Mexico	21,428	3.6
2	USA	44,791	7.5
	Other America:	31,704	5.3
29	Agrentina	4,286	0.7
35	Puerto Rico	3,065	0.5
	Other America	24,353	4.1
	E.Asia/Pacific (EAP)	**87,025**	**14.7**
30	Australia	4,167	0.7
6	China	22,765	3.8
15	Hong Kong	11,703 V	2.0
26	Indonesia	5,034	0.8
32	Korea	3,684	0.6
28	Macau	4,890	0.8
21	Malaysia	7,138	1.2
22	Singapore	6,608	1.1
20	Thailand	7,192	1.2
	OtherEast Asia/Pacific	13,884	2.3
	Europe (CEU)	**351,612**	**59.2**
	Central/Eastern Europe	83,479	14.1
37	Bulgaria	2,795	0.5
12[2]	Czech Republic	17,000	2.9
8	Hungary	20,670	3.5
9	Poland	19,410	3.3

(1)	(2)	(3)	(4)
36	Romania	2,834	0.5
14[3]	Russin Federation	14,587	2.5
	Other Central/Eastern Europe	6,173	1.0
	Northern Europe	39,314	6.6
25	Ireland	5,280	0.9
38	Norway	2,746H	0.5
5	UK	26,025 V	4.4
	Other Northern Europe	5,263	0.9
	Southern Europe	98,507	16.6
18	Greece	8,987	1.5
4	Italy	32,853	5.5
17	Portugal	9,900	1.7
3	Spain	41,295	7.0
	Other Sourthern Europe	5,472	0.9
	Western Europe	118,244	19.9
11	Austria	17,090A	2.9
24	Belgium	5,753A	1.0
1	France	61,500	10.4
13	Germany	15,205A	2.6
23	Netherlands	6,546A	1.1
16	Switzerland	11,097	1.9
	Other Western Europe	1,053	0.2
	East Mediterranean	12,068	2.0
19	Turkey	7,966	1.3
	Other East Mediterranean	4,102	0.7
	Middle East (CME)	**15,256**	**2.6**
40	Bahrain	2,669	0.4
33	Egypt	3,675	0.6
34	Saudi Arabia	3,458	0.6
	Other Middle East	5,454	0.9
	South Asia (CSA)	**4,477**	**0.8**

1. A = arrivals at accommodation establishmkents reporting; H=arrivals at hotels reporting; V=visitor arrivals (includes day visits).
2. Former Czechoslovakia.
3. Former USSR.

Source: WTO National Reports (some preliminary); modified from BaRon (1997).

- Canada to USA, a flow of 15 million;
- USA to Mexico, a flow of 14 million;
- USA to Canada, a flow of 12 million;
- France to Spain, a flow of 12 million;
- Germany to Italy, a flow of 10 million;
- Germany to Austria, a flow of 10 million;
- Hong Kong to China, a flow of 10 million;
- Switzerland to Italy, a flow of 10 million;
- France to Italy, a flow of 9 million;
- Germany to Spain, a flow of 7 million;
- Mexico to USA, a flow of 7 million;
- UK to Spain, a flow of 7 million;
- Austria to Italy, a flow of 6 million.

While such patterns are well established in international tourist travel, the growing significance of EAP and outbound/intraregional travel needs to be recognised. Although the existing Europe–Americas dominance of flow remains marked, the growth of arrivals in other regions is a noticeable feature of the 1980s and 1990s. Although WTO (1992) did provide a summary of tourist transport, WTO stopped publishing tourist transport statistics in their summary and full compendium of tourism statistics in 1996, so it is unfortunately no longer possible to investigate the role of transport and arrivals. This exemplifies the problem facing tourism researchers in developed countries and particularly in developing countries (Weaver and Elliot 1996; O'Hare and Barrett 1997), where inadequate data exists beyond general aggregate statistics that do not investigate the tourism-transport interface. However, occasional market studies published in *Travel and Tourism Analyst* do focus on particular tourism flows between WTO regions (e.g. see Cockerell 1994 on flows from Europe to the Asia Pacific region.)

Other Statistical Sources on International Tourist Travel

At a transnational level, the EC (now the EU) is also an important source of statistical information on tourist transport (Jefferson and Lickorish 1991). In the past, the EC has undertaken

Table 11.12
Mode of Transport Used by European Holidaymakers

	Car (%)	*Train (%)*	*Plane (%)*	*Boat (%).*	*Motorbike or bike (%)*	*Coach (%)*
By origin						
Belgium	77	6	10	1	8	7
Denmark	59	14	18	11	3	4
France	81	15	6	2	2	7
Germany	61	16	17	3	1	7
Greece	78	4	13	25	1	0
Ireland	51	11	31	18	1	6
Italy	73	15	5	5	2	11
Luxembourg	62	10	19	4	0	15
Netherlands	70	8	14	5	6	14
Portugal	76	17	3	3	1	16
Spain	70	16	5	2	0	12
United Kingdom	59	11	24	8	0	14
EU member stares	68	14	13	5	1	10
By destination						
Own country	78	14	1	8	1	8
Other country	52	11	32	6	2	13
Non-EU Europe	53	15	29	17	0	18
Ourside Europe	35	19	86	1	0	15

Note: Totals exceed 100 owing to multiple responses.

Source: EC Omnibus Survey, cited in Page (1993d: 12).

various studies of tourist travel, most notably the 1986 Omnibus Survey *The Europeans and their Holidays,* which examined the travel patterns in member states and recognised the overwhelming importance of carborne travel. Although Table 11.12 is dated, it remains one of the comprehensive sources of data on tourist modes of travel between member states. More recently, the EC publication *Transport, Communications, Tourism Statistical Yearbook* (Eurostat 1987) recorded generalised time series statistics on tourist travel in relation to:

- transport infrastructure in member states;
- distances covered by various modes of transport;
- definitions and explanations of tourist travel on railways, roads, waterways and aircraft by country;
- summary information on tourism demand.

However, it is now too dated to provide detailed insights into the high level of intraregional tourist travel (i.e. international tourist travel within the EC). For example, in 1989 there were 220,779,000 tourist trips in the Europe/Mediterranean region, the majority undertaken by West Germans (25.5 per cent), French (9.5 per cent), British (9 per cent), Dutch (5.4 per cent), Swiss (5.3 per cent) and Italians (4.9 per cent). For these trips, air and road travel assumes an important role.

For more detailed analyses of tourist use of transport systems in the EC, such dated figures have to be complemented by international travel surveys undertaken by member states. These are well documented in accessible sources such as Latham (1989) and Jefferson and Lickorish (1991) and the technical, issues associated with these surveys need not be reiterated here. In the UK, the most important government survey of international tourist travel is the International Passenger Survey (IPS) which began in 1961 and is a stratified random sample of tourists arriving/departing at the UK's main ports of entry. Latham (1989 : 64) identifies its principal aims as the collection of :

- data on the government's travel account (expenditure by. incoming tourists and outgoing visitors) which is used to calculate tourism's contribution;
- detailed information on visitors to the UK and outbound travellers to overseas destinations;
- information on international migration;
- data on the routes used by tourists to assist shipping and aviation authorities.

These statistics are published annually in a revised format as the *International Passenger Survey* (HMSO 1990), although for a commercial annual subscription (now in excess of £ 20,000), companies can purchase the raw data from the IPS survey and additional questions can he added to the survey at a cost to transport operators. In addition, other organisations publish summaries of transport statistics (e.g. Porter 1997) of travel to and from the UK and the Department of the Environment, Transport and the Regions (DETR) produces the UK transport statistics, although they do not distinguish between tourist and non-tourist use of transport. Ad hoc studies, such as the former UK *Long Distance Travel Survey* and the *National Travel Survey* 1993/95 (see HMSO 1997a) also provide more detailed insights into the use of tourist transport. For example, the *National Travel Survey* 1993/95 indicated that on average, each person in the UK travelled 871 miles a year, comprising 29.6 journeys a year (excluding commuting). Although few tourism surveys specifically target tourist transport as me primary focus, these sources of data can be used to understand the nature of international tourist use of different forms of transport.

From this discussion of data sources on tourism demand, it should be evident that up-to-date market intelligence is essential for tourist transport operators, particularly in a situation where demand is increasing at a rapid rate. For this reason, attention now turns to a case study of outbound travel from Japan to illustrate the type of data sources used by researchers, and the need to consider the extent to which demand is shaped by a variety of factors (e.g. government policy, cultural traits and the perception of tourism and leisure time) :

CASE STUDY : The Demand for Outbound Tourist Travel and the Transport System in Japan

One of the main areas of expansion in outbound travel in the 1980s and 1990s occurred in the Asia-Pacific region, which comprises the established industrial and newly industrialised countries of South East Asia, most notably Japan (Edwards 1992; C.M. Hall 1997). The continued growth in outbound travel from these markets has attracted a great deal of interest from tourist transport operators, especially global airlines, since these markets have been growing at a time of relative stagnation in many of the mature outbound travel markets in North America and Western Europe. Japan (Figure 11.2) is an interesting example as it was the third-largest generator of international tourism expenditure in 1996, after North America and Germany. Japanese outbound travellers spent US$ 37,977 million in 1996 (BaRon 1997). It is a lucrative market which many international tourist destinations have nurtured, given that Japan's 123 million population constitutes a dominant source market for international tourism. In 1996, the Japanese took 16.7 million overseas trips. According to Nozawa (1992), Japanese travel to destinations in the Asia-Pacific' regions is set to expand in the late 1990s, with Australia, Canada, New Zealand and Switzerland ranked as the most desirable destinations (see Page 1989a for a discussion of Japanese outbound travel to New Zealand). Within Western Europe, the UK, France and Italy were also 'desirable destinations for Historical . . . sightseeing and folklore tours for Japanese tourists' Nozawa 1992: 232) and in the Asia-Pacific region, destinations such as Thailand, Singapore and Hong Kong have remained popular (Morris 1990). In addition, Pacific Island destinations have proved popular locations for tourism development and investment (Page 1996; Hall and Page 1996). This case study examines the situation in Japan in the 1980s and 1990s and the significance of a government policy designed to expand outbound tourist travel. Emphasis is placed on the factors associated with is a boom in outbound travel and the constraints imposed by the existing tourist transport system, which is inhibiting further growth. This is followed by a critical discussion of the situation in the 1990s and the significance of government policy and its long-term effect on Japanese travel. It is pertinent, however, to commence with a discussion of sources of data on international tourism demand in Japan and the historical evolution of outbound travel to place the case study in a broader context.

Data Sources on Japanese Outbound Travel

According to Pearce (1995), one of the main sources of data available to assess international travel by Japanese tourists is the passport applications generated by the Ministry of Justice's Immigration Bureau prior to 1970. Since there were restrictions on outbound travel from Japan prior to 1970, this data provides evidence of the purpose of visit and main country visited' (Pearce 1995). After 1970, restrictions on travel and multiple visa applications were gradually lifted, making the data more difficult to analyse, and therefore recent trends are calculated using a number of statistical sources. The Ministry of Justice still collates passport applications, but the Japanese National Tourist Organisation reanalyses the data to ensure they are consistent

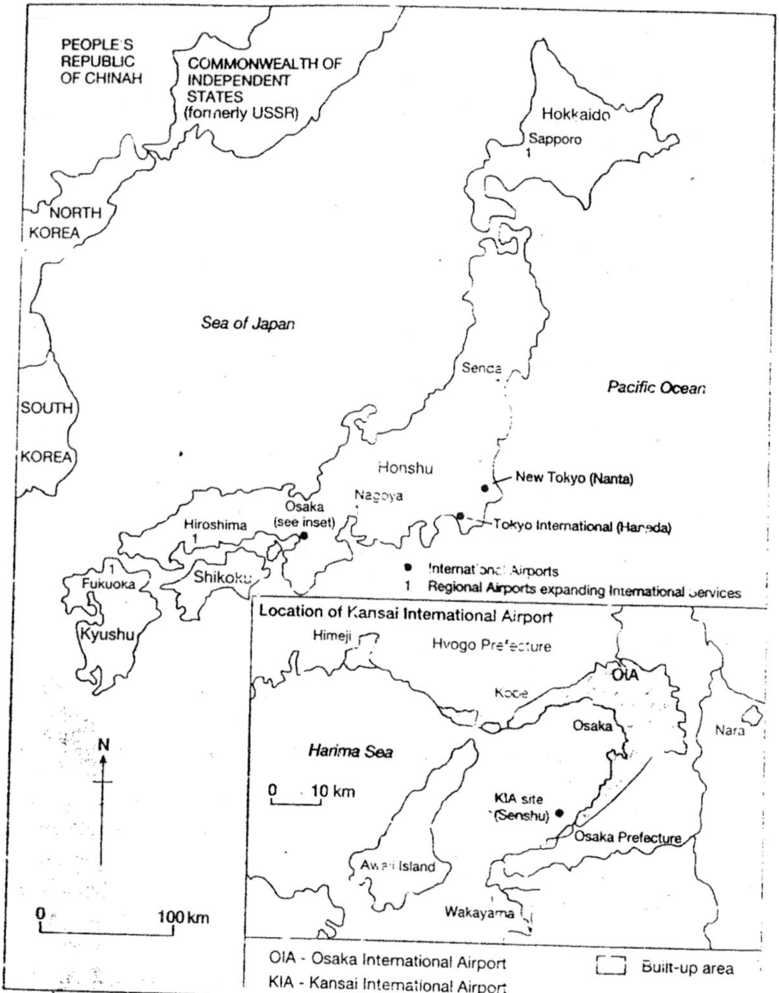

Fig.11.2 : Japan: location map and Kansa International Airport (redrawn from Page 1994)

with the methodology employed by organisations such as WTO. The Ministry of Transport, responsible for the formulation and implementation of tourism policy, collects tourism data for policy purposes. It is the main source of data for the transport and travel trade. Other bodies which produce useful research data include:

- The Japan Travel Bureau (JTB), which is Japan's premier travel company and produces regular reports on tourism market trends together with an annual report on the Japanese travel market;
- The Market Intelligence Corporation, which surveys air travellers quarterly at key airports, generating data for reports and other bodies such as JTB (Morris 1994).

The Evolution of Tourism Demand

Pearce (1995) documents the evolution of Japanese outbound travel between 1964 and 1981, when the number of tourists travelling increased from 100,000 to over 4 million (Tokuhisa 1980). A number of factors can be attributed to this rapid expansion in demand:

- a continued growth in international trade and the generation of wealth from activities in the Japanese economy;
- increased personal affluence for that population and additional disposable income to spend luxury items like travel;
- the liberalisation of currency restrictions in 1964;
- the easing of administrative procedures to obtain a passport and visa;
- improved aircraft technology which facilitated easier access to overseas destinations;
- the development and marketing of package holidays which reduced the price of travel.

Since 1981, outbound tourist travel has expanded at an even greater rate than in the 1970s, with the number of outbound trips more than doubling from 5 million to 11 million between 1986 and 1991. And in 1996, outbound travel reached 16.1 million trips. This growth has caused a great deal of debate among analysts over the extent to which it was stimulated by government policy rather than the result of an underlying trend towards international travel in Japanese society. For example, Polunin (1989) interprets this expansion as a result of an underlying growth within Japanese society which was only marginally influenced by official policy. The significance of Polunin's (1989) analysis is that whilst encouraging a growth in demand, the government has failed to match this with an expansion in the supply of tourist transport infrastructure to accommodate growth. In contrast, a recent synthesis by Burns (1996) questions the validity of such arguments. For this reason, it is useful to examine the role of government policy in stimulating the demand for outbound travel, followed by the range of underlying factors which Polunin (1989), Nozawa (1992) and Burns (1996) cite as influential in shaping demand.

Government Policy and Outbound Travel in Japan

In 1986, the Japanese government announced its Ten Million Programme which sought to encourage a doubling of outbound travel between 1986 and 1991. The rationale for this programme has been interpreted in various ways, including:

- the promotion of international citizenship among Japan's population;
- a response to growing international pressure for Japan to reduce its trade surplus generated through its balance of payments;
- a strong export-led economy in the 1970s and 1980s.

Polunin (1989) suggests that this policy was little more than a public relations exercise since outbound travel was already expanding by over 11 per cent in 1986 and this trend continued with expansion in excess of 20 per cent in 1987 and 1988. However, the significance of this policy statement was that the Japanese tend to regard government bureaucrats as well-intentioned partners in progress. . . . Thy respond positively to being told what to do. The Ten Million Programme says that travel is desirable and indeed expected' (Polunin 1989 : 6). In this context, the Ten Million Programme may be viewed as legitimising outbound travel in Japanese society where there have been cultural barriers to travel, since the work ethic has traditionally militated against long holidays. Government policy endorsed outbound travel and positively encouraged travel as a way of addressing international criticism of the accumulating trade surplus.

More recently, the government's Ten Million Programme has been expanded to incorporate the Two Way Tourism, 21 Programme, designed to nurture incoming tourism to Japan. This has focused on attracting the growing Asian outbound markets by emphasising the unique culture, history and traditions of Japanese society. This policy aimed to boost the existing $ 3,435 million receipts from inbound tourists in 1991 to offset the $ 23,983 million spent by outbound Japanese travellers. Yet for the tourist transport operators in Japan it is interesting to ascertain what factors facilitated the Japanese travel boom in the late 1980s and the effect of expansion in demand for the tourist transport system.

Evaluating the Ten Million Programme and the Expansion of Outbound Travel from Japan

Polunin (1939) argues that the growing internationalism of Japanese society has encouraged a growth in outbound tourism, as Japan developed a more outward-looking position in the world economy, accompanied by increased international investment in overseas countries. Such a change in outlook led to a greater awareness in Japanese society of the desirability of overseas travel. Nozawa (1992) argues that the 1989 annual White Paper on leisure activity in Japan found that 32 per cent of respondents would like to travel abroad if given an extra day off a week. This reflects a shift in emphasis within Japanese society from the work ethic, as in 1987 'average annual Japanese working hours were 2150 hours compared with typical US hours of 1924 (Nozawa 1992 : 228). Hard work and loyalty to one's company have traditionally resulted in long working hours and few official overseas holidays. However, a number of specific factors appear to have stimulated a Japanese travel boom in the 1980s:

- Japan's gross national product outperformed the world average in the 1980s, creating additional disposable income available for discretionary spending on tourism and leisure services in Japan;
- In 1986, the state ended Japan Airline's (JAL) monopoly of international scheduled services (Polunin 1989) and some of the capacity constraints of the late 1970s; the 1980s were characterised by additional airlines offering extra scheduled services. In 1991, there were 52 scheduled

airlines operating to 32 destinations and a further 43 seeking traffic rights. Yamauchi (1997) examines the gradual libralisation of air transport policy in Japan and the effect on international, travel, particularly the consequences for Japanese airlines.

- In 1987, the International Tourism Institute of Japan was formed to assist the government in the the promotion of outbound travel, providing tourism consultants to developing countries on projects assigned by the Ministry of Transport (Nozawa 1992).
- The Japanese government encouraged the Ministry of Labour to reduce the working week from 48 to 40 hours in 1988 to generate additional leisure time for overseas travel. It was followed by the promotion of a 'Long Holiday Week' and a 'Tourism Week' to encourage outbound rather than domestic travel.
- The year 1988 was deemed 'the year of liberalisation for Japanese tourism' (Nozawa 1992 : 227), with a streamlining of emigration procedures and tax privileges for outbound travel (see Morris 1990).
- The Japanese government has negotiated bilateral visa waivers for short-stay visitors in other countries, most notably the USA in 1988, which stimulated an increase in demand for visits to this destination.
- Overseas investment by Japanese tourist transport enterprises has been characterised by diversification into overseas hotels (Morris 1990), as Japan's international carriers (e.g. JAL and All Nippon Airways) secured a stake in the major destinations served by these airlines (see Go and Murakami 1990). For example, Morris (1990) noted that 60 per cent of hotel rooms in Hawaii were owned by Japanese companies.
- A 'Working Holiday Scheme' for young Japanese travellers was developed for Australia and subsequently expanded to New Zealand and Canada.
- State investment in international airports and the promotion of regional airports for the use of charter flights on inclusive tours has only had a marginal impact on

capacity constraints at Narita and Osaka international airports.

However, Burns' (1996) seminal study argues that while the Ten Million Programme achieved its numerical, objectives ten months ahead of its target, the programme was an abject failure in social terms. Burns (1996) analysed the Ten Million Programme and identified four elements:

- a publicity campaign by the government and tourism industry to encourage Japanese people to take more holidays abroad;
- the promotion of overseas school tours to develop the idea of international citizenship;
- assistance with public relations for foreign national tourism associations based in Japan;
- a campaign to promote longer holidays.

In his assessment, Bums (1996) examines the mechanisms employed by the Japanese government to achieve its objectives. He concludes that no underlying cultural change occurred in Japanese society in terms of holiday-taking. The amount of time which the Japanese population spend at work has remained high. Their perception of holidays remains a barrier, with the 9–15 days' paid leave to which employees are entitled is often viewed as emergency paid sick leave or to use for attending, events such as funerals. In the 1990s, just over 10 per cent of the Japanese population travelled overseas. Burns (1996) highlights the paradox of the Ten Million Programme as statistically significant, but in policy terms it was a smokescreen to give the illusion that the country was reducing its trade surplus with its trading parties.

Unfortunately, the demand for outbound travel and its continued expansion in the late 1980s and 1990s has not been matched by the supply of airport capacity. One simple explanation is that airport development requires 3 long-term programme which is phased in over a number of years (see Doganis 1992). The expansion in demand of over 20 per cent per annum in the late 1980s would be difficult to accommodate in any tourist transport system. Hunt (1988) notes that a Bank of Japan study on Japanese airports found 1.5 million tourist trips were deterred by capacity constraints (e.g. Narita, Tokyo, Osaka and Itami airports only had one runway). According to Nozawa (1992) this was compounded by a curfew on night flying, constraining existing capacity by 30 per cent. In addition, the expansion of Narita airport, involving the construction of two extra runways and a new terminal, was delayed until 1995. Among Japan's regional airports which operate as international gateways, an absence of long runways, terminal facilities and associated services has constrained expansion. In Osaka an innovative solution to the problem has been the construction of the New Kansai International Airport on a floating island.

Kansai International Airport

Therivel and Barrett (1990) examine the construction of this new airport, focusing on the environmental impact of developing a 24-hour service in a country where land is a scarce commodity. Kansai International Airport (KIA) is located in Central Japan, and provides much-needed access to Asia (Morris 1990). The KIA project was conceived to avoid the complaints and problems associated with Osaka International Airport, which was built near a densely populated area and attracted considerable public criticism due to noise pollution. The planning of KIA can be dated back to the 1960s. Based on a feasibility study of sites in 1968, an Aviation Deliberation Council (ADC) examined seven sites in the Osaka region, with a view to their being able to:

- handle domestic and international flights;
- offer 24-hour airport operator;
- provide comprehensive environmental protection;
- offer the possibility of further expansion;

Source: Therivel and Barrett (1990 : 82).

It was not until 1974 that the Japanese Ministry of Transport released the ADC report and this identified a site 5 km off Senshu as the preferred location. Despite opposition from the local authorities concerning the environmental impact of such a project, a decline in the local economy in the mid-1970s prompted a greater consideration of local planning gains from the project (Therivel and Barrett 1990). In 1982, following environmental reports, the project was approved and the KIA Company was formed. The Company's plans sought:

- 511 ha of reclaimed land;
- a 3,500 m runway;
- terminals and associated buildings;
- capacity for 16,000 take-offs and landings per annum;
- a second phase to expand the site by 1,200 ha with two additional runways of 3,000 m and 3,500 m.

Source: Therivel and Barrett (1990: 83).

The airport received planning permission after a complex environmental review process and opened in 1994, fifteen months behind schedule due to landfill problems associated with reclamation works. This has meant that the project was ever budget at ¥ 1.4 trillion, which may jeopardise the second phase expansion with its estimated cost of ¥ 1.8 trillion. But what are the prospects for improving international airport capacity in other regions of Japan in the 1990s?

The Ministry of Transport's Five-Year Airport Development Plan (1991 – 95) advocated that a further ¥ 3.19 trillion was needed for investment in airport infrastructure. However, almost 60 per cent of the budget has already been allocated to projects at Narita, Haneda and the KIA, and to the upgrading of regional airports which suffer from a lack of long runways, terminal facilities and associated services. For example, in the early 1990s new airports were opened at Fukushima and Hiroshima.

Lessons from the Japanese Experience

- Facilitating an expansion in the demand for outbound travel requires appropriate investment in tourist transport infrastructure so that inadequate supply does not constrain demand.
- The rhetoric and actions of government policy need to be set in a rational framework where the demand for outbound travel is sensitively managed to avoid congestion and a decline in the 'tourist travel experience'. Deregulating and liberalising air travel in Japan was not a short-term solution to expanding capacity, as airports are seriously constrained in terms of the volume of traffic they can accommodate. Morris (1994: 63) argues that 'the airport iog jam that has long hindered the development

of the outbound market will be eased by the opening of the new airport in Kansai in 1994'.

- Measures to facilitate outbound travel need to be phased in as new airport capacity comes on stream, but Bums (1996) is critical of existing measures which are viewed as 'window dressing'.
- Despite the lead time and cost of airport investment, an expansion in outbound travel was achieved in the timespan of the five years envisaged in the Ten Million Programme.

Prospects for the Japanese Outbound Market: Implications for Tourist Transport Systems

It is evident from the number of operators seeking to develop airline operations to serve Japan and the Asia-Pacific region that the Japanese outbound market offers considerable potential for the new millennium. Morris (1990) forecast that the outbound market would double by the year 2000, reaching 20 million trips and averaging annual growth rates of approximately 10 per cent. Nozawa (1992) argued that market research in Japan suggests outbound travel would expand in the following market segments:

- outbound travel by the female traveller market, especially in the 20-39 age group among office professionals (single females with a high discretionary income);
- Japanese housewives using package tours;
- older married couples aged 45 or more (full mooners) with the 'greying' of its population;
- the 'silver market' (the over 60s);

and these are markets which were discussed by Page (1989a) within the context of New Zealand.

Outbound Japanese tourists are likely to require more sophisticated package tours and independent travel on scheduled airlines. Since the Japanese tourist is preoccupied with quality in service provision, airlines and providers of tourism services will need to be conscious of the needs and 'tourist experience' sought by these travellers. Repeat travel among the Japanese to destinations they visited on package tours is growing, particularly in New Zealand. As sightseeing and touring dominate their itineraries, these offer potential niche markets for transport service providers in destination areas. The tendency among Japanese tourists for shorter stays abroad and the complex motives that influence their travel remain important factors which tour operators and tourist transport systems must try to take into account if they are to nurture the Japanese market (Morean 1983; Moore 1985). An understanding of the objectives and values of such travellers (e.g. the desire for service quality and safety) and compliance with these demands will influence the perception and image of specific tourist transport system in the 1990s and the airlines tourists choose to fly on. Transport operators serving Japan not only need to recognise the dimensions of demand in inbound and outbound tourism markets, but also to consider how future demand will be accommodated in tourist transport systems. The Japanese case study shows that infrastructure was unable to balance the demand with adequate supply.

Yamauchi (1997) identifies the difficulty which foreign airlines have in entering the Japanese market due to government policy and airport congestion problems. New proposals to allocate airport slots at Hareda airport, after the completion of a new runway, may mark a shift to a more transparent and competitive approach to air travel. But a very traditionalist approach to international aviation could continue to add to constraints on making travel more available and cost-driven for the benefit of consumers.

Attention now turns to the significance of the demand expressed as market segments before considering tourism forecasting to understand future patterns of tourist demand for travel. This will help to develop a sophisticated analysis to enable transport planners and policy makers to recognise the opportunities for tourist transport systems so that adequate infrastructure is provided to meet demand.

Analysing Tourism Demand : A Market Segment Approach

In the previous case study, the discussion of growth in the Japanese outbound market focused on the prospects for specific market segments. This approach has found a great deal of support among research companies and tourist transport operators who seek to understand how they may be able to target niche or broadly defined markets to understand their travel requirements. In a growing global marketplace with transport operators seeking to offer new products to customers, research adopting a market segment approach can provide another source of data to assess the demand for travel. For this reason, three markets, (business travel, VFR and the senior market) are now outlined to illustrate the value of such specialist studies in assembling data on a specialist form of demand.

Business Travel in the 1990s

Within the literature on tourism demand, comparatively little attention has been devoted to business travel Much of the research has been in the form of specialist reports by agencies such as American Express in the 1980s and a range of studies by market intelligence organisations and analysts. Rowe (1994) is an excellent example of an in-depth market intelligence report combining secondary sources of travel data and a blend of primary research commissioned to examine the business issues and prospects for this activity. Rowe (1994: 1) defines business travel as 'non-discretionary trips made for a work-related purpose'. Rowe's key finding is that the global volume business travel is probably underestimated in WTO statistics. The data in Table 11.13 is based on estimates from WTO in 1992 and illustrates the poorly documented nature of the subject. While Rowe's (1994) study is instrumental in explaining the extent of business travel by industry sector and the average company travel expenditure, it also provides detailed insights into the nature of demand. Macroeconomic influences have a major impact on the demand

Table 11.13
WTO Estimates of Business Travel by Region

Region	*Business-related arrivals (000s)*
Europe	47,108
Americas	8,082
East Asia-Pacific	7,079
South Asia	405
Africa	2,524

Source : WTO (1992) cited in Rowe (1994).

for this form of travel, although other factors also influence the rate of growth, such is the role of trading blocs. According to Rowe the fastest growth in global business travel is likely to occur in Central and South America, the Middle East and all parts of the Asia-Pacific region. Table 11.14 highlights the regions of forecast growth in business travel within the East Asia-Pacific (EAP) region.

The UK VFR Market

The VFR market segment has only recently attracted attention. According to Beioley (1997), VFR constituted 29 per cent of UK domestic tourist trips in 1995, which equates to 39 million trips. This generated £ 3.25 billion of revenue, equivalent

Table 11.14
Future Growth Circles for Business Travel in the East Asia-Pacific Region

Growth circle	*Participating countires*
• Golden quadrangle	S.W. China, Burma, Thailand and Laos
• Japan Sea economic zone	Japan, North and South Korea, N.E. China and the Russian Far East
• Growth circle	Taiwan and the neighbouring Chinese province of Fujian
• Growth circle	Hong Kong, Guangdong and Macau
• Growth cirlce	South China, Vietnam, Cambodia, North East Thailand and Laos
• Yellow Sea economic zone	Maritime China, Zhanjiang and Liaoning province
• The Straits growth triangle	Singapore, Malaysia's Johor and Indonesia's Riau province
• Northern growth triangle	North Malaysia, South Thailand and Northern Sumatra
• Growth circle	Malaysia and Indonesian-governed area in Borneo, the South Philippines and North Sulawesi
• Growth circle	Southern Sulawesi and Australia's Northern Territory.

Source : Modified from Rowe (1994) based on *Asia Inc. Business Magazine.*

to 13 per cent of the UK's total tourism spend. The interesting feature which Beioley identifies is the dominance of such trips by young people (under 30 years of age) who have a strong reliance upon public transport. Overseas tourist visiting the UK for VFR purposes tend to stay longer than non-VFR visitors. In fact, within the domestic VFR market, 33.1 million trips were spent in the homes of friends and relatives in the UK. In terms of mode of transport used, rail companies in the UK estimate that between 30 and 50 per cent of traffic is leisure–oriented (Beioley 1997), with some airlines (e.g. Ryanair) viewing VFR leisure travel to/from Ireland as comprising 70 per cent of their business. Similarly, scheduled carriers such as Qantas view VFR business as comprising 50 per cent of their market. In geographical terms, much of the VFR demand in the UK is located in the larger cities (14.8 million trips) compared to small towns (9.7 million trips), countryside areas (6.8 million trips), London (4.8 million trips) and coastal towns (3.6 million trips). It is evident from Beioley's (1997) study that there are a group of market segments and understanding the demand for VFR travel is a more complex task than was hitherto the case.

The Senior Market

In recent years, researchers have begun to focus on the increasing significance of one market segment that has exhibited many growth characteristics, notably the elderly or senior market (Viant 1993). The senior market is invariably defined as those travellers in middle age (55 years and over). Their significance is illustrated by Smith and Jenner (1997) who argue that international arrivals by this group will exceed 100 million in 1997, accounting for one-sixth of global trips. This is a recognition of the 'greying' of the population base of many Western nations, with the 55+ age group growing steadily in the USA and Europe and also in Japan. As a market segment, this group is normally described as possessing a significant disposable income and an expectation of increased mobility reflected in greater international travel habits. Smith and Jenner (1997: 44) cite a US magazine, *Seniors Travel Tips,* which notes that seniors account for '80 per cent of luxury travel' 70 per cent coach tours, 65 per cent of cruises, 32 per cent of overnight stays in hotels and 28 per cent of foreign travel, control 50 per cent of discretionary income, and 44 per cent of passports'. This is a clear indication of the market's significance in North America and its contribution to domestic and international tourism demand.

Table 11.15
Senior Population Aged 55 or Over for Main Tourism-Generating Countries, 1997

Country	*Total population (000)*	*Population 55+ (000)*	*Senior population (% share)*
Austria	8,054	2,101	26.1
Belgium	10,204	2,725	26.7
Denmark	5,269	1,349	25.6
France	58,470	14,678	25.1
Finland	5,109	1,254	24.5
Germany	84,068	23,846	28.4
Greece	10,583	2,988	28.2
Ireland	3,556	695	19.5
Italy	57,534	16,559	28.8
Japan	125,717	35.221	80.0
Luxembourg	422	104	24.6
Mexico	97,563	9,043	9.3
Netherlands	15,653	3,603	23.0
Portugal	9,868	2,535	25.7
Spain	39,244	10,257	26.1
Saudi Arabia	20,088	1,331	6.6
Sweden	8,946	2,436	27.2
Taiwan	21,656	3,288	15.2
UK	58,610	14,971	25.5
USA	267,955	55,913	20.9

Source: US Bureau of the Census, International Data Base, cited in Smith and Jenner (1997: 47).

Smith and Jenner (1997) indicate that there is a dearth of research on this topic following a series of ad hoc reports by the European Travel Data Centre and the Aviation and Tourism Consultancy report on the subject in 1992. WTO do not collate any comprehensive data on this market, which means researchers have to look to other sources, and in some cases make estimates of demand. While Smith and Jinner (1997) debate the semantics of what is a senior traveller they provide a useful overview of the senior population by main tourism-generating countries (table 11.15). This highlights the volume and variable proportion of the senior population in each country (see Smith and Jenner 1997 for individual profiles of the senior travel market by country). On the basis of estimates derived from their research, Smith and Jenner (1997) consider that:

- On average the senior pupulation comprises 25 per cent of the population in most countries, with Germany, Italy, France, the UK and Spain having the largest populations in this age group in the EU.
- The older people become, the less inclined they are to travel. For example, in the EU, the senior market (aged 55 - 59 years) made 2.4 domestic trips a year and 0.8 internacional trips on average. By age 75, the number of domestic trips drops to 1.3 domestic and 0.5 international trips.
- In 1993, there were an estimated 49 million senior arrivals in the EU, many of which were intraregional and by 1996 this had riosen to 60 million trips.

Table 11.16
Transport Used by Seniors on International Trips in the EU, 1996

Mode of transport	*Share of market(%)*
Air	
Scheduled	17
Charter	14
Car (private/rental)	27
Coach/Bus	24
Train	7
Cruise/Ferry	10
Other	1
Total	100

Source: Estimates by Smith and Jenner (1997)

- The senior market is far less seasonal than otelhr tourism markets, given its flexibility to travel in the non-peak period.
- Almist one-third of trips made by the senior market in Europe were by air and they also favour other land-based forms of transport (e.g. coach travel) which they perceive to be safe. Table 11.16 outlines the use of transport by this market and also highlights the interest in cruising.

A range of specialist senior travel organisations exists which nurture such travellers (e.g. the Saga group in the UK) while outbound North American educational tours have also seen significant growth in recent years (e.g. the Elderhost group). Smith and Jenner (1997) rightly point to the future growth prospects of this market, expecting a 30 per cent growth in the EU to 83 million arrivals by the year 2000. At a global scale, they forecast a growth to 136 millin arrivals in the year 2000.

It is apparent from a consideration of the significance of three types of demand expressed through market segments that researchers often need to move beyond aggregate data sources produced by WTO and OECD to derive more specific data and information. This often involves developing matching data sets to produce estimate of tourism demand, as in the case of the senior market. Transport operators and planners therefore need to have a detailed understanding of tourism demand and the difficulties associated with data sources used to understand demand. The implications here are significant when attempting to predict future patterns of demand through forecasting.

Forecasting the Demand for Tourist Transport

According to Jefferson and Lickorish (1991 : 101), forecasting the demand for tourist transport is essential for commercial operators, 'whether in the public or private sector. . . [as they] . . . will seek to maximise revenue and profits in moving towards maximum efficiency in [their] use of resources'; Archer (1987) argues that:

> no manager can avoid the need for some form of forecasting: a manager must plan for the future in order to minimise the risk of future or, more optimistically, to maximise the possibilities of success. In order to plan, he must use forecasts. Forecasts will always

be made, whether by guesswork, teamwork or the use of complex models, and the accuracy of the forecasts will affect the quality of the management decision. (Archer 1987: 77)

Reliable forecasts are essential for managers and decision-makers involved in service provision within the tourist transport system to try and ensure adequate supply is available to meet demand, while avoiding oversupply, since this can erode the profitability of their operation. In essence, 'forecasts of tourism demand are essential for efficient planning by airlines, shipping companies, railways, coach operators, hotelier, tour operators . . .' (Witt *et. al.*, 1991 : 52).

Forecasting is the process associated with an assessment of future changes in the demand for tourist transport. It must be stressed that 'forecasting is not an exact science' (Jefferson and Lickorish 1991 : 102), as it attempts to make estimations of future traffic potential and a range of possible scenarios, which provide an indication of the likely scale of change in demand. Consequently, forecasting is a technique used to suggest the future pattern of demand and associated marketing activity is required to exploit the market for tourist transport services.

According to Jefferson and Lickorish (1991 : 102) the principal methods of forecasting are:

- 'the projection by extrapolation, of historic trends' (i.e. how the previous performance of demand may shape future patterns);
- 'extrapolation, subject to the application of . . . [statistical analysis using] . . . weights or variables';
- and structured group discussions among a panel of tourism transport experts may be used to assess factors determining future traffic forecasts (known as the Delphi method).

Bull (1991) recognises that the range of tourism forecasting techniques are determined by the methods of analysis they employ. There are two basic types of forecasting method: those based on qualitative techniques, such as the Delphi method, which Archer (1987) argues are considerably less rigorous than quantitative forecasting methods, using techniques developed from statistics and economic theory.

Bull (1991 : 127-28) classifies the quantitative techniques forecasters use in terms of the degree of statistical and mathematical complexity based on.

- time-series analysis of trends (e.g. seasonality in travel) which involve simple statistical calculations to consider how past trends may be replicated in the future
- economic theory models, used in econometrics (see Witt and Martin 1992).

Clearly, in an introductory book such as this, there is insufficient space to consider the detailed technical aspects of forecasting which are reviewed in a number of other good sources (e.g. Archer 1987; Witt: and Martin 1992; Witt and Witt 1995; Frenchtling 1996; Sinclair and Stabler 1997). The important issue to recognise here is that in forecasting, a number of variables are examined which relate to factors directly and indirectly influencing tourist travel. These variables are considered according to their statistical relationship with each other. Bull (1991 : 127) notes that the most common variables used are:

- number of tourist trips;
- total tourist expenditure and expenditure per capita;
- market shares of tourism;
- the tourism sector's share of gross domestic product.

Depending on the complexity of the methodology employed, the forecasting model may examine one dependent variable (e.g. tourist trips) and how other independent variables (e.g. the state of the national and international economy, leisure time, levels of disposable income, inflation and foreign exchange rates) affect the demand for tourist trips.

Approaches to forecasting can also be classified according to what they are attempting to do. For example, time-series models of tourism, using statistical techniques such as moving averages (see Witt and Martin 1989: 6) may be easy and relatively inexpensive to undertake, but they are 'non-causal'. This means that they do not explain what specific factors are shaping the trends: they only indicate what is happening in terms of observed trends. In fact, there is also evidence that non-causal techniques have been more accurate than more complex econometric models

(Witt *et al.*, 1991). Econometric models are termed 'causal' since they are searching for statistical relationships to suggest what is causing tourist trips to take a certain form, thereby producing particular trends. Thus, the level of complexity involved in causal modeling is considerably greater.

Usyal and Crompton (1985) provide a good overview of different methods used to forecast tourism demand, concluding that:

> Qualitative approaches when combined with quantitative approaches enable forecasts to be amended to incorporate relevant consumer demand data. When asked alone quantitative models have conceptual limitations. Typically they are philosophically blind. . . . Lack of appropriate data means that they are unable to incorporate an understanding of consumer motivations and behaviour which explain tourism demand and may cause it to shift unpredictably in the future. (Usyal and Crompton 1985: 14)

Ultimately, forecasting attempts to establish how consumer demand for tourist transport has shaped previous trends and how these may change in the future, often over a five- to ten-year period. At a world scale, the detailed study by Edwards (1992) *Long Term Tourism Forecasts to the Year 2005* and subsequent updates remains an invaluable and widely cited source which examines the future demand for tourism. This can be used to assess how the demand for tourist transport will change on a global basis and within different countries over the next decade. A useful discussion of the significance of using forecasts of tourist use of a new transport system can be found in Page and Sinclair's (1992b) analysis of the demand for Channel Tunnel rail services. Nevertheless, such reports remain highly technical and only of particular use to economists who understand the techniques and methods used to forecast tourism (see Frechtling 1996). However, industry organisations such as the Air Transport Action Group commission specialist agencies to produce forecasts. For this reason, some of their key findings from their North America Traffic Forecasts 1980 – 2010 (Air Transport Action Group 1994) are now, examined.

Air Transport Traffic Forecasts to the Year 2010

The Air Transport Action Group (ATAG) was established in 1990 as an industry coalition aimed at developing 'economically beneficial aviation capacity improvements in an environmentally responsible manner'. It is concerned to lobby bodies to ensure the future growth in air travel can be accommodated through appropriate investment in airports and air traffic management. The organisation recognises that its impact has been greatest in Europe, North America and Asia through a range of publications it produces. Most of its reports are also available on the Internet (http://www/atag.org/atag/Index.htm). Given ATAG's values and objectives, the report it commissioned from IATA in 1993 provides a detailed analysis of North American traffic forecasts to 2010 (http://www.atag.org/NATF/Index.htm). While there is not space here to examine the report in detail, as a source of data it derives forecasts based on total passenger numbers in North America between 1980 and 1993. The report is extremely detailed and differentiates between various, elements of existing and future demand by US and non-US citizens and also between US and non-US carriers. Some of the key findings are interesting given the implications that ATAG identifies for its members, government agencies and private business interests:

- Air traffic in North America is heavily dominated by domestic travel and the USA accounts for approximately 80 per cent of passenger traffic, followed by Canada (4 per cent) and Mexico (3 per cent). Intra-NAFTA (North American Free Trade Area) traffic constituted 5 per cent and international traffic 8 per cent.
- Future growth rates for international traffic to and from the USA on routes to the year 2010 are forecast to be 8.2 per cent on Pacific routes, 5.6 per cent on Atlantic routes and 6 per cent on Latin American routes.
- Domestic travel in the USA is expected to rise from 450 million passengers in 1993 to over 700 million in 2010.
- IATA forecasts that the number of international passengers travelling to and from the USA will reach 226 million by 2010, a 187 per cent increase on 1993 figures of 78:8 million passengers.
- As a consequence of these growth rates, ATAG identifies the following supply-side issue: delays at US airports will increase from 23 to 33 airports by the year 2002, based on cumulative annual delays of over 20,000 hours a year.

Thus ATAG provides a range of reports on air travel in key markets which utilise IATA, ICAO and other data sources to assess demand. Its reports are easily accessed on the Internet and the detailed analysis of the North American market by domestic and international routes is a useful starting point to consider the relationship between demand, supply and the role of forecasting. Such research also highlights the significance of using various data sources and techniques to assess future demand. As Witt and Witt (1995) conclude in their seminal review of tourism forecasting methods, future developments in forecasting need to make improvements in model building and to use a range of methods to produce forecasts.

Conclusion

This chapter has shown that the demand for tourist transport can be examined from a range of accessible data sources published by the WTO and OECD, which may be complemented by more detailed studies by individual researchers, consultancies and transport operators interested in understanding the needs of their customers. The demand for tourist transport can be directly influenced by government policy to expand both incoming tourism and outbound tourism (e.g. Japan), although this has important consequences for infrastructure provision and the supply issues in tourist transport which are dealt with in subsequent chapters. In the case of China, the demand for domestic travel is of a scale which many planners, operators and researchers would find difficult to visualise and conceptualise. Growth in demand has major implications for infrastructure and the use of transport modes. Even a minor growth in demand in China has major consequences for tourist travel, given the large base population and distances involved in domestic trips. While data on domestic tourism in China is notoriously difficult to access outside of China, existing studies do point to the significance of diverse data sources in reconstructing patterns of demand and expected future growth. In this respect, WTO data can only be a rudimentary starting point for any analysis of demand. As the case study of Japan and the discussion of market segments reveal, a variety of other data sources (which do not always correspond with each other) are vital in understanding the human dimension of tourism demand.

The Ten Million Programme promoted by the Japanese government appeared to overlook the constraints imposed by airport capacity, despite the licensing of new carriers and routes to serve the Japanese market Many airline companies have set their sights on penetrating this emerging market for outbound tourism in the 1990s, at a time of relative stagnation in other mature travel markets. Such strategies are based un forecasts of the likely growth in the Japanese outbound market since companies need to establish how future investment programmes in new routes and infrastructure can be justified. Yet as Burns (1996) argues, statistical growth in tourism is not necessarily an indication of widespread cultural and cognitive changes towards holiday and overseas travel. The Japanese outbound market would have considerable growth potential if it was able to develop a holiday-taking culture commensurate with its disposable income. It is not surprising that large tourist transport operators employ forecasting experts in-house and use a variety of transport analysts to ensure that they receive the best sources of market intelligence to understand how tourism markets are performing and changing to remain competitive. Such information inevitably remains confidential, even though forecasting is not an exact science which is able to offer definitive answers on how particular tourist markets will perform over a five- to ten-year time span.

Yet the demand for tourist transport should not be viewed in isolation from supply issues. The tourist transport system operates through the interplay of government policy, consumer demand and the supply of transport services.

12

The Demand for Tourism

Introduction

Importantly, however, neither chapter has fully explored *why* it is that tourism has become such a widespread leisure activity particularly in developed, western nations. That is, although a variety of conditions must be in evidence for people to be able to participate in tourism (and for particular countries or destinations to be attractive to tourists), these do not alone explain why it is that people decide to 'consume' tourism, as opposed to other products or services, or what form that tourism will take. To put it another way, even though most people may have the ability to be tourists, it does not follow that they will all do so or, indeed, seek similar tourist experiences.

For example, roughly 60 per cent of the adult British population take a holiday (defined as four or more nights away) each year; conversely, 40 per cent do not take a holiday, a proportion that has remained the same for almost twenty years. Thus, the growth in tourism in the UK (domestic and outbound) is primarily accounted for not by more people participating in tourism, but by existing tourists taking additional holidays. At the same time, of course, the market for tourism is neither uniform nor homogenous. Different tourists seek an enormous variety of different tourism experiences, and are influenced or motivated to do so by an equally diverse variety of factors. Thus, for tourism businesses to be able to market their products effectively, to identify and target specific markets or segments and to satisfy their needs, some understanding of the complex and dynamic nature of the demand for tourism is necessary.

Therefore, purpose of this chapter is to explore the demand for tourism at the level of the individual tourist. In particular, it focuses upon:

- the tourism demand process;
- tourist motivation;
- factors that pattern or influence the nature of tourism demand;
- transformations in tourism demand.

What is Demand?

Tourism demand can be defined in a number of ways. Most commonly, it refers to the actual, measurable participation in tourism as a whole, or specific types of tourism, and it is presented in the form of statistical data. It is referred to as expressed, effective or actual demand. Thus, the actual demand for international tourism to the UK is roughly 25 million visitors, this being the annual number of overseas visitors who have visited the UK in recent years. In addition to expressed, actual demand, however, there are three other categories of demand:

- *Suppressed demand* – there may be significant numbers of tourists who wish to visit the UK, but are unable to do because of time constraints, a lack of money, or some other factor that prevents then from fulfilling their wish. Thus, their demand is suppressed until such time that their circumstances allow them to become part of the actual demand for tourism to the UK.
- *Latent demand* – in addition to suppressed demand, there are undoubtedly tourists who would visit the UK but do not because of a lack of knowledge or a lack of awareness of the means and opportunities for visiting the country. Latent demand may also exit if potential tourists feel that the services or products but they desire are not currently provided by the tourism industry.
- *No demand* – there will always be those who do not wish to travel, who will never demand tourism.

For travel and tourism businesses, therefore, the challenge is to maintain and increase their share of actual demand at the same time as converting latent demand to actual demand. Similarly, the aim of national tourist organisations is, primarily, to satisfy latent demand. It is also evident that, globally, the total demand for tourism (expressed plus suppressed plus latent) is significantly higher than actual demand, the main growth opportunities being in those countries and regions where, currently, demand is suppressed.

The Tourism Demand Process

The demand for tourism, as for most products or services, is far more complex than is immediately evident. That is, the apparently simple process of deciding to go on a holiday and then purchasing one is influenced at every stage by a variety of tangible and intangible factors, from the obvious and measurable constraints of time and money to the more subjective individual needs of the tourist. Thus, although the desire to travel can be seen as the result of having 'itchy feet', 'or the 'travel bug' – a condition referred to by Michael Palin in his book 'Around the World in 80 Days' as *dromomania* - in reality, such is the diversity of influences that determine the demand for tourism that explaining why people travel is a difficult, if not impossible, task. Indeed, it has been observed that most tourists, themselves are unable to identify what motivates them into going on holiday (Krippendorf 1987) whilst, within tourism studies, there is no common theory or understanding of the tourism demand process (Jafari 1987). Nevertheless, for travel and tourism businesses to be able to plan, develop and market their products effectively to satisfy the needs of tourists, then it is necessary to understand the nature of the tourism demand process.

As a starting point, it is important to note three related points. Firstly, many tourism texts refer simply to 'tourist motivation' when considering the demand for tourism. However, 'the term tourism demand should not be equated with tourism motivation. Tourism demand is the outcome of tourists' motivation' (Pearce 1992: 113) and is, in fact, only the first step in the demand process. Secondly, the tourism demand process is not a one-off event in people's lives. That is, although the actual holiday may only last one or two weeks, the overall experience, including anticipating the holiday, selecting and purchasing it, and remembering it afterwards, may represent a continual, cyclical process in people's lives, with previous experiences influencing the nature of subsequent holiday decisions (see Figure 12.1).

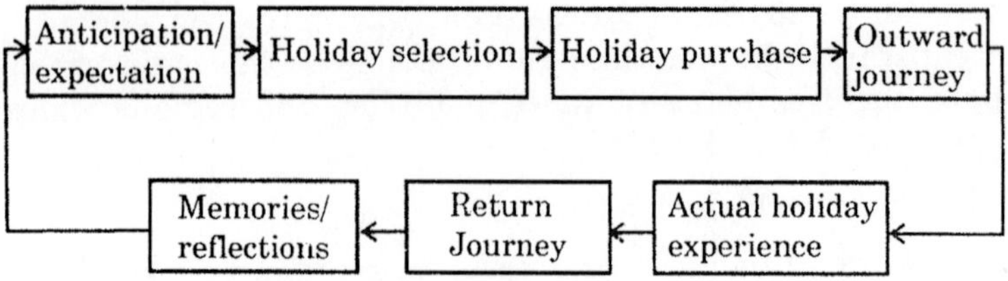

Fig. 12.1 : The Tourism Demand Cycle.

In this model, each element is an important part of the overall demand process, with certain aspects, such as anticipating or dreaming about the holiday, being an exciting and satisfying (if not more so!) than the holiday itself.

Finally, the demand for tourism should not be viewed in isolation from other demand processes or from the broader socio-cultural setting within which it occurs. Not only does tourism 'compete' with other products and services for a share of an individual's usually finite disposable income, but also a number of factors, such as values, tastes, fashion and 'consumer culture', influence behaviour. As Solomon observes, 'consumption choices simply cannot be understood without considering the cultural context in which they are made' (Solomon 1994: 536).

Collectively, these points suggest that the demand for tourism is highly complex. It is related to both personal preferences and constraints and external socio-cultural influences, as well as being dynamic and evolving in line with the tourist's own experience and expectations. A number of authors have attempted to develop models of this complex process (see Goodall 1991 and, more generally, Cooper *et al.* 1998, some of which are simple, unidirectional linear models, whilst others are more sophisticated. All, however, follow the basic premise that, once they have decided to purchase a holiday, tourists go through a process of acquiring information, deciding what holiday would best satisfy their needs and, subsequently, evaluating the extent to which those needs were met. Moreover, each stage in this process is shaped by a variety of personal and external factors. Figure 11.2 summarizes this tourism demand process.

Inevitably, perhaps, this model over-simplifies the tourism demand process, although it does highlight the principal elements of consumer decision-making. Thus, prior to any purchase decision, the consumer (tourist) must feel or recognise a need which may be satisfied by the consumption of a particular product or service. The choice of product/service selected is then determined both by personal and external social factors and by the choice on offer (i.e. the attraction of different destinations and the way in which it is sold or packaged), as well as the experience of previous holidays. At the same time, however, the entire process is influenced by broader cultural factors, in particular the role of consumption in society.

These elements of the tourism demand process are usefully summarized by Gilbert (1991: 79), as follows:

(a) *Energisers of demand* – These are the various forces, including motivation, that act as a trigger setting off the tourism demand process.

(b) *Filterers of demannd* – these are all the factors, such as time, income and demographic characteristics, that constrain choice or 'filter out' inappropriate products.

(c) *Affectors of demand* – the actual choice of holiday will be affected by the attributes and image of different destinations.

(d) *Roles* – the role of the tourist as a consumer (who is making the decision and 'how' they consume) will also determine the final choice of holiday.

Of course, any attempt to explain the overall tourism demand process is fraught with difficulty, particularly as most consumers are unlikely to follow, whether consciously or unconsciously, a logical decision-making process. For example, many holidays are undoubtedly bought as last-minute, impulse purchases whilst, more generally, going on holiday (buying on trust, experiencing unusual environments, and so on) is hardly rational behaviour. Indeed, the annual mass rush for the sun has been likened to the behaviour of lemmings (Emery 1981)! Nevertheless, it is

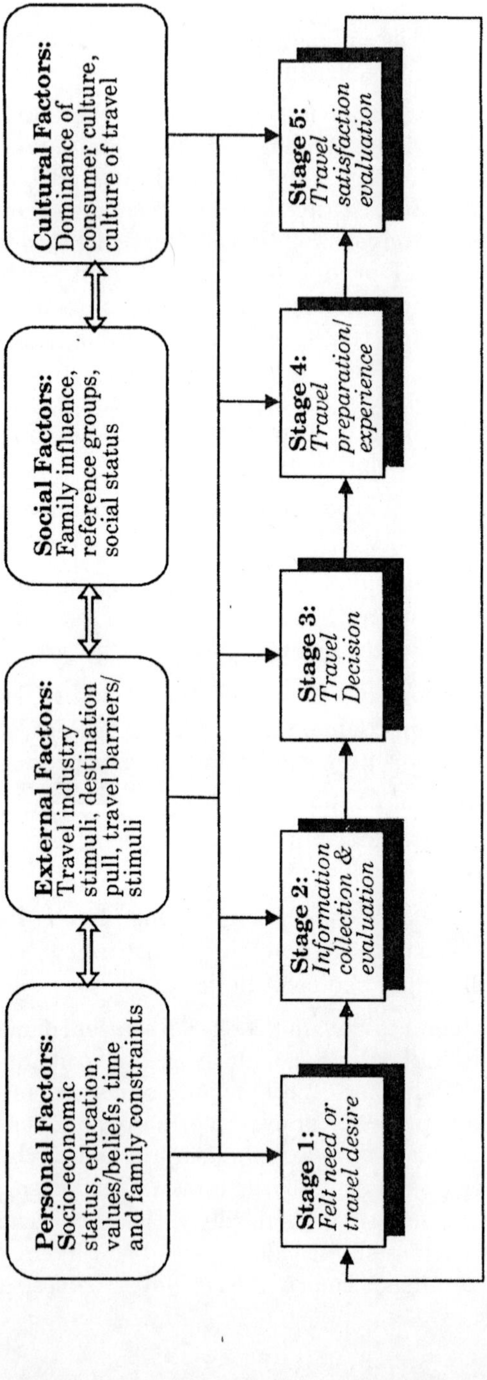

Fig. 12.2 : The tourism demand process.

important to appreciate specific influences on the decision-making process, and it is with these that the following sections are concerned.

Tourist Motivation

Motivation is the most important yet, at the same time, most complex elements of tourism demand. Certainly, without motivation there would be no demand for tourism: 'the importance of motivation in tourism is quite obvious. It acts as a trigger that sets off all events in travel' (Parrinello 1993). In other words, it is motivation that provides the link between a need and action to satisfy that need; it is motivation that translates a need into goal-orientated consumer behaviour. However, much less clear is how needs emerge in the first place and how the satisfaction of those needs can be related to tourism in particular. For example, there are those who argue that motivation is purely a psychological concept and, therefore, that tourism demand is the result of intrinsic, psychological needs, such as relaxation, love and affection, and so on (hence the common reference to Maslow's 'hierarchy of needs' in many tourism texts).

Conversely, there can be no doubt that the motivation for tourism is also socially determined. That is, it is society that, in one way or another, creates the need within people to travel, to participate in tourism. For example, society 'expects' people to take a summer holiday and, in a sense, tourism is 'social therapy, a safety valve keeping the everyday world in good working order' (Krippendorf 1986). Undoubtedly, for most people it is the need to escape, from work, from the 'rules' of society or whatever, that provides the primary motivation to go on holiday whilst a variety of socially-determined factors also influence the type of holiday people take.

It is not surprising, therefore, that the literature on tourist motivation encompasses a broad spectrum of ideas and approaches. By way of summary, Dann (1981) identifies seve different perspectives on motivation that have been adopted:

(a) *Travel as a response to what is lacking yet desired* – The motivation for travel lies in the desire to experience something new or different. People become tourists because their own physical and cultural environment cannot fulfil this need.

(b) *Destinational pull in response to motivational push* – This approach highlights the importance of push factors in tourist motivation (see below). Such factors may be determined by the tourist's home environment or by an individual's own psychological needs.

(c) *Motivation as fantasy* – Tourists may be motivated by the perceived opportunity to indulge in forms of behaviour that would not normally be 'allowed' in their usual home/work environment.

(d) *Motivation as classified purpose* – In contrast to push factors, this approach views the purpose of a trip as the primary motivating factor.

(e) *Motivational typologies* – Typologies of tourists are often used as models of tourist motivation. However, they may be more accurately seen as factors that influence the nature of tourist behaviour rather than a primary force behind the initial need to consume tourism

(f) *Motivation and tourist experiences* – This approach suggests that tourist motivation is largely determined by the expected experience in relation to the home environment, in particular by the promise of authenticity.

(g) *Motivation as auto-definition and meaning* – The ways in which tourists define and respond to situations, rather than simply describing their behaviour, is seen by some as one way of explaining tourist motivation.

It is neither possible nor appropriate here to review all of these (see, for example, Sharpley 1999). Nevertheless, certain points which more fully explain the role and nature of tourist motivation deserve emphasis.

Push Versus *Pull Factors*

In order to clarify the importance and position of motivation in the tourism demand process, a distinction must be made between what are called 'pull' and 'push' factors. Pull factors refer to all the knowledge, information, images and perceptions that an individual has of a particular holiday or destination. These 'destination-specific attributes' (Goodall 1991: 59) include tangible factors, such as accommodation facilities, beaches, entertainment facilities, the prospect of good weather, and so on, whilst more subjective factors include how fashionable the resort is.

Conversely, push factors influence, or push, the individual into wanting a holiday in the first place. These 'person-specific motivations' are the needs that push an individual into wanting a holiday or trip of a particular type, or a holiday as opposed to another product or service. Thus, only when a need or push has been recognised do pull factors come into play; push factors motivate the individual to buy a holiday, whereas pull factors determine which holiday or destination is chosen to best satisfy the individual's needs.

The distinction between push and pull factors is of fundamental importance to understanding the role of motivation within the demand for tourism. For example, the choice of a beach holiday might be explained by the 'pull' of the climate and the likelihood of getting a suntan. However, the true motivation may well result from the need to be seen with a suntan; the push is to get a suntan that can be shown off when the tourist returns home. Similarly, the motivation to visit exotic destinations may not be the desire to see a particular place, but the opportunity to say that you have been there (reinforced by the opportunity to send the ubiquitous post card or to take holiday photos to show at home!). In short, 'the key to understanding tourist motivation is to see vacation travel as a satisfier of needs and wants' (Mill and Morrison 1985: 4). The task then is to consider what creates these needs.

Intrinsic Versus *Extrinsic Motivation*

Although a number of different approaches are evident in the literature, there are two distinct perspectives which are of particular use and which, for the most part, embrace much of the existing theory and knowledge of tourist motivation. At the same time, they also recognise the traditional dichotomy between motivation as a psychological or a sociological concept.

Intrinsic Motivation

The basis of intrinsic motivation is that all individuals possess a variety of unique personal needs, the satisfaction of which has long been considered the primary arousal factor in all motivated, goal-oriented behaviour, including tourism. Therefore, the understanding of human motivation is, from an intrinsic motivational perspective, dependent upon what those needs are and how they can be fulfilled or satisfied.

One of the best known and most widely referred to theory of motivation is, of course, Maslow's hierarchy of needs. Maslow originally proposed five classes of needs, from basic physiological needs through to self-actualisation, each of which must be satisfied before the individual is motivated by the next level in the hierarchy. Given its simplicity, Maslow's model has been adapted to different contexts, including tourism, in order to explain human behaviour. For example, a similar framework of tourist motivation was developed by Pearce and Caltabiano (1983), who suggest that hierarchical needs, ranging from biological (rest and recuperation), through relationship and special interest needs to self-actualisation, can be used to explain tourist behaviour.

More simply and generally intrinsic psychological needs have been collectively referred to as 'ego-enhancement' motivational factors (Dann 1977), which suggest that people are motivated to participate in tourist in the expectation of intrinsic psychological rewards. In other words, people are motivated to travel or to go on holiday to have their ego or confidence boosted, to personally and psychologically gain from tourism and to feel better about themselves. This may be achieved whilst travelling (for example, by staying at an hotel that provides levels of service or luxury not normally experienced during the tourist's day-to-day life at home) or on return (as before, the opportunity to show off the suntan). A number of other psychological motivations have also been listed by Krippendorf (1987), who includes compensation and social integration, escape, communication, broadening the mind, self-determination, self-realisation, and happiness as intrinsic needs that may form the basis of tourist motivation.

Extrinsic Motivation

In Contrast to intrinsic motivation, extrinsic motivational factors are those forces and pressures which emanate from an individual's social and cultural environment and which may, to a lesser or greater extent, influence that individual's needs and motivations. In a general sense, this may simply be 'society' as a whole. That is, for most people, tourism represents the opportunity to escape from the pressures, strain or even boredom of everyday life, to unwind and relax or to seek excitement and new experiences. Indeed, it is probably true to say that tourism has become an essential ingredient in an individual's life cycle in modern society–in order to survive modern life and society, an individual must, periodically, escape from it. In this sense, modem tourism has achieved the status of a new religion; it is a kind of sacred Journey which provides physical and spiritual refreshment.

More specifically, however, both the need or desire to go on holiday, and the nature of the experience sought, may be directly influenced by external (as opposed to intrinsic, psychological) factors which become translated into needs within the individual, are summarised in Figure 12.3.

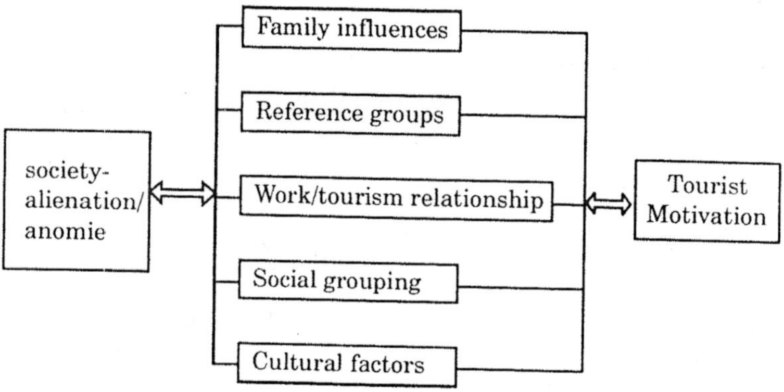

Fig. 12.3: Extrinsic motivational factors.

Inevitably, not all of these extrinsic factors will influence an individual tourist. Indeed, if it were actually possible to accurately ascertain the factors and influences that determine an individual's motivation to participate in tourism (an unlikely event given the fact that most tourist do not recognise – or are not prepared to admit - what actually motivates them), it is likely that there are as many forms of tourist motivation as there are tourist. Nevertheless, it is safe to suggest that, for the most part, tourists, are motivated by a combination 'escape' and 'ego-enhancement' needs and, therefore, the challenge facing the tourism industry is to recognise and satisfy these needs with products and experiences that are attractive to tourist.

Factors that Pattern or Influence the Nature of Tourism Demand

According to the model of the tourism demand process (Fig. 12.2), once an individual is motivated to purchase a holiday or trip (i.e. the tourism demand process has been 'energised'), he or she then goes through a process of collecting information, from brochures, travel agents, advertisements, guide books, word of mouth and personal experience before making a travel decision. That decision is, partly, based on the extent to which a particular trip, holiday or destination satisfies the individual's needs (for example, a skiing holiday for someone who seeks a healthy life-style), but also partly according to constraints or factors which limit or shape the eventual choice. These are the 'filterers' and 'affectors referred to earlier and are, in effect, a set of both tangible or measurable factors and subjective, psychographic factors. (The latter category includes the tourist's attitudes, values and beliefs which, perhaps inevitably, also impact upon motivations, but for the sake of simplicity we shall consider them here separately from motivation.) Thus, although a skiing holiday has been identified as the ideal holiday, the actual destination, length and time of holiday and other variables will be subject to a number of factors.

Tangible Demand Factors

There are number of tourism enabling factors. Principally, these factors can be grouped under the headings of 'time', 'money' and 'technology', increases or advances in which have been the driving force behind the historical growth in tourism. At the same time, the development of a sophisticated travel tourism industry, greater public sector support, changes in the structure of the tour operating industry, improvements in information and ancillary services, such as insurance, and innovation in product design have all, the 'macro' level, contributed to the expansion of tourism.

Some, if not all, of these have also had an impact on tourism demand at the individual, micro level and it is important to consider these and other factors that act as filters and affectors in the tourism demand process.

Mobility

As a prerequisite to tourism (which by implication involves travel), an individual must benefit from mobility. In one sense, this means having the freedom to travel, something that the populations of the industrialised, western world have long enjoyed – subject to visa restrictions in destination countries – but which those in many other countries have only recently begun to enjoy. At the same time, however, mobility may be taken more literally as the physical ability to travel. Thus, in the UK domestic market, car ownership is a significant influence on mobility whilst, more generally, the extent to which facilities are provided for those with disabilities has a significant impact on tourism demand.

Employment and Income

As already noted, the nature of an individual's work may be related to the desired type of holiday experience. However, as tourism is an expensive activity that requires a certain level of income before participation is possible, employment plays a more fundamental role in the demand for tourism. More simply stated, with the exception of certain groups, such as those with independent means or retired people on private or occupational pensions, it is usually necessary, for at least one family member to be in employment to pay for a holiday.

However, simply having a job and income does not guarantee the ability to participate in tourism. Although it is safe to assume that, as income rises, so too does the demand for tourism, it is vital to consider tourism as an item of expenditure on the household budget. In other words, although some level of gross income is necessary before a holiday can be afforded, tourism is usually a discretionary, or non-essential, form of expenditure. All households have certain outgoings that cannot be avoided – the mortgage or rent, income and local tax, expenditure on food clothing, transport, and so on – and only when these have been paid can some (or all!) of the remaining, discretionary income be spent on tourism. At the same time, all households have different discretionary income levels. A 'double-income-no-kids' household may have significant sums of money to spend on tourism compared with a young family; conversely, they may have committed themselves to very high mortgage before having children and therefore have little spare cash for holidays.

This suggests that the effect of income on tourism demand must be considered at the individual level although, when average levels of discretionary income fall, such as during a recession or when interest rates are high, it has been found that it is the amount spent on a holiday, rather than the number of holidays, that decreases. This suggests, in turn, that tourism is becoming an essential (i.e. non-discretionary) element of household expenditure.

In addition to discretionary income levels, it is important to note two other economic factors that influence the demand for tourism:

(a) *Absolute cost of tourism* – The ability to pay for a holiday is dependent on not only levels of income, but also the 'real' cost of the holiday. Thus, if holidays become cheaper in real terms, then it is likely that overall demand will increase or that the demand will shift to more exotic/luxurious types of holiday or destination. Certainly, the average price of package holidays out of the UK fell during the early 1990s, contributing, to the growth in international tourism, whilst the inclusion of cruising in package holiday brochures significantly increased demand for a once exclusive form of holiday.

(b) *Relative costs* – As a result of exchange rate fluctuations and local economic conditions in the destination, the demand for particular destinations can rise and fall. In the mid-1990s, for example, the French franc was relatively strong against sterling and, as a consequence, the number of British visitors to France fell dramatically. Conversely, the strong pound over the last two years has made many countries much more affordable to British tourists, particularly those which have devalued their own currencies.

Paid Holiday Entitlement

Related to employment and income, the amount of paid holiday that an individual enjoys is also a major determinant of tourism demand. Since the Holidays with Pay Act was passed in Britain in 1938, ever-increasing numbers of employees have benefited from greater amounts of paid holiday time. For example, by 1969, 97 per cent of all full-time manual workers in Britain received two weeks paid holiday; by 1988, 99 per cent received four weeks, with many of those in the professions enjoying even longer paid holidays. Thus, paid holiday entitlement has inevitably had a positive impact on the demand for tourism, in particular permitting additional holidays to the traditional two-week summer break, although more flexible work practices, such as 'flexi-time', have also enabled people to take more short-break holidays.

Of course, not all countries enjoy the same levels of paid holidays. It tends to be more generous in developed countries, although the USA is less generous than many European countries. Much also depends upon the number of public or 'bank' holidays which are more numerous in some countries than others, whilst the availability of paid holidays does not always guarantee that all employees take full advantage of their entitlement. Equally not all paid time off will be spent on holiday, suggesting that, overall, there is not an entirely clear relationship between the levels of paid holiday and the demand for tourism.

Education

Typically, a positive relationship exists between levels of education attainment and the propensity to travel (Cooper *et al.* 1998: 43), although it is probably fairer to suggest that it is not participation in tourism itself, but the *type* of tourism demanded, that varies according to education. Therefore, it is likely that the more educated tourist is more likely to seek out new destinations, new, experiences and, perhaps, view tourism itself as an education.

Demographic Factors

Inevitably, the demand for tourism is affected by a variety of demographic variables, including age, stage in the family life cycle, race and gender. Thus, parents with young children are constrained by destination choice and by time if the children are at school, whilst older people (or 'empty-nesters') enjoy more flexibility, particularly if they are retired and can travel at times to suit themselves. Race is also an important variable. Increasingly, international tourist flows follow historical patterns of migration, with a significant demand for tourism between, for example, Britain and the Indian subcontinent or Australia/ New Zealand and Britain, whilst some forms of Tourism are entirely determined by race/culture, such as the annual pilgrimage to Mecca. Gender is, generally, a less significant determinant of tourism demand although women travellers may be discouraged from visiting certain countries as a result of local cultural or religious practices.

Values, Attitudes and Beliefs

As suggested above, all stages of the tourism demand process are influenced by a potentially large variety of factors which determine not only the comparison of alternatives and choice of holiday, but also the actual and evaluated holiday experience. In particular, these factors include demographic variables : 'it is commonly believed that tourist behaviour [is] affected, if not determined, by the tourist's age, sex, marital status, education, disposable income, place of origin and other similar factors' (Pizam and Calantone 1987). However, although such factors are useful for segmenting markets and as a basic predictor of how particular groups may consume tourism, they reveal little about *why* tourists behave in particular ways.

As a result, it is increasingly recognised that so-called psychographic or life-style variables, which include values, attitudes, opinions and interests, are more important influences in the tourism decision-making process. In other words, although certain descriptive variables, such as demographic characteristics, may limit or affect the eventual holiday choice, the entire decision-making process is framed and guided by values, attitudes or beliefs upon which the individual bases most, if not all, forms of behaviour and decisions.

The most powerful of these influences are, according to Rokeach (1973), values. Whereas an attitude refers to the application of a number of beliefs to a specific situation or object, a value 'refers to a single belief of a very specific kind' (Rokeach 1973: 18). In other words, values are concerned with acceptable or appropriate forms of behaviour end-states that an individual aspires to and, thus, govern that individual's interests, attitudes, consumption behaviour and other activities that define a lifestyle.

According to Rokeach, not only do individuals carry these beliefs or values that determine their modes of behaviour, but they also organise them into a value system. This represents a continuum of the relative importance of the different values they hold, which then guides behaviour and decision-making according to different situations. Thus, an individual who embraces 'pleasure' as a higher value and 'environmental concern' as a lower value may normally buy environmentally friendly products except in the case of a holiday, were pleasure will be the dominant desired end-state. Rokeach himself devised a 'value survey' of 18 'instrumental' and 'terminal' values; which includes values such as 'pleasure', 'freedom', 'exciting life' and 'self-respect', all of which of direct relevance to tourism as well as reflecting the two primary motivational factors of escape/avoidance and self-reward/ego-enhancement. Indeed, many of Rokeach's terminal values are likely to be dominant in the tourism decision-making process (see Figure 12.4)

A comfortable life	Inner harmony
An exciting life	Mature love
A sense of accomplishment	National security
A world at peace	Pleasure
A world of beauty	Salvation
Equality	Self-respect
Family security	Self-recognition
Freedom	True friendship
Happiness	Wisdom

Figure 12.4: Rokeach's terminal values

Source: Rokeach (1973: 359 - 40)

A more simple version of a value scale for segmenting consumer behaviour is the Values and Lifestyle Scale (VALS) that divides American consumers into nine lifestyles or types under four categories based upon their self-images, aspirations, values and beliefs (Figure 12.5)

Need Driven Groups:	*Outer Directed Groups:*
Survivor lifestyle	Belongers lifestyle
Sustainer lifestyle	Emulator lifestyle Achiever lifestyle
Inner Directed Groups:	*Outer/inner Directed Groups:*
I-am-me lifestyle	Integrated lifestyle
Experimental lifestyle	
Societally-conscious lifestyle	
Self-directed lifestyle	

Figure 12.5: VALS categories.

Here, there are evident links between these groups and sub-groups of consumer types and different forms of tourist behaviour, suggesting that the VALS scale represents a useful predictor of tourism demand. For example, inner directed, societally-conscious consumers are, perhaps, likely to favour 'appropriate' forms of tourism, such as eco-tourism, whilst outer-directed groups are more likely to choose holidays or trips that offer the opportunity for status enhancement.

Surprisingly, perhaps, few empirical studies have been made into the influence of values on tourism demand in particular (see Sharpley 1999: 171), Those that have been undertaken have demonstrated that values are indeed related to holiday or destination choice criteria and different forms of actual behaviour. At the same time, however, they suggest that values alone are not a sufficient criterion for predicting behaviour. Not only does the importance place on specific values vary according to context but, within tourism, there is a greater likelihood of value conflict. That is, values of socially acceptable behaviour may, for example, conflict with hedonistic-type values. Thus, the importance of values to the study of tourism demand lies in their contribution – as one of a number of factors – to a greater understanding of how and why tourists make particular consumption decisions, rather than underpinning the entire process.

Consumer Culture and Tourism

For the most part, research into the tourism demand process in general, and, tourist motivation in particular, has been highly tourism-centric. That is, attention has been largely focused on the actual tourism decision-making process and the factors, at the level of the individual, that influence that process. 'Conversely, until recently, less importance has been placed on exploring the significance and meaning of tourism as a form of consumption in general, and the ways in which the consumption or styles of tourism may be influenced by cultural transformations and developments in the tourist's home environment in particular.

To put it another way, it is certainly important to understand the process that tourists go through in purchasing a holiday and to appreciate the factors that shape or direct that process. However, to focus specifically on the needs and wants of individuals and how tourism may satisfy these needs and wants is to overlook the broader cultural forces that influence not only tourism, but all forms of consumer behaviour. Tourism is but one of innumerable forms of consumption in a world where people's lives are increasingly defused by their consumption habits; that is, people consume, or buy, products and services not only for utilitarian need satisfaction, but also to give 'meaning' to their social existent. Tourism is no exception and, therefore, it is important to understand the role of this 'consumer culture' in general on the consumption of tourism in particular.

What is 'Consumer Culture'?

Consumer culture may be defined as the character, significance and role of the consumption of commodities, services and experiences within modern societies. Its existence as a cultural phenomenon implies that consumption, as a social activity, has become culturally significant. More simply stated, the emergence of a dominant consumer culture reflects a shift in power from the producer to the consumer. Whereas throughout the twentieth century, up to the early 1970s, the consumer was obliged to accept what was produced by manufacturers (indeed, the success of mass production as pioneered by Henry Ford – hence the term 'Fordist' production – was dependent on willing mass consumptions, more recent years have witnessed the emergence of 'consumer power', with producers having to respond to frequent changes in taste and fashion.

In part, this has come about as a result of changes in the social and economic system in postindustrial societies that have enabled the practice of consumption to assume a leading role in people's lives. These changes include:

- the large, widely-available and ever-increasing range of consumer goods and services;
- the popularity of 'leisure shopping';
- the emergence of consumer groups and consumer legislation;
- pervasive advertising; and
- widely available credit facilities.

Collectively, these factors have provided the consumer with enormous choice and, hence, power (Lury 1996).

However, it is not only the practice of consumption that has underpinned the emergence of consumer culture. It has long been recognised that commodities, whether goods or services, have a meaning or significance beyond the basic economic exchange or use value. Therefore, when people buy things, not only do they buy commodities that fulfil a particular function, but also they acquire things which create or shape their social life. In short, people consume products and services not only for their basic use but also to say something about themselves. The obvious example is, of course, that car which, fundamentally, is a convenient means of travelling from one place to another. However, the car is also, arguably, one of the most powerful status symbols of modern times.

Collectively, the practice and significance of consumption can be thought of as 'the active ideology that the meaning of life is to be found in buying things and pre-packed experiences' (Bocock 1993: 50). That is, people add meaning to or embellish their day-to-day existence through consumption of goods and services, and tourism is no exception to this process. In other words, tourism has long had a significance beyond its 'utilitarian' value of providing rest, relaxation, escape, education, and so on, with people choosing different modes of transport, types of holidays or destinations for other reasons. Most typically, people consume tourism as a means of classification or self-identity creation, to classify themselves in relation to other people and to establish social status. As one commentator has observed, 'while travel has remained an expression of taste since the eighteenth century, it has never been so widely used as at present' (Munt 1994). Thus, people may choose to holiday at an all-inclusive resort in the Caribbean, such as Sandals, in order to feel exclusive, or to have a holiday in Agia Napa in Cyprus to be part of the 'club scene'.

The implication for the travel and tourism industry is that, increasingly, it is having to develop more specialised, niche products to satisfy the demands of tourists who are no longer satisfies with the standard 'off-the-shelf' package holiday. Thus, eco-tourism holidays, all-inclusives, fly-cruise holidays, more distant or exotic destinations and more individualistic holidays (albeit within the framework of the traditional package of flights, transfers and accommodation) are becoming more widely available, offering the aura of status or luxury though at a relatively affordable price. In other words, although tourists are undoubtedly motivated by the desire to escape, rest, relax and have fun, their consumption of tourism experiences is framed by a cultural dimension of which the industry is becoming increasingly aware.

Changes in Demand: Shift to the New Tourist?

As evidence, perhaps, of the influence of consumer culture on the demand for tourism, there is little doubt that tourists are becoming more discerning, more quality and value conscious, more individualistic and, generally, more experienced in the practice of consuming tourism. In other words, it would appear that tourists are increasingly rejecting the standardised package for holidays or tourism experiences that do not conform with the image of a mass produced/consumed (and, by implication, down-market) product.

Certainly, changes in the demand for tourism over the last decade tend to support this view. In general, tour operators and other tourism businesses are having to develop more specialised products for niche markets. Mention has already been made of the introduction of 'package-cruises' by major tour operators in the early 1990s, but other notable trends include:

- an increasing demand for activity-based holidays;
- significant growth in the '(eco-tourism' market – this is considered by many to be the fastest growing sector of international tourism;
- an expansion of the long-haul holiday/package market;
- the increasing popularity of theme parks and holiday parks;
- a consequential relative drift from traditional sun-sea-sand holidays to cultural tourism, urban and rural tourism;
- growth in the short-break market;
- a relatively greater incidence of independent, as opposed to organised (packaged) holidays.

This list is, of course, by no means exhaustive. The important point here, however, is that some would claim that these changes in the demand for tourism are themselves evidence of the emergence of the 'new' tourist. For example, Poon (1993) suggests that 'old', mass tourism, characterised by maas produced, mass marketed and standardised holidays, were consumed by inexperienced, 'sun-lusting', unadventurous tourists. Conversely, she argues that the new tourist is, for example, more flexible, more experienced, has more special interests, if environmentally sensitive, is more independent and seeks variety, adventure and quality. Similarly, others suggest that tourists are becoming 'greener', that they are demanding holidays that are more environmentally appropriate (the growth in demand for eco-tourism usually being cited in support of this argument). This latter point is certainly open to debate although, as argued elsewhere, there is little evidence to suggest that tourists do in fact take environmental factors into consideration when buying a holiday (Sharpley 1999; Swarbrooke and Horner 1999). Indeed, with reference to the previous section on consumer culture, it has been suggested that eco-tourism (which tends to be exclusive and expensive and usually occurs in more exotic destinations) should actually be called 'ego-tourism' (Wheeller 1992)!

Whether or not the new, 'good' tourist exists, two points should be emphasised. Firstly, the package tour remains highly popular, suggesting that significant numbers of tourists are satisfied with the convenience, safety and value of the traditional package holiday. Secondly, however, there is no doubt that people have become more experienced tourists. They are less willing to accept poor quality or service and poor value for money, they understand their legal rights as consumers, and they increasingly seek more individualistic holidays, albeit within the framework of the package. Thus, tour operators are becoming obliged to focus more on quality, service, diversity whilst, at die same time maintaining the relatively low prices that underpin the success of the tour operating business. Whether this can be achieved through greater efficiency or, as is more likely, through increases in the average price of holidays remains to be seen.

Conclusion

This chapter has considered the tourism demand process, focusing in particular on the variety of influences and forces that determine why and how people 'consume' tourism. Emphasising the fact that motivation does not equate with demand - the demand for tourism is, in effect, the outcome of tourist motivation - it has demonstrated that there are no simple answers to the question 'why do people participate in tourism?'. Indeed, such is the variety of influences, both tangible or measurable, such as income or time, and socio-cultural, that each tourist goes through a unique, personal demand process. Nevertheless, it is vital that tourist businesses understand and appreciate this variety of influences on tourism demand in order to be able to continue to satisfy the changing needs of tourists.

13
Tour Operations

Introduction

Since the early 1950s, when Vladimir Raitz established Horizon Holidays and offered what is considered to be the first charter flight-based package holiday (Yale 1995: 38), tour operators have played a dominant role in the production and distribution of tourism. Not only have they made a significant contribution to the growth and democratisation of international mass tourism, but also they have come to occupy a strategically dominant position within the international tourism industry. Indeed, as Ioannides (1998: 139) suggests, tour operators act as 'gatekeepers' to the industry, being able to exert 'enormous influence over the geography of origin-destination tourist flows and, ultimately, the fortunes of individual destinations'.

At the same time, and despite the more recent growth in demand for independent holidays, inclusive tours/package holidays remain as popular as ever. Thus, although inclusive tours represent a declining proportion of total overseas holidays taken by British tourists (Table 13.1), the total number of overseas holidays continues to grow, as does the number of inclusive tour holidays, albeit at a slower rate. In fact, an estimated 17 million inclusive tours were taken by the British in 1999, only slightly below the record 17.4 million in 1998; of these, 13.7 million, or 81 per cent, were holidays by air (Mintel 2000). The number of licensed tour operators also continues to grow; in the UK, for example, there are now in excess of 1400 Air Travel Organisers

License (ATOL) holders. However, the majority of these are small, specialist companies and it is the large, international operators that are best known and which, over the last decade, have achieved a dominant position within the industry.

Table 13.1
Independent/Inciusive Overseas Holidays Taken by British Tourists (millions)

	1986	*1990*	*1995*	*1997*	*1986 - 97 % change*
Total overseas holidays	17.5	20.5	26.0	26.5	+51
Of which:					
independent holidays	6.5	9.0	11.0	11.5	+77
inclusive tour holidays	11.0	11.5	15.0	15.0	+36
Inclusive tours as % of total	62.8	56.1	57.7	56.6	

Source: Adapted from Pender (2001 : 7).

The purpose of this chapter is to explore the structure and activities of the tour operating sector. In particular, it focuses upon:

- The role of the tour operator in the production and distribution of tourism.
- The structure of the industry and the benefits of integration,
- The planning and creation of a package holiday.
- The importance of consumer protection.
- Quality management in tour operating.

Firstly, however, it is important to define what is meant by the term 'tour operating'.

Tour Operations: A Definition

Perhaps the best way of explaining the nature and scope of tour operating is to define the product of tour operating – that is, the inclusive tour or package holiday.

The Package Holiday

According to Section 2(1) of the EU's Package Travel, Package Holidays and Package Tours Regulations 1992 , a package holiday is legally defined as:

'the pre-arranged combination of at least two of the following components when sold or offered for sale at an inclusive price and when the service covers a period of more than 24 hours or includes overnight accommodation:

(a) transport

(b) accommodation

(c) other tourist services not ancillary to transport or accommodation and accounting for a significant proportion of the package.'

Thus, although package holidays are, perhaps, most commonly thought of in terms of charter flights to summer sun destinations, there is in fact an enormous variety of types of package holiday. Package holidays by air, for example, can be subdivided into travel by scheduled carrier (known as ITX) and travel by charter flight (ITC).

For simplicity, different types of package tour can be characterised by:

- *Mode of transport* – in addition to air inclusive tours, the transport element of a package holiday may involve travel by ship (ferry, cruise liner, hovercraft, chartered yacht, etc.), rail, coach (travel to or around the destination) or hired car or bicycle. Some packages can also be characterised by the holidaymaker providing their own transport such as walking, cycling and domestic self-drive holidays.
- *Mode of accommondation* – the accommodation element of a package may be a room in an hotel, guest house or other serviced accommodation, a self-catering apartment or villa, a tent or caravan, or may even be combined with the transport element, such as a cabin on a cruise ship.
- *Services provided* – a package may include only the basic flight, transfer and, say self-catering accommodation. At the other extreme, it may be 'all-inclusive', where all meals, drinks and, perhaps, activities and entertainment are provided.
- *International vs. domestic* – although most usually associated with outgoing international tourism (for example, UK tourists taking holidays overseas), an important sector of the market is incoming inclusive tours,

organised by either overseas operators or operators based within the UK. At the same time, package holidays are also sold to the domestic market, typically based on coach travel or self-drive.

- *Length of holiday* – the length of a package holiday may vary from a short-break of between one and three nights to away to longer holidays (i.e. four or more nights away). Typically, this is the 7, 10 or 14 night holiday, although some tour operators offer extended winter-sun holidays for the retired market.
- *Distance to destination* – The majority of package holidays are taken within Europe – 90 per cent of inclusive tours from the UK are to Europe, with Spain accounting for over 30 per cent of the market (Mintel 2600) – and are, therefore, to 'short haul' destinations (normally considered to be up to four hours flying time). However, long haul destinations, including North America, the Caribbean, the Far East and Australia, are becoming increasingly popular.

Overall, then, the package holiday is a much broader concept than is immediately apparent. Indeed, even a six-month overland trip through, for example, South America, which would include return flights, transport in trucks and/or local transport, and basic accommodation and food is, in fact, a package holiday. Adventure tour operators offering these types of holiday are, however, unlikely to refer to them as such – ironically, they are usually referred to as 'independent travel'.

It is also evident that a package holiday need not necessarily. include air travel. However, the majority of inclusive tours are by air and therefore, it is with these operators that this chapter is principally concerned.

The-tour Operator

Following on from the above definition of an inclusive tour/ package holiday, a tour operator (or what the ED Package Travel regulations refer to as a 'tour organiser') is clearly an individual or organisation who buys the various components of the package (usually in bulk), combines them to produce the package holiday, and then sells it to the customer either directly or through a travel agent. This implies, of course, that a travel agent who assembles a holiday for an individual customer can also take on the role of a tour operator.

In a sense, therefore, a tour operator is a wholesaler, occupying an intermediary position in the chain of distribution between producers (principals) and the retailers, although some would argue that, by assembling a variety of products into a single, new product, tour operators themselves are producers. In practice, this intermediary role reflects the activities of the majority of smaller operators; however, as we shall see shortly, the larger tour operators own both certain elements of production, such as airlines and hotels, and retailers (travel agencies), reinforcing their role as 'gatekeepers' referred to above.

The Role of Tour Operators

Tour operators exist and are, by and large, successful because they fulfil an important function within the tourism industry. In other words, tour operators are needed by both principals and customers and, undoubtedly, they remain in business by satisfying the needs of these two groups.

The Needs of Principals

The attraction of tour operators to tourism producers or principals, specifically airlines, hotels and ground operators (for example, local coach operators or tour organisers in the destination) is their ability to reach customers and their access to distribution channels to sell their products. In other words, tour operators are able to provide principals with business which they might not otherwise be able to attract. For example, many hotels in tourism destinations are smaller, independent businesses which possess neither the necessary resources for marketing nor the reputation to attract customers. Thus, tour operators provide an essential link between destination accommodation providers and the major tourism generating markets. Through bulk purchasing, they are also able to provide, subject to certain conditions, a guaranteed level of business for hotels over particular periods, such as the summer season. Similarly, for airlines, particularly scheduled flights which must operate irrespective of the number of seats booked, tour operators play an important role in filling seats which may otherwise go unsold (Holloway 1998 : 192 – 194).

In both cases, the ability of tour operators to provide a guaranteed level of sales through their marketing power, their access to large numbers of potential customers and their brand image, enables principals to cover their high levels of fixed costs and to plan more effectively in what is traditionally, a volatile and uncertain business where demand and supply are rarely in balance.

The Needs of Customers

Although the advent of the Internet has allowed tourists to assemble their own package more easily and quickly, tour operators still offer a number of significant benefits to customers:

- *Price* – as a result of bulk purchasing and their dominant position in the chain of distribution, tour operators can usually negotiate prices that are much lower than those which an individual tourist could secure. Although the 'no-frills' airlines, such as easyJet, have significantly reduced the cost of flights to many destinations, package holidays are still a cheap way to enjoy overseas holidays.
- *Convenience* – by combining all the elements of the holiday into a single package (and then selling it through the brochure), tour operators make it much easier for tourists, who normally do not have the necessary expertise, knowledge, time or access to principals, to purchase holidays. Indeed, the convenience of 'one-stop' holiday shopping has probably been, alongwith price, one of the most important factors in the development of mass, package tourism.
- *Reliability* – travel and tourism, particularly overseas travel, inevitably involves an element of risk and uncertainty for the tourist. In other words, by travelling from an environment (their home) with which they are familiar to one (the destination) with which they are not – they may not speak the local language, be familiar with local customs, and so on – they are putting themselves at risk. At the same time, as the tourism product can be 'pre-tested', they may be unsure about the quality of the experience that they are paying for. Conversely, the tour operator, through the package holiday, provides an element of reliability and quality, as well as an aura of safety, to the

potential tourist. In short, the package holiday is relatively safe and predictable although, in practice, the quality and service promised in the brochure may not always be provided. In such circumstances, the tour operator also offers.

- *Consumer protection* – since the introduction of the Package Travel Regulations in 1992, tour operators are liable for all aspects of the holidays which they assemble and sell. Therefore, in buying an inclusive tour from a tour operator, tourists enjoy rights and a degree of protection that would not be available to them if they were holidaying independently.

If the importance of tour operators to both principals and consumers was to diminish, then they would be in danger of disintermediation. That is, if tourists were increasingly able to deal directly with airlines and hotels at a reasonable cost and if principals were able to attract a sufficient customer base of their own, thereby reducing their often total dependence on intermediaries, then tour operators would, in effect, be overlooked in the chain of distribution. However, there is no evidence to suggest that this is likely to occur to any great extent in the near future.

The Structure of the Tour Operating Sector

The tour operating sector of the UK travel industry is currently dominated by four major tour operators – Airtours plc, Thomson Travel Group, Thomas Cook and First Choice Holidays plc – who between them control around 60 per cent of the market for package holidays. However, as already noted, there are over 1400 'air' operators alone who require a license (ATOL) from the Civil Aviation Authority (CAA) and, although this figure also includes licenses provided to 'flight-only' operators, the CAA figures probably provide the best guide to the proliferation of smaller tour operators in the UK. At the same time, there are, of course, many other types of tour operators, including outgoing/incoming international operators and domestic operators, which utilise other forms of transport. As a result, it is impossible to estimate accurately the total number of tour operators in the UK. Here, we are concerned primarily with air tour operations.

The current structure of the tour operating sector is characterised by:

- An élite group of about 10 vertically integrated tour operators which collectively account for 70 per cent of the air holiday market. This group includes the 'big four', alongwith other well-known companies, such as Unijet Travel and Virgin Holidays.
- A central group of established, medium sized operators which enjoy strong a strong, niche market presence. These carry between 100,000 and 300,000 passengers a year. As discussed shortly, however, in recent years, a number of these have come under the ownership of the majors – for example, Direct Holidays is now part of the Airtours group.
- A very large number of small, specialised operators, carrying up to 100,000 (but usually fewer) passengers, which focus on particular markets or destinations.

Table 13.2 lists the top 20 ATOL carriers in the UK in 2000.

Table 13.2
Top 20 ATOL Tour Operators[1] in the UK, 2000

Operator	*Passengers carried*	*Operator*	*Passengers*
Thomson Holidays	4,172,570	Gold Medal Travel Group	369, 680
Airtours	3,106,646	Direct Holidays	303,297
JMC Holidays	2,915,009	British Airways Holidays	287,302
First Choice Holidays	1,895,469	Kuoni Travel	261,136
Unijet Travel	917,800	Specialist Holidays	257,960
Avro	601,808	Lotus International	211,433
Trailfinders	592,827	Libra Holidays	199,460
Virgin Holidays	394,339	Travel 2	176,104
Thomas Cook Retail	287,145	Kosmar Villa Holidays	161,483
Cosmosair	374,681	Panorama Holidays Group	146,851

Source: ATOL (2001a).

1. It is important to note that an ATOL is awarded to individual tour operators, not to the parent company. Thus, for example, Airtours are licensed separately from Direct Holidays and Panorama, although all are part of the Airtours group.

Two principal factors have led to the present structure. Firstly, recent years have witnessed increasing concentration (or horizontal integration) within the sector, with the larger companies increasing their market share by purchasing smaller operators. Secondly, the sector has also been characterised by vertical integration, with the larger tour operators owning and/ or controlling their own airline and travel agencies.

Over the two decades, this process of horizontal and vertical integration has led to significant transformations in the structure and ownership of the tour operating sector. Not only have some companies been able to grew into large, multinational corporations (Airtours, for example, started off as a small travel agent in the north-west of England, Pendle Travel, which, first set up tour operating division in 1980), but some of the largest of the UK operators have themselves been taken over by overseas groups – the Thomson Travel Group, for example, is now owned by the German company Preussag AG, the world's largest tourism group.

At the same time, it has also resulted in a number of spectacular failures, the first being the collapse of Court Line/ Clarksons Holidays in 1974 which stranded 50,000 tourists abroad. Similarly, International Leisure Group (ILG), the owners of the then second largest tour operator in the UK, Intasun, collapsed in 1991. Usually, such failures result from one or more of the' following factors:

- Over rapid growth based upon excessive borrowing to finance expansion.
- Insufficient, profit resulting from price cutting to maintain market share.
- External factors such as fuel prices rises or political instability.

For example, the terrorist attacks in the USA on September 11th 2001, and the subsequent drop in demand (by December 2001, an estimated one million UK tourists had cancelled or re-arranged their overseas travel plans, whilst summer 2002 bookings remained 50 per cent down on the previous year) are expected to lead to a number of operator failures.

Fig. 13.1
The Four Major UK Tour Operators: Who Owns What

	Tour Operations	*Retail Operations*	*Cruise Operations*	*Airline Operations*
Airtours plc	Airtours Holidays Panorama Bridge Travel Service Cresta Holidays Eurosites Tradewinds Worldwide Jetset Europe Leger Holidays Holidays for Less (Aspro) Direct Holidays Manos	Going Places (729 outlets) Travel World (138 outlets) Late Escapes Go Direct Flightdeck Holidayline	Airtours Sun Cruises The Carnival Corporation	Airtours International
Thomson Travel Group	Thomson Holidays Portland Direct Skytours Club Freestyle Just Port Philip Group Austravel Budget Travel Thomson Breakaway Thomson Ski, Lakes & Mountains	Lunn Poly (794 outlets) Callers Pegasus (34 outlets) Sibbald Travel (12 outlets) The Travel House (61 outlets) Team Lincoln Budget Travel Manchester Flights	Thomson Cruises	Britannia Airways

Fig. 13.1 : *(contd.)*

	Tour Operations	*Retail Operations*	*Cruise Operations*	*Airline Operations*
	Crystal Holidays Jetsave Jersey Travel Service Tropical Places Greyhound International American Holidays Something Special Hols. Spanish Harbour Hols. Magic Travel Group Simply Travel Headwater Holidays	Thomson preferred agents – aligned independents (2,500 outlets)		
Thomas Cook	JMC Thomas Cook Holidays Neilson Club 18-30 Time Off Style Holidays Sunworld Ireland Skiers World British Airways Holidays (50 : 50 venture)	Thomas Cook shops (700 outlets) Thomas Cook Plus (6 travel warehouses) Thomas Cook Direct ARTAC Worldchoice Partnership (800 outlets)	None	JMC Airlines

Fig. 13.1 : (contd.)

	Tour Operations	Retail Operations	Cruise Operations	Airline Operations
First Choice Holidays plc	First Choice Holidays Eclipse 2wentys Sovereign First Choice Ski, Lakes & Mountains Unijet Flexi Conference & Incentives Flexiski Skibound Ski Partners Travelbound Schools Abroad Sunquest Hayes and Jarvis Meon Group Sunsail Crown Holidays Falcon (Ireland) JWT (Ireland)	Travel Choice and Travel Choice Express (200 outlets) Travel Choice Direct Bakers Dolphin (78 outlets) Holiday Hypermarkets (32 outlets) Hays Travel (partner - 23 outlets) Holiday Express (partner - 22 outlets)	First Choice Cruises Alliance with Royal Caribbean International from summer 2002	Air 2000 Viking Aviation (Seat broker)

The changing structure of the tour operating sector over the last decade is outlined by Holloway (1998: 199-200), whilst Figure 13.1 details the most recent patterns of ownership with respect to the four major UK tour operating groups.

As is evident from Figure 13.1, each of the four major tour operators are highly integrated organisations, ecah owning a significant number of tour operating companies/brands, retail outlets, and an airline. Not shown here, however, is the wider extent of their activities. Airtours, for example, has a significant interest in tour operations in Scandinavia, America and Germany, whilst Thomsons, as well as owning overseas operations in the Nordic region, also controls a number of specialist holidays companies including Crystal Ski, Austravel, Breakaway (short and city break holidays) and Headwater Holidays (adventure holidays) which come under the banner of its Specialist Holiday Group. Until relatively recently, Thomson was also a major player in domestic tourism in the UK with its Holiday Cottages Group which has now been sold.

Whilst the actual structure of the tour operating sector is of interest (and, of course, dynamic), of greater importance in the context of this chapter is the reason why this concentration and integration has occurred within the industry. Therefore, the following section explores the factors that have brought about the present patterns of ownership and control.

Tour Operating: Integration

The benefits of both horizontal and vertical integration can be explained from two perspectives. Firstly, and in a practical sense, integration provides a number of benefits to tour operating businesses, as follows:

Horizontal integration (i.e. across one level of the chain of distribution) provides a tour operator with:

- economies of scale (bulk purchasing, marketing economies, etc.);
- increased market share;
- the opportunity to strengthen through expansion;
- the opportunity to strengthen through diversification (new products).

Vertical integration (i.e. linking with organisations at different levels in the chain of distribution provides a tour operator with:

- economies of scale;
- continuation of supply – tour operators depend upon a supply of hotel beds and airline seats;
- the ability to control quality – given their liability under the Package Travel Regulations, it has become increasingly important for operators to control the quality of all elements of the package;
- control over, distribution (retailing) and merchandising - it is more likely that an operators products will be sold if it owns its own retailing operation.

Secondly, integration can be explained more broadly as a means of surviving and growing within a highly competitive and dynamic industry such as tourism.

Integration as a Competitive Strategy (see Dale 2000)

According to Porter (1980), there are five major forces within the competitive environment which any organisation must be aware of and react to in order to survive (see Fig. 13.2)

According to this model, the most challenging competitive conditions occurs when new entrants are likely, when buyers and suppliers are able to exercise control over the market place and when there are many substitutes. To a great extent, this reflects the potential characteristic of tour operating industry and, therefore, Porter's model can usefully explain both horizontal and vertical integration as a logical response to competition within tour operating.

New Entrants

Tour operating has, traditionally, been an easy industry to enter; that is, there are relatively few barriers to entry. Not only does it require little capital, but there is easy access to suppliers and retailers, whilst there is little chance of retaliation as the industry is comprised mainly of hundreds of other small businesses. Therefore, for existing companies to survive and make a profit in the face of the threat of new entrants, companies need to either grow or specialise; a quick way to achieve this is, of course, by acquiring other companies (i.e. horizontal integration).

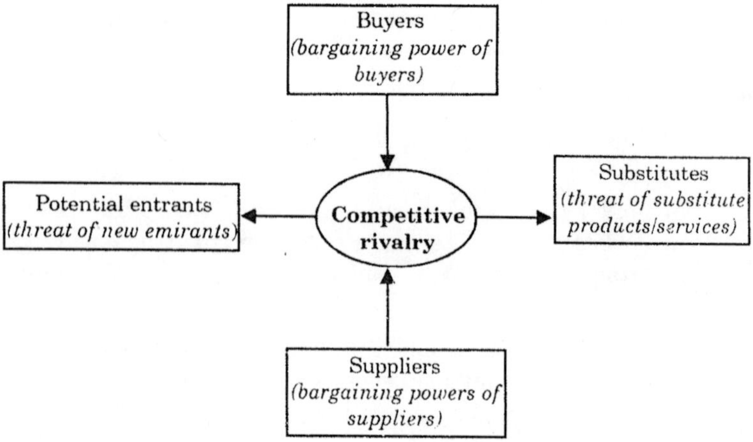

Fig. 13.2 : Portion five forces model.

Buyer Power

Tour organisers and travel retailers can be viewed as 'buyers' within the chain of distribution, each with the potential to exert a powerful-influence on their suppliers. Tour organisers 'buy' the required elements of their package holiday (accommodation, flights, ground handing etc.) from principals and depending on their 'buying power' can exercise considerable control over them, At the same time, however, retailers can also exercise power over tour organisers in their role as buyers. Although holiday products are not bought and sold in the same way as tangible goods, the larger of the national and regional holiday retail chains, such as Lunn Poly and Going Places, are, given their access to a wide customer base, able to exert power over tour operators through their selection of which holiday companies products to sell. This retailer power can be reinforced in the following situations where:

- there are too many tour operators trying to place their products with too few retailers;
- they have a brand that is stronger than that of the smaller operators;
- backward integration with a tour operator can increase the power of an agency over non-integrated operators.

This power is often manifested in higher commissions being demanded to 'stock' a particular, tour operators holidays, or in the directional selling (the favouring through, for example, the ranking of brochures) of a particular operator's products. Thus, in order to compete, tour operators must either secure distribution channels – that is, integrate vertically downwards – or seek alternative distribution methods. For example, First Choice have, in recent years, sought to expand their retail operations (see Figure 13.1), whilst Airtours bought Direct Holidays in 1998 in order reach the customer directly.

Of course, as mentioned, many tour operators themselves enjoy buyer power over the principals, particularly when they are larger and can choose from a large number of suppliers. This is most often the situation faced by destination accommodation providers who cannot hope to have a strong brand than, or better access their generating markets than, the tour operators who buy from them. Nonetheless, it is possible for very well-established, high quality hotels to achieve such a good reputation in popular resorts that it can pick and choose between potential buyers. This is known as supplier power (see below).

Supplier Power

The suppliers, such as airlines, hotels and ground handlers, have power over tour operators when:

- there are few or just one large supplier;
- the supplier enjoys strong brand recognition amongst potential tourists;
- the supplier integrates forward with another operator;
- tour operators are insignificant to the supplier's overall business.

This supplier power is particularly evident in the case of airlines and their relationship with non-integrated operators. They might supply them with the least desirable seats or flight times or, given the fact that seats on aeroplanes tend to be less plentiful than hotel beds, not supply them at all. Indeed, as the industry has become more integrated, independent operators have found it increasingly difficult to secure seats on airlines owned by other tour operators.

Hotels may also have power over tour operators, particularly the larger hotel groups in popular resorts. In response, tour operators can integrate backwards, buying their own airline, hotels and, in some cases, ground handling operations, in order to guarantee both the supply and the quality of these elements of the package holiday. Alternatively, smaller tour operators may seek alternative sources of supply, such as new destinations. or grow (through horizontal integration) to gain more buying power.

Tour operators can also wield considerable supplier power over travel agents in deciding whether or not to distribute their holiday offering through them. Many tourists would, for example, expect to be able to buy a well-recognised brand such as Thomson or Airtours from their agent and would take their business elsewhere if they could not.

The Threat of Substitute Products

Within tourism, an enormous variety of substitutes exist for anyone tour operators products. These can include, for example:

- Domestic holidays for overseas holidays.
- Skiing holidays for summer sun holidays.
- Short breaks for one long holiday.
- Activity holidays for beach holidays.
- All-inclusive holidays for self-catering.
- One destination/country for another.

A particular challenge for tour operators is where independent travel becomes a substitute for the package holiday, rendering the tour operator's product obsolete. More usually, however, the main problem facing tour operators is that their products can be easily substituted. Not only are there many other companies offering similar products, but tourists are increasingly seeking new or different types of holidays or more exclusive, up-market experiences.

In order to survive, integration is once again a key strategy. That is, many operators have diversified, through integration, into 'substitute' areas in order to keep their customers. Thomsons, for example, offer a wide range of specialist expertise through those companies they have acquired which now form their Specialist Holiday Group, First Choice satisfy the demand for more exclusive holidays through their acquisition of Hayes and Jarvis, whilst Bridge Travel has given Airtours a toothold in the city-break market. Additionally, operators are adding more benefits or quality to their existing offerings, something that is likely to occur more frequently as opportunities for strategically beneficial integration diminish. It is also worth noting that non-holiday products can also substitute for a holiday purchase, making it especially important that holiday companies improve on the personal benefits to be gained from a holiday and deliver them.

Competitive Rivalry

Finally, competitive rivalry is most likely to occur when:

- Competitors are the same size.
- There are high fixed costs and, thus, there is a high level of competition to cover these costs.
- Markets are undifferentiated – most companies sell the same products to the same customers.
- In order to gain competitive advantage, extra capacity must be bought in large quantities.

These characteristics largely reflect the current structure of the (integrated) tour operating industry. As a result, the large operators compete aggressively for market share and, certainly in recent years, their focus has been upon growth through integration and pricing strategies. However, as there are now fewer opportunities for large scale integration, particularly in the British if not the European context, following the blocking of Airtours' bid for First Choice, it is likely that other strategies, such as the development of quality, will come to the fore.

Tour Operations

As we have already seen, there is an enormous variety of tour operators, ranging from the large, integrated, multinational organisations, such as the Thomson Travel Group, to small, specialist companies with, perhaps, up to six core staff. As a result, the way in which tour operations function will also vary enormously according to a number of factors, such as the type and scale of operation, destinations offered and the season of travel. Thus, for example, a small company offering up-market, long-haul winter-sun holidays faces a different set of challenges compared with a large company operating in the highly competitive, short-haul summer sun market.

Nevertheless, most tour operators follow a largely similar process in the planning and construction of a package holiday. In other words, for a particular package holiday to be commercially viable, a tour operator is likely to follow a pattern of steps or stages from initially considering an idea through to the actual sale of the holiday. Prior to embarking on this process, however, a tour operator should consider its overall business objectives and strategy.

Tour Operations: Objective and Strategy

As in any business, it is essential that the planning and development of a new product does not occur in isolation from the major business objectives and the strategic direction of the company. That is, decisions regarding product development, such as the creation of a new package holiday, should meet the longer-term objectives of the company and the strategies designed to achieve those objectives.

The principal short-term objective of most tour operators is, of course, to make money and stay in business, thereby fulfilling their obligations to shareholders, employees, banks, customers and other stakeholders. However, other business objectives may vary according to the characteristics of different companies and their managers, For example, a smaller operator may focus upon becoming a specialist, niche market supplier, whilst the objective of larger operators may be to consolidate or increase market share. At the same time, all operators will have longer-term and inter-related objectives, such as market positioning, desired profit levels, or the scope and Scale of the business.

Whatever the overall objectives of a tour operator, its strategy is likely to be directed towards a combination of two related elements:

Profit – all companies seek to make a profit. However, if an operator wishes to earn higher profits, not only will it need to manage its finances effectively, but its strategy will focus on reducing costs and achieving higher margins on each holiday that it sells.

Market share – if an operator seeks to increase its market share, the challenge is to increase the number of holidays it sells; that is, it will seek to increase its capacity. Capacity estimations are one of the most vital decisions in tour operating, Each year, an operator's ATOL is renewed according to projected numbers of tourists but, perhaps more importantly the extent to which capacity targets are met determines the profit levels of a company. The reason for this is that, in order to increase capacity and, hence, market share, a tour operator must increase the number of beds and aircraft seats that it agrees to 'buy' from principals. However, it is almost impossible to predict the numbers of holidays which will be sold – unforeseen events or the activities of competitor operators may reduce expected demand – and, frequently, operators suffer from over-capacity. That is, they often have unsold holidays, meaning that they have to operate yield management systems to set late, discounted prices which will attract customers but which, at the same time, minimise potential losses. Not surprisingly, therefore, increases in market share are usually achieved at the cost of reduced profit levels.

The trade-off between profit margins and market share is illustrated by the example of Airtours. In 2000, the company raised its capacity by 15 per cent in the UK market, whilst in other markets, particularly Germany, it had severe over-capacity – in fact, the German operator Fti, wholly owned by Airtours, lost some £ 100 million in 2000. Therefore, Airtours' strategy for 2001 was to consolidate its position and increase margins rather than seek market growth, with a 30 per cent reduction in capacity (800,000 passengers) in its German operation.

To summarize, then, the initial decision to develop a new package holiday must be guided by the tour operator's overall business strategy, with the most appropriate type of package being selected to meet the company's objectives. Once this decision has been made, a set of key stages must be followed, determined to a great extent by the 'calendar' of tour operating.

Tour Operations: Creating the Package

Depending upon the nature of a particular package holiday, the planning and creation of a package holiday through to its sales may take anything from nine months to three years. Within this period, however, a number of key activities must be undertaken including research, capacity planning, finance and administration, sales and marketing and tour management. Although a detailed consideration of these is beyond the scope of this chapter (see Yale 1995; Cooper *et al.* 1998: 257 – 268; Holloway 1998: 209 – 223), they can be summarised within the context of a 'typical' tour operating calendar for a 'summer sun' product.

Year 1: (August to December)

Prior to developing a product, *research* must be undertaken to determine choices of destinations, types of holidays, prices, capacity, and so on. Usually, such research will include:

- a review of the company's performance and objectives (see previous section);
- market trends and growth – changes in demand, tourist flows, etc.;
- existing products and competitive supply – the activities of competitors; are there any gaps in the market?
- destination research – essentially, a feasibility study to determine ease of access, extent of existing tourism infrastructure and services, and the local legal and political climate.

Once answers have been found to these questions, the tour operator can then devise a marketing strategy that balances the objectives of the company with the product development opportunities revealed by the research.

Year 2

The second year of the calendar embraces what is, in effect, the creation of the package. Four fundamental activities are undertaken at this stage:

Capacity Planning

In line with company objectives and strategy, target capacity figures must be planned which, in turn, determine the characteristics of the package according to type, size and frequency of operation. Once the specifications of the package have been set, the operator then negotiates with principals {hotels and airlines} in a process known as contracting.

Accommodation may be contracted in one of two ways:

1. *allocation* – beds are contracted on a sale or return basis, with any unsold rooms being returned to the hotelier with between 2 to four weeks notice. The advantage of allocation is that the risk is transferred from the operator to the principal. For example, following the 11th September terrorist attacks on the United States, many tour operators – quickly sought to drop allocation bookings to long-haul destinations around the world. The disadvantage of allocation bookings is that hoteliers will often make contracts with a number of operators in order to cover themselves. This sometimes leads to double booking, when operators find that the rooms they have contracted are occupied by another operator's clients.
2. *commitment* – the operator pays a non-returnable deposit on rooms whether they are sold or not (and the hotelier may not offer the beds to another operator). Such contracts may be based on a cheaper rate then allocation, but are more risky. Therefore, the operator must be relatively certain of selling its holidays.

Contracting aircraft seats is a crucial activity. Not only is about 40 per cent of the final holiday price is paid for the aircraft seat, meaning that unsold seats may result in significant losses, but - also, for many destinations, aircraft seats are less plentiful than hotel beds. Thus, for popular destinations, it may be difficult for smaller operators to acquire the seats they require.

Aircraft seats are contracted in a number of ways. As already noted, the larger operators have their own airline and will focus on maximising the use of the aircraft. They may also sell blocks of seats to other operators. For the majority of other operators who do not enjoy this benefit, seats can be contracted either on scheduled flights (ITX) or on charter flights (ITC). ITX flights are usually more expensive and are, therefore, most commonly used by specialist, niche operators. ITC seats are cheaper, and can be booked in a variety of ways depending on the nature of the operation.

- a block of seats on a flight;

- the whole plane for a specific flight (whole plane charter);
- an aircraft for the whole season (time charter);
- with air crew (wet lease) and without (dry lease).

Financial Planning

The high street prices for mainstream package holidays are usually estimated between eight months and twelve months before the holiday is actually taken, based on current and forecasted exchange rates, inflation and fuel prices. Thus, operators are subject to a variety of risks. These financial risks also include insurance costs (raised following the terrorist attacks in the USA on September 11th, 2001), destination and UK taxes, and so on. Therefore, effective financial management is an essential requirement. Moreover, the actions of competitors, available supply to particular destinations, market demand and will all need to be taken into account. Therefore, in reality, prices can change at the latest possible moment before launch. Thus, all brochure details are often printed well in advance, with the exception of pricing panels which are overprinted later. Depending upon the take up of sales, alternative pricing strategies may need to be employed, subsequent edition brochures may be printed and/or systems of 'flexible pricing' may be adopted. Here, customers are invited to enquire as to the latest discount available on particular holidays. (Perhaps the most extreme form of price flexibility is the Internet holiday auction).

Sales and Marketing

The most popular means of selling package holidays remains the brochure. Brochure production usually starts a number a number of months before launch date and can only occur once the previous stages of the package creation process have been undertaken (although, as noted below, operators may re-negotiate contracts with suppliers for subsequent editions of brochures). Both the timing of the brochure launch and its distribution are crucial. Larger operators selling mainstream holidays will seek maximum exposure by distributing brochures widely (particularly through their own retail chain), and will try to beat their competitors to the launch. In recent years, this has resulted in brochures being launched ever earlier (sometimes summer-sun brochures have been launched during the Spring of the previous year!), with discounting schemes designed to attract the early booker. Conversely, specialist operators usually have a more limited distribution, thereby reducing costs and conveying a sense of exclusivity (see Cooper *et al.* 1998: 262).

At the same time sales reservation systems must be made ready to take bookings, and sales promotions and advertising to the trade and to the public will need to be timed to coincide with the brochure/product launch. Moreover, as bookings are generated and competitors' brochures are launched, it may be necessary for an operator to re-negotiate with suppliers if it finds that its products are more expensive – tour operators are now able, with the appropriate computer software, to calculate what their competitors have paid for the different elements of the package.

Hence the marketing role is not confined to brochure production and promotion alone. It is central to the whole process of product development and planning. It involves research and communication across all departments from the initial exploratory research stage through interim performance and sales measurement to the monitoring of customer feedback and competitor performance. All of this information will be used to determine future development of the product.

Administration

During the second year, a number of administrative activities are undertaken. These include:

- recruiting and training reservation staff;
- setting up the reservations systems;
- recruiting resort staff;
- processing initial bookings.

Year 3

A number of activities occur during the third stage of the tour operation calendar, broadly reflecting the patterns of the holiday season. Throughout the main season, for example, sales will be monitored, capacity will be adjusted where possible and yield management systems will be implemented to maximise sales of holidays. Indeed, many operators will review sales figures daily and will sell off excess capacity at a discount. More specifically, the following destination management activities will occur:

- *holiday management* – tourists are met, transferred to resort and welcomed.
- *brochure accuracy reports* – representatives will assess the accuracy of the details presented in the brochures with respect to, for example, the facilities available, as well as more specific quality/safety aspects, such as the depth of the pool, fire exits, and so on.
- *customer care* – representatives attend to the needs of tourists, sort out problems, accompany local tours when appropriate, and so on.
- *account payments to suppliers* – the operator will pay the principals, usually by an agreed date.

Monitoring quality – most operators distribute customer questionnaires in order to determine the performance of the representatives and the customers satisfaction with the various elements of the package. The results of these feed into the planning

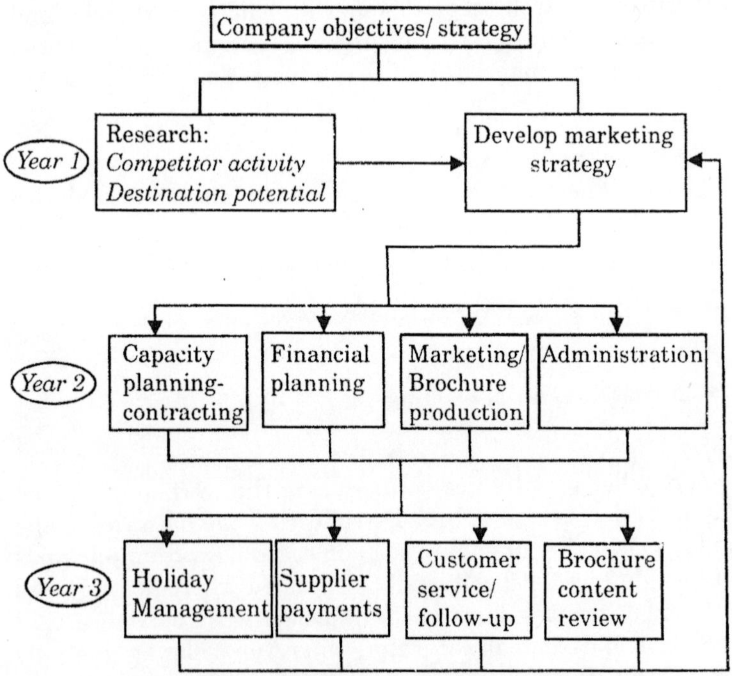

Fig. 13.3 : A Typical tour opeating 'calendar'.

process for the following year. At the same time, tour operators must respond to any correspondence or complaints received from customers once they have returned from their holidays. Indeed, as the next section shows, customer care/protection has become an increasingly important element of tour operating.

Inevitably, the tour operating process is more complex than presented here. Moreover, it is a continual process of research, planning, product development, review and monitoring so that, in reality, no clear boundaries exist, in a temporal sense, between the different activities and functions. Nevertheless, the tour operating calendar as outlined here can be summarized as in Figure 13.3.

Tour Operating : Consumer Protection

There are two reasons why consumer protection is of importance in the context of tour operating. Firstly, holidays are normally bought on trust. That is, tourists spend usually significant sums of money on a product that cannot be tried out or even viewed before purchase. At the same time, of course, package holidays are a combination of different elements, some of which are provided by local businesses in the destination, and as a result, it may be difficult for the operator to ensure consistent quality. Therefore, it is inevitable that holidays do not always meet with tourists expectations or do not match up with what is promised in the brochure. In other words, the nature and complexity of the package holiday are such that tourists often do not receive what they have paid for or, more precisely, what they believe they have paid for.

Secondly, less frequently but more seriously tour operators go out of business. Although major business failures, such as the collapse of Court Line/Clarksons in 1974 and ILG in 1991, are relatively rare, a significant number of operators fail each year. In fact, between January 1986 and March 2001, 303 licensed operators failed, leaving a total of 181,814 tourists stranded overseas and well over a million people unable to take the holidays they had paid for (ATOL 2001b).

Thus, Tourists require two forms of protection :

- protection designed to ensure that (a) tour operators provide the scope and standards of service as described in the brochure and (b), should they fail to do, mechanisms for gaining redress or compensation; and

- protection against tour operator failure that either (a) provides for repatriation or continuation of the holiday should the company fail while a tourist is overseas or (b) provides refunds for holidays paid for but not yet taken.

To a great extent, both forms of protection are provided for in the form of regulations that restrict the activities of tour operators or define their liability for the degree and quality of services provided. In terms of consumer law – that is, legal measures that seek to protect and assert the rights of consumers – tour operators have become subject to an increasingly complex array of both UK and EU legislation designed to shift the emphasis from the tradition of *caveat emptor* (buyer beware) to producer liability. Perhaps the most important element of this is the European Package Travel Directive, which has provided the principal legal framework for tour operators within Europe since 1990 (this is enshrined in UK law *via* the Package Travel, Package Holidays and Package Tours Regulations, 1992). Not only do the Regulations set out in detail what an operator may or may not do, but they also make the operator liable for any problems with any part of the package contracted out to other suppliers. As a result, tour operators have become obliged to focus on improving the quality and reliability of their products (see below), whilst it has become easier for the travelling public to assert their rights (of which they are becoming increasingly aware) as consumers.

Protection Against Tour Operator Failure

Following the collapse of Fiesta Tours in 1964, stranding some 5,000 tourists abroad, it became evident that some form of protection against the financial failure of tour operators was necessary. In response, the following year the Association of British Travel Agents (ABTA) established a 'common fund' based on 50 per cent of its membership subscriptions in order to reimburse or repatriate tourists affected by any future failure. ABTA fully expected the government to introduce legislation to regulate tour operators but, when this did not occur, it established 'Operation Stabiliser'. This controversial scheme meant that ABTA tour operators could only sell their packages through ABTA travel agents and vice versa, whilst tourists would only be protected if they had bought their holiday from an ABTA agency (see Yale 1995: Chapter 10).

Operation Stabiliser was removed in 1993 as a result of the Package Travel Regulations which, amongst other things, require all travel organisers to be 'bonded'; that is, to have sufficient funds or security to refund customers or cover the cost of repatriation in the event of financial failure. This regulation extended to *all* packages (which come within the definition of a package as set out in regulation 2(1) of the Package Travel Regulations) a system first introduced in the UK by the Civil Aviation Authority (CAA) in 1972, which required all tour operators using charter flights or block-booked scheduled seats to apply for an Air Transport Organisers Licence (ATOL).

The ATOL system is still the principal statutory consumer protection scheme applied to air travel. Under the Civil Aviation (Air Travel Organisers Licensing) Regulations 1995, anyone – other than airlines themselves – selling either air inclusive packages or air seats must apply for and receive an ATOL. Failure to do so is a criminal offence with a fine of up to £ 5000 and two years in prison. The purpose of the ATOL system is to protect the customer against the failure of tour operators by refunding those who have paid but not yet travelled or by repatriating those stranded abroad.

Businesses that are required to apply for an ATOL include package tour operators, group and conference travel organisers, seat consolidators and many travel agents. Protection through ATOL is assured as far as possible because:

- All those applying for an ATOL must undergo stringent financial health checks – an ATOL is granted for only 12 months.
- Before being granted an ATOL, all travel organisers must arrange a bond with a recommended insurance company which is sufficient to reimburse or pay for the repatriation of customers in the event of the company failing. Under the Package Travel Regulations, this bond should amount to 25 per cent of a company's annual turnover although for companies that are members of an approved body, such as ABTA, this can be limited to 10 per cent.
- If an insolvent company's bond is insufficient to cover the cost of claims, the shortfall is made up from the Air Travel

Trust Fund. Set up in the 1970s and originally funded by a 2 per cent levy on holidays, the Fund is administered by the CAA and, although it is in significant deficit, it is guaranteed by government. Since 1986, roughly one third of all failures have drawn on the Fund which has paid out a total of £ 42 million.

As a legal requirement for air travel organisers, the ATOL system protects up to 28 million passengers from losing money or being stranded abroad, and more details about the system and the different types of ATOL can be found on its web site (www.atol.org.uk). There are some exceptions - most notably, airlines do not require an ATOL and, therefore, a traveller who buys a ticket on a scheduled flight direct from the airline is not covered. However, for those on package holidays, ATOL is an effective system which, in combination with consumer legislation, provides tourists with significant degree of protection. Conversely, tour operators are having to function in an increasingly regulated environment, particularly with respect to consumer legislation, and, as we now consider, this is one of the reasons why operators are increasingly focusing on the quality of the products they provide.

Quality Management in Tour Operating

Having long enjoyed a dominant position within the international tourism system, tour operators now face a number of challenges to the future success of their business.

- *Competition* – the tour operating sector has become increasingly competitive. Not only are the smaller, specialist operators threatening to erode the market share of the 'big players', but that market share remains largely based on price, undermining the longer-term drive for increased margins.
- *Sophisticated tourists* – people have become more experienced as consumers of tourism products and now seek a variety of benefits other than a low price in the holidays they purchase. In particular, non-price factors, such as quality of services provided, have become more important – indeed, as early as the 1970s it was predicted that price competition would become subordinate to quality competition.
- *Consumerism* – in most industries, increasing attention is

being paid to the rights of consumers and tourism is no exception. Recent years have witnessed a dramatic growth in media interest in the quality of tourism, with numerous newspaper articles and television programmes, for example, highlighting 'tourism disasters' and the ways in which tourists can claim compensation.

- *Legislation* – linked to consumerism, the increasingly regulated environment described above has resulted in tour operators paying out large amounts in compensation to dissatisfied tourists each year. According to a recent survey (Holiday Which? 2001), the most common reason for being unhappy with a tour operator was the service provided by holiday representatives, while in previous surveys, hotel quality has been rated the most disappointing aspect.

Collectively, these factors have led to a new awareness of the need for quality within the tour operating sector. Not only are large sums of money paid out; perhaps needlessly, each year compensating tourists for poor quality, but also quality has emerged as a minimum requirement for market entry and an important means of gaining competitive advantage. However, it has been suggested that the majority of problems and challenges facing tour operators *can* be addressed by management (Gilbert and Joshi 1992).

There is, then, little doubt that the implementation of quality management systems is, in theory, both desirable and necessary in the context of tourism. However, two questions must be addressed:

- how, in general, can quality management be achieved in a service industry?
- how applicable are quality management models to the specific challenges to the tourism industry?

Approaches to Quality Management

As Hope and Muhlemann (1998) point out, all service industries possess a number of characteristics that complicate the management process. These characteristics are widely referred to in the tourism literature and represent challenges for quality management:

Simultaneity – as the delivery and consumption of a service occur simultaneously, there is little or no chance for problems to be sorted out without the customer being aware. Therefore the challenge is in providing effective damage-limitation and recovery.

Heterogeneity – no two customers or service providers are the same, therefore, a standard, agreed level of quality is difficult to attain.

Intangibility – performance measurement, a key element of quality management, is difficult.

Perishability – a particular service cannot be stored if unsold by a particular date. This can produce a pressured selling environment which can lead to a mismatch of customers and products.

The management of quality in tourism is further complicated by the fact that the tourism system covers three separate regions – the generating region, the transit route, and the destination – each of which requires appropriate service delivery, Nevertheless, a number of models have been proposed that are potentially applicable to tourism (see Gilbert and Joshi 1992: Hope and Mühlemann 1998 for more detail), the most useful of which are summarized as follows:

(a) Gronroos (1982, cited in Gilbert and Joshi 1992) argues that consumers' image of service quality is determined by the extent of the gap between the service they expect and the service which they perceive that they get. This image is created by a combination of technical quality or 'hard factors' (such as the quality of this meal the customer receives, the bed they sleep in, etc.) and functional quality or 'soft factors' (that is how the service is transferred to the customer). Thus, it is suggested that quality, as perceived by the customer, can be improved by focusing on elements of functional quality, such as the behaviour, attitudes or appearance of staff, as well as attempting to influence customer expectations.

(b) Similarly, Parasuraman *et al.* (1985) suggest that service quality is represented overall by the gap between expected and perceived service and that four 'subgaps' contribute to this:

(i) the gap between expected service and the management's expectations of customer expectations; more simply, a failure on the part of management to understand what customers expect.

(ii) the gap between management perceptions of customer expectations and the service quality specifications – the setting of low or inappropriate standards.

(iii) the gap between service quality specifications and service delivery; that is, poor employee performance.

(iv) the gap between service delivery and external communications to customers. In other words, and as frequently occurs in tourism, inconsistencies exist between the quality image portrayed in promotional literature and the actual service provided.

Thus, researching and addressing these gaps can provide the foundation for developing quality orientated strategies that work towards greater 'fit' between expectations and actual experiences.

(c) A broader approach is provided by the concept of Total Quality Management (TQM). TQM is 'a management philosophy embracing all activities through which the needs and expectations of the customer and the community, and the objectives of the organisation are satisfied in the most efficient and cost-effective way by maximising the potential of all employees in a continuing drive for improvement' (Hope and Mühlemann 1998). At the centre of TQM are key 'processes' which link the supplier with the customer, and the quality/efficiency of these processes can be influenced by the use of appropriate systems, tools and teamworking

According to Hope and Mühlemann (1998), the factor that links all models of quality management, and that is of particular importance to an international service industry such as tourism, is people, That is, the success of any quality initiative is dependent upon the ability of staff to respond add adapt to demands for increased quality in the delivery of services. Thus, human resource issues, including staff selection, training and empowerment, as well as the implementation of appropriate rewards schemes, are fundamental to the management of quality.

Quality in Tour Operating?

The final question to consider is the extent to which quality management is a viable objective in tour operating. In other words, although the need for quality is evident in order to address the challenges of competition, consumerism and legal considerations, the extent to which the tour operating sector can respond to this need is less certain.

On the one hand, there is no doubt that human resource policies can be tailored towards recruiting, training, and empowering staff, whilst performance-related rewards schemes may provide a useful incentive – much depends; however, on the overall company culture and management philosophy.

On the other hand, a number of factors potentially militate against the successful implementation of quality management. The characteristics of services referred to above represent an initial hurdle, as does the international nature of tour operations. More specifically:

- The external environment at the destination influences tourists' perceptions of quality. This may include the behaviour of other tourists, the standard of attractions and facilities or even the general local ambience.
- Despite increasing integration within the sector, parts of the package are not directly owned by operators. As a result, operators have less control than is necessary to manage quality, with limited influence, for example, over the employment policies of hotels.
- As with all services, the human element of tourism is subjective. That is, different people have different perceptions of quality, whilst the nature of work within tour operating, particularly at the destination, suggests that consistent quality is difficult to achieve. For example, tour reps often tend to be younger, seasonally employed individuals with relatively little training. As a result, they may have little loyalty or commitment to the company and to a philosophy of quality.

More generally, tourism is about dreams–it could be argued that rarely, if ever, are tourists' expectations fully satisfied. Nevertheless, there is little doubt that, as tourists become more experienced, more discerning and more demanding, tour operators will have to pay greater attention to the issue of quality. However, this is only likely to be achieved at the cost of more expensive holidays.

14

Tourism Distribution

Introduction

This chapter is concerned with the means and mechanisms used by organisations within the travel and tourism industry to distribute their products. Distribution is a fundamental concern for the industry as, quite simply, the tourism product needs to be made available to, and be purchased by, consumers (tourists). Owing to its very nature, consumers need to be able to access the tourism product at multiple points of sale away from the places of service production. Unlike manufacturing, the product cannot be physically transported to the consumer and, therefore, distribution within travel and tourism is concerned with the provision of customer access to the product rather than physical transportation of goods.

The principal focus of this chapter will be on the role of distribution in enticing customers to destinations and making the product accessible. However, it must nevertheless be remembered that distribution also refers to physical location or locational analysis. Locational analysis is used to determine the best sites for the distribution of facilities, such as hotels and resorts, and the identification of such sites is becoming increasingly important as the continued growth of tourism has led to intensive competition for prime sites. It is also of crucial importance to the small-to-medium tourism enterprises that constitute the bulk of the travel and tourism industry. For these small businesses, locational analysis can determine the size of their service production and also their main sales point (Pender 1999).

What is Distribution?

Distribution is the means by which the product is made available and accessible to customers. It involves getting sufficient and appropriate information to the right people at the right time and at the right place in order to allow purchase decisions to be made, and providing the mechanism whereby consumers can make and pay for purchases. The distribution system needs to be efficient, positive and dynamic. In the tourism industry context, distribution can be defined as 'an operating structure, system or linkage of various combinations of travel organisations through which a producer of travel products describes and confirms travel arrangements to the buyer' (McIntosh 1995).

Distribution in the Wider Picture

Within marketing, distribution is synonymous with one of the classic four 'Ps' of the marketing mix – 'Place'. It plays a key role in the success of the other elements in the marketing mix and, importantly, distribution choices have implications and ramifications for the other elements of the marketing mix, as distribution does not exist in isolation. If, for example, travel agents are used as a means of distributing the tourism product, it might well have cost implications and lead to increases in prices. These travel agents have to be serviced with brochures to ensure that they are aware of the products available - i.e. promotion. If brochure supplies were not kept up to date, consumers entering travel agents in response to advertising campaigns may be persuaded to book alternative holidays. Thus, as with all elements of the marketing mix, there is a need for flexibility and fluidity. There is a need to adapt to changing consumer patterns, expanding markets, maturing products, entering of new competition and new and innovative distribution channels emerge (Kotler *et al.* 1996).

Characteristics of the Tourism Product

The unique characteristics of tourism also need to be considered when examining distribution. These characteristics are:

Intangibility

. This as a key feature that separates the tourism product and other services) from virtually all other forms of retailing as the product cannot be seen or touched prior to purchase. This not only heightens the role of information in representing the product, but also it can pose particular difficulties for those whose job it is to market tourism. Furthermore, the purchase of a package tour has been described as 'a speculative investment' (Holloway 1995). Thus, it also involves a high degree of trust on the part of the purchaser, particularly because holidays are likely to be one of the most expensive purchases made in the year. Within the distribution process, the brochure takes on a crucial role as it is one means of illustrating the holiday and making it 'real' to the consumer.

Perishability

If the service is not sold, then the business can never be recovered as an empty room or train seat cannot be put into storage for later consumption. Unsold revenue is lost and, therefore, effective and efficient communication of such information is vital so that loads and yields are maximised and losses minimised. There is a need to be able to provide last minute distribution of unsold products as services cannot be stored for future sale. Within the UK travel and tourism industry, the late booking market has also evolved through developments in information technology, such as call centres and, of course, the Internet.

Dynamism

Tourism destinations are usually in a constant process of change as they grow, develop and adjust to the market. In this sense, the tourism product is always an unfinished product as it is always responding and adjusting to planning and marketing imperatives and opportunities. The use of communication and information technology allows for such changes and is having a considerable impact on the methods of distribution available. This characteristic also impacts upon the location of tourism services within resorts and destinations.

Heterogeneity

It is difficult for suppliers to provide the same standard or level of service at every consumption occasion, as standards and quality vary over time and under different circumstances. As almost all services provided to tourists have to be delivered at the time and place at which they are produced, one consequences is that the quality of the social interaction between the provider of the service and the consumer is part of the 'product' being purchased by tourists. If certain aspects of the social interaction are unsatisfactory, then what is purchased is, in effect, a different service product. At the same time, tourists tend to have high expectations of what they should receive, since 'going away' is an event endowed with particular significance. For distribution, this can place an increasing importance on the service provided by the elements of the distribution channel – the suppliers, travel agents and tour operators.

Inseparability

This refers to the overlap between the production and performance of the service and its consumption. It means there is an inseparability in buyers minds, as those who provide the service are the service, and buyers are often unable to judge the quality of a service prior to purchase. Such services cannot be produced anywhere; they have to be produced and consumed in very particular places and so part of what is consumed is, in effect, the place in which the service producer is located. Consumers will see buying the product as part of the overall experience, although the purchase of a holiday from a travel agent has no direct relevance to the service provided by a tour operator.

These characteristics of the tourism product highlight the crucial role of the distribution function in tourism. When a tour operator, such as Thomson, have an unsold package holiday they may well decide to have the holiday advertised as a late booking *via* a travel agency chain such as Luna Poly, as once the departure date has gone the holiday is lost as it is perishable. Equally, the inseparability of the product places further emphasis on the importance of the travel agent as the consumer sees them as the face of the holiday and it is, therefore, crucial they retain good communications with the tour operator. In the example of Thomsons and Lunn Poly, as they are integrated and part of the same group, it may well be easier to retain such links of communication.

The special characteristics of the tourism product also mean that the distribution of tourism is different to that of manufactured goods. In manufacturing, goods are transported to the consumer whilst, in tourism, it is the consumer that is transported to the product. This difference is extremely important as it means that information assumes a vital role, with subsequent implications for the method of distribution. Indeed, consumers are unable to physically inspect the product/service and are, therefore, forced to rely on information about the product. In turn, suppliers not only provide the product but also provide information on price, quantity, times (arrival and departure), quality, supplements, conditions of purchase and booking procedures.

Channels of Distribution

Distribution channels are the sequence of firms or organisations involved in the moving of the service from the 'producer' to consumer (Cowell 1991). They vary according to size and types of organisation, and larger principals (i.e. those producers at the top of the chain – in tourism, this includes airlines, hotels, and so on) tend to use more than one form of distribution channel. The travel and tourism distribution process can be visualised as a model (see Figure 14.1):

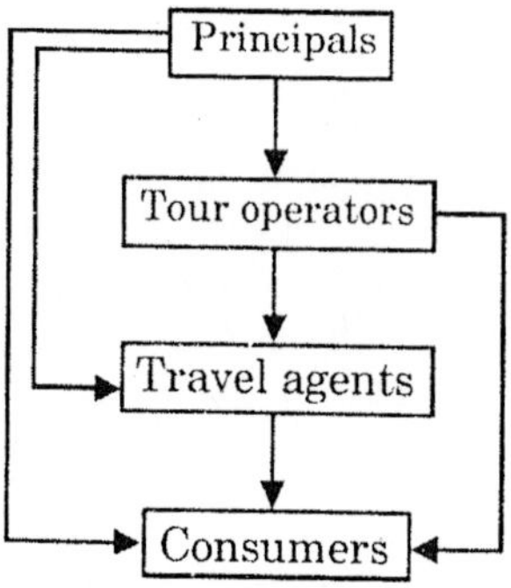

Fig. 14.1: Channels of distribution within travel and tourism industry.

There are a number of routes that can be taken through the distribution model to ensure the tourism product reaches the consumer. The principals, such as the transport and accommodation providers, can choose to sell direct to the consumers or go *via* an intermediary to tour operator and/or travel agent – whilst tour operators have two options of selling direct or selling through travel agents. (Of course, extensive vertical integration within the travel and tourism industry, means that tour operators are now often principals, as well as owning distribution businesses – travel agencies – further down the chain). With domestic tourism, it is common for tourists to purchase directly because they usually have good product knowledge and ready access to telephones to make reservations.

The distribution channel in tourism creates the link between the producers of tourism services and their customers, with tour operators frequently playing a pivotal role in distributing and channelling international tourism products to the consumer. Indeed, since tourism products are experimental and consumed on site, tour operators are an integral link in the distribution system (Mill *et al.* 1992). The relationship is one of reliance and need throughout the channels of distribution to ensure the consumer is purchasing the product required. Principals rely on tour operators to supply them with tourists and to honour contractual obligations - a tour operator, for example, may well be committed to filling all of a hotels rooms during the peak summer season. It is important, therefore, that the tour operator is able to fulfil this as otherwise the hotelier might have unfulfilled capacity and so lose revenue.

Equally, consumers rely on the tour operator to package and distribute the package holiday so that they do not need to do so themselves. They rely on the tour operator to provide accurate and sufficient information about the holiday to facilitate an informed purchase, so that when the tourist arrives at the destination their expectations are realised.

The traditional package holiday involves the principals selling to the tour operator who combines the elements of the holiday (transport and accommodation) into a package to be sold to consumers *via* travel agents or direct. If selling *via* a travel agent, the information regarding the package holiday be passed onto the travel agent to enable the product to be purchased, but built travel agents themselves do not hold any stock. In principle, they merely facilitate information dissemination and ensure that the consumers' needs are addressed by the particular holiday being booked.

The tourist industry and market is diversified and fragmented and, perhaps inevitably, the different market segments and principals involved influence the nature of different channels of distribution. In recognition of this, Bottomley Renshaw (1997) has adopted a sector approach to distribution and proposes separate models of distribution for airline travel, surface transport, accommodation and inclusive tours. As an example, Figure 14.2 shows the possible channels of distribution open to an hotel chain. Additionally, the changing needs and perceptions of consumers has also had significant impact on distribution.

Distribution Choices

According to Holloway (1995), the three most important factors which influence distribution choice are cost, control and level of service, whilst Lumsdon (1997) further identifies the nature of the market, resources commitment and competitor activity as influencing channel choices. Additionally, the market coverage required, the costs involved of distribution, the effectiveness of generating sales for motivation and image channels, the characteristics of the destination and tourism service and economic concentration all need to be considered when an organisation is choosing the most appropriate distribution strategy for it products.

The importance of making the right distribution choices cannot be overstated and, undoubtedly, an effective distribution strategy can be a competitive weapon. This can be clearly seen with First Choice which, following its UK expansion and distribution strategy from 1998 to 2000, became a fully vertically integrated travel group. It increased its competitiveness through buying into travel agents and, most notably, acquired full control of Holiday Hypermarkets in May 2000. Holiday Hypermarkets had been a joint venture between West Co-operative Society, United Norwest Co-operative Society and First Choice. First Choice Holiday Hypermarkets now 'holds the number one position in the growing town travel retailing sector with 33 sites across the UK, as at June 2001' (First Choice 2001).

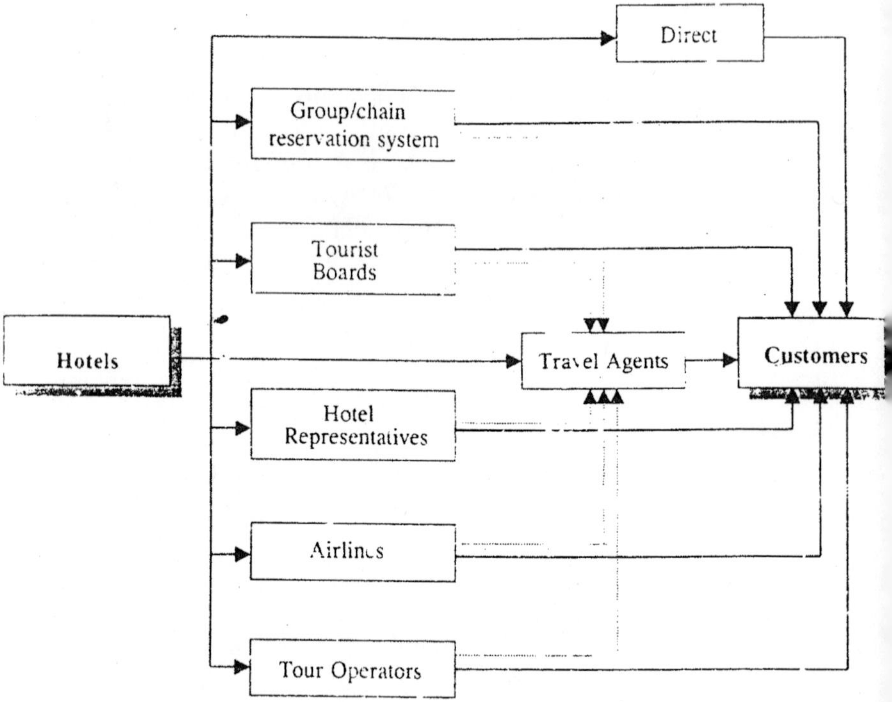

Fig. 14.2: Chain of distribution in the accommodation sector.

Channel decision must be based on an analysis of the market, the product, the producer and competitive factors, with the overriding decision being where, when and how consumers choose to buy the good or service. Within this, the dynamic nature of distribution strategies and, hence, the need for reassessment must be acknowledged; that is, it is important to determine what services consumers in various target segments desire and, by determining what channels are most appropriate or productive, to consider whether a new strategy is needed. Following First Choice's strategy from 1998 to 2000 of acquiring a presence in the retail travel agent sector, their stated aim is to now to 'further develop distribution capabilities and increase the percentage of sales *via* direct routes to market' (First Choice 2001). Thus, along–with a significant number of tour operators. First Choice see the potential of electronically distributing travel products, be it *via* the Internet or digital television, for example.

In formulating a distribution strategy, there is a need to take into account the degree of intensity required. This can be intensive, exclusive, or selective (Holloway 1995).

Intensive Approach

This involves the use of many outlets to distribute the product. It can, therefore, incur considerable costs in terms of print runs for brochures and level of support and is, perhaps, best suited to the general, mass market type holiday. So, in theory, a basic package holiday to Ibiza could be sold *via* all travel agents in the UK. Conversely, it is unlikely to be appropriate for more specialised, niche market products, such as the booking of luxury self-catering accommodation and exclusive package holidays as offered by BA Holidays and Kuoni. Generally, however, an intensive approach is increasingly less likely with tour operators and travel agents becoming integrated, as there is a greater tendency for tour operators to favour aligned travel agents and visa versa.

Selective Distribution

Here, the supplier selects a limited range of outlets and employs minimum criteria to be met by them. These criteria might include travel agents meeting financial guarantees, minimum staffing qualifications and minimum turnover, or it may involve the use of travel agents which are owned by or linked to tour operators. Airtours UK Leisure Group, which includes Airtours Holidays, Aspro, Panorama, Direct and Manos Holidays, are distributed *via* Airtours plc retail network, which encompasses Going Places and Travelworld on the high street, and the Holidayline telephone distribution business (integration is further discussed below). Targeting can also be done *via* specialist tour operators, such as Sunvil, which focuses on a limited number of destinations where their travel products are either sold direct or *via* their own retail travel agents. Not only can targeting can be done *via* the type of holiday on offer, be it luxury and exclusive, but it can also be done by age range and customer type. For example, Saga Holidays focus their direct marketing activities on people aged 50 and over (althougn an accompanying spouse or partner may be aged 40 or over). These particular types of products are specific to customer type and may be favoured by a number of specialist independent travel agents.

Exclusive Distribution

Exclusive distribution is rare in travel and tourism but occurs when a supplier grants exclusive rights to an agent to sell its products. It can sometimes occur with destinations or tourism offerings that offer themselves to an exclusive set of customers, such as island resorts or hotel complexes. This is the case with Sandals, which is a collection of ten all-inclusive resorts, which are purely for couples, whilst private island resorts such as Guana Island (www.guana.com) and Musha Cay (www.mushacay.com) offer highly exclusive destinations.

Whilst these decisions concern the extent of the distribution strategy, as, for example, whether to use multiple chains of travel agents or a selective number of independent travel agents, there are other ways of expending distribution. Integration and co-operative distribution systems can lead to the opening up of new and more extensive distribution channels .

Integration

Significant features of the UK travel and tourism retail industry in recent years have been both the 'march of the multiples, and vertical/horizontal integration. The 'multiples', that is, the large national and regional chains of travel agents (such as Lunn Poly and Going Places) enjoy, as a result of their size, great negotiating power which enables them to control terms and lay down expectations and wants to principals. At the same time, however, bias can also result from vertical integration, as the retail outlets might favour the tour operator they are linked with by racking brochures in prominent positions and promoting their holidays more strongly to customers when face to face selling. This situation can be further complicated by horizontal integration, as with Thomson's ownership of Lunn Poly and Callers Pegasus, the latter formerly being an independent chain of retail travel agents in the north east of England.

Co-operative Distribution Systems

Co-operative distribution systems include franchises and consortia. Franchises are an arrangement whereby a business grants an organisation the right to use their name and market its product in exchange for a fee. The franchisee benefits from the right to an established brand name and centralised marketing support whilst franchisers benefit from a rapid expansion of sties and a central fund. Within the travel and tourism industry, Holiday Inns are the oft-cited example of successful franchising operation. Consortia involve organisations uniting for marketing purposes whilst they retain their independence. This can result in joint brochures being produced, or access to central reservation systems, whilst for travel agency consortia a significant benefit is the negotiation of higher rates of commission for group members.

Worldchoice, formerly ARTAC, and Advantage Travel Centres are examples of travel agency consortia, and represent the largest networks of independent travel agents in Europe. Membership of Worldchoice leads to certain benefits, such as the offering of an overbranded Lakes and Mountains brochure produced with Airtours, increased negotiating power in setting commissions from tour operators, and private health care and motor insurance for agents. Advantage Travel Centres have developed a sophisticated web site that offers consumers online booking, holiday search facility and links to other consortium members, with the option for consumers to deal directly through a local travel agent by searching the online database. In America, the Virtuoso travel agency consortium provides marketing, sales, technology support, and exclusive services and products to leading independent luxury and adventure travel agencies.

Direct Sale Versus *Intermediaries*

In making distribution channel choices, one simple yet important question must be addressed – that is, whether to sell direct or *via* intermediaries. The tourism product lends itself to direct selling. The product cannot be seen, touched or physically inspected before purchase, which means that the consumer is, essentially, dependent on information. This information can just as easily be obtained directly from a supplier as through a third party and nowadays, tour operators are increasingly combining direct sale operations with those brands which are sold *via* travel agents. Airtours, for example, own their own travel agent, Going Places, a web site booking facility (mytravelco) and a direct sell tour operator, Direct Holidays.

In the promotion of products sold direct, there are associated price advantages to the consumer from buying direct whilst tour operators benefit from not having to pay commission to travel agents. Travel agents are sensitive regarding the publication of direct telephone numbers within tour operator brochures, which are available *via* the travel agency network, and the offering of cheaper prices when booking direct. One such instance was when First Choice was accused by a travel agent of offering a special discount to a client booking direct, as it makes it very difficult for agents to compete when tour operators undercut them (Richardson 2000). Direct Holidays, in their advertising campaign which clearly refers to cutting out the middleman (i.e. travel agents) to cut the costs, have annoyed travel agents to the extent that they requested that ABTA suspend Direct Holidays membership (Travel Trade Gazette 2001).

Direct Sell : Costs and Benefits

For direct sell, the fixed costs that are incurred are higher, such as the initial investment in infrastructure and information technology. There are also issues of concern for tour operators choosing direct sell, such as how to make late availability known to potential customers. Travel agents offer an easy and viable means of advertising last minute offers as seen with advertisements in the windows of high street travel agents. If a tour operator found there was excess availability on a package holiday, it would be expensive to mailshot customers from their database. Technological developments have also facilitated the growth of call centres and travel agents, such as Freedom Direct, have exploited Teletext as an alternative means of advertising last minute special offers, allowing customers to then book the holiday *via* their call centres.

Conversely, for tour operators selecting direct sell, costs might be reduced in terms of brochure production, as there would not be the need to gear the brochure runs to supplying intermediaries and the numbers needed would be more in line with consumer demand. Direct sell operations also, of course, place the control over sales in the hands of the product providers, thus helping to induce brand loyalty since the company is advertising itself direct to the consumer. With greater control of the system, this can lead to greater responsiveness to the needs of the consumer and the current selling position, with additional sales opportunities through relationship marketing and increased profit levels through the elimination of the travel agent's commission. For the customer also, buying direct from the producer can lead to greater control as they are dealing directly with the company packaging the product. There can also be time savings and greater accuracy, as the customer is communicating with the knowledgeable tour operator rather than a travel agent who might not be familiar with that particular product. For consumers, it could also be assumed that they gain from lower prices as there is no commission payable to a travel agent, although research undertaken by Holiday Which round that only one direct sell operator, Eclipse was actually cheaper than a high street agent for a comparable holiday (Mintel 2000). However, as discussed below, the 'traditional' travel agent still offers advantages over direct forms of retailing.

Categories of companies that sell direct include those that sell direct exclusively, those that sell both direct and *via* a travel agent, travel agents selling direct and credit card companies selling direct. In addition, direct selling offers new opportunities to established operators, which handle the business of third parties. For example, Thomas Cook Direct runs the newly formed First Direct Travel which was launched by the phone banking service First Direct and an established operator also handles the Barclays Travel Shop Direct (Mintel 1998).

Direct sell affords a greater degree of control and some principals, such as airlines, are by nature geared to it. Airlines are selling a simple, singular product and they have successfully exploited the opportunity afforded by the internet with the use of e-ticketing and have cut commissions to travel agents so making it less profitable for airline tickets to be sold by travel agents. Some operators have turned to direct sell following dissatisfaction with the level of service travel agents have offered them. For a large number of smaller and independent tour operators, the issue of racking and difficulties of getting a prominent position in travel agents mean they resort to direct sale as the easiest option.

Intermediaries: Costs and Benefits

Intermediaries – travel agents, tour operators, tour retailers, specialist brokers, business agents and tour wholesalers – can provide a practical solution to the problems of distribution as they allow for a variety of economies. The tour operator can focus on the delivery of an appropriate package without the worry and hassle of selling it to consumers as an experienced intermediary can do this for them. If there is under capacity, they are simply turn to the intermediaries to sell the package as a last minute special offer and, in using intermediaries, they can take advantage of the relationships the intermediaries have developed with their customers.

At the same time however, the use of intermediaries can result in the incurring of extra costs, such as commission payments and higher costs of brochure production, and less control and difficulties with the level of service. Nevertheless, the distribution sector of tourism is much stronger, and travel intermediaries have far greater power to influence and direct consumer demand, compared to their counterparts in other industries. Unlike other products that flow from producer to consumer, tourists flow to the product. This inverted distribution system relies on intermediaries to perform much more than simple delivery services with, for example, travel agents being seen as the 'reassuring human fare' of the travel industry.

Thus, the changing structure of the tourism industry and the development of new technology has undoubtedly led to difficulties for travel agents. Airlines have, for example, been cutting commissions and attempting to cut out the middleman by selling direct and effectively using call centers and the Internet to do so. This is especially the case for the 'no-frills' airlines such as Ryanair and Easyjet, whilst many tour operators are developing direct sell operations as in the case with Airtours and their purchase of Direct Holidays. Similarly, Thomson Cook has Thomas Cook Direct, First Choice has Eclipse and Thomson has Portland Direct. Although these operations tend to only sell a selection of the holidays featured in the main brochures, to their parent companies and where the same holidays do feature there is often a different in the prices offered (Mintel 2000). Nevertheless although some would claim that the days of the travel agent (in particular the independent, as opposed to chain, agency) are numbered, the travel agent, as the following section suggests, will continue to play an important role in travel distribution.

The Role of the Travel Agent

Although it is not within the scope of this chapter to be able to enter into a full discussion on the role of travel agent (see Bottomley Renshaw 1997), travel agents are a key intermediary and, as such, deserve some attention. Travel agents are distinctive from other types of retailars as they carry no stock and so bear little financial risk, never purchase products but act on behalf of consumers, and receive commission on sales from their 'suppliers' (i.e. from the principals upon whose behalf they act as agents). This means that the contract of sale is not between the customer and the travel agent, but between the customer and the principal. Travel agents can also emphasise products which earn higher commissions, whilst the issue of racking is another contentious area allowing for favouritism. There can be extreme problems in getting brochures racked by the travel agents, and there are also costs such as servicing the agent, commissions, overrides and other incentives and information technology. The wide variety of products available in travel agents also require extensive knowledge and skill. Therefore, the level of service can be variable as the average travel agent cannot know everything and anything about all products on sale.

The role of the travel agent is dependent on the products sold, the customers, the degree of specialisation of the agency, the demand within the area and the levels of commission offered. It must also be noted that the role of the travel agent has developed differently in different counties, as in America, for example, they have developed a role as packager of holidays. The discussion here, however, is mainly concerned with the situation as it is in the UK.

There are about 7000 travel agents in the UK, including leisure and holiday agents and business agencies (Mintel 2000). Leisure and holiday agents can either be general agencies or specialist agencies. General agencies sell all types of products from Inclusive Tours to coach tickets and airline tickets but, by dealing with such a wide range of products, associated problems can arise. The focus tends to be on low cost and low revenue business, such as coach tickets, whilst the staff can fail to develop specialist knowledge as they have to know about everything and anything. As a result, some travel agents specialise in particular types of holidays, such as those to long haul destinations (for example Austravel), student travel (for example STA Travel) or flight only (for example, Trailfinders and FIightbookers).

High street travel agents do not tend to specialise in business travel, although they do provide flights to business clients, mainly daily return fares within the UK or to mainstream Europe. Conversely, business agencies sell to commercial clients and not the general public. The UK business travel market is significant, valued at around £ 10.5 billion in 1998 (Mintel 2000). It is also a highly lucrative market, with hotel groups and airlines relying on revenue that is generated from this target audience, although the success of the low-cost/no-frills airlines such as Ryanair, Easyjet, Go and Buzz, as well as the opportunity for businesses to save on travel costs by booking direct, is a threat to the continued success of business agencies. Other areas of concern for business travel agencies include commission cuts, passenger service charge and the introduction of management fees. Major business agencies include American Express, Business Travel International UK, Hogg Robinson, Carlson Wagonlit and Rosenbluth. Medium sized players in the UK market include Britannic Travel, Portland Travel, Seaforth Travel and The Travel Company.

Organisation of the Travel Agency Sector

The travel agency sector in the UK can be crudely divided into multiples and independents and a dominant feature since the 1980s, as with the tour operator sector, has been increasing concentration and consolidation. This phenomenon has been referred to as the 'march of the multiples'. The multiples travel agencies are usually integrated with tour operators and round a third are owned by the top three high street chains (Mintel 2000). Indeed, in 1999 the top four travel companies (Thomson, Airtours. Thomas Cook and First Choice) accounted for around 70 per cent of the retail travel agency market by volume. Renshaw (1998) identifies how the increase in power and weight for companies' means they can control terms and lay down expectations and wants to principals. Bias can also result from vertical integration, as the retail outlets might favour the tour operator they are linked with. This is referred to directional selling, as travel companies sell their own inclusive tours through their own travel agents in preference to other alternatives. Mintel (2000) research has shown this is common practice (Mintel 2000), despite it being the subject of a Monopolies and Merger Commission investigation in the UK. The 1997 investigation cleared the integrated operators of anti-competitive practices and, since then, the degree of vertical integration has increased substantially (Mintel 2000). A succession of takeovers and mergers occurred and the major companies now own a wide portfolio of tour operators, airlines and, significantly, travel agents.

Not surprisingly, independent travel agents, such as Bath Travel, Althams Travel Services, Dawson & Sanderson, and Phoenix Travel, claim that directional selling is against the public interest because consumers are not given a real choice of product or price. Similarly, the Campaign for Real Travel Agents claims the multiples are just becoming distribution points for the major tour operators (Mintel 2000). Certainly, it is increasingly difficult for the independent sector to remain competitive and, as a result, the number of such agencies is constantly falling (Mintel 2000). Those that remain have realised that, unless they specialise in niche products (such as cruises and golf packages), their future will remain threatened.

A further challenge to independent travel agents is the emergence of online specialist travel agents, whilst the major multiples have also started to offer their own in-house online offers. Mintel (2000) research has shown that direct sales, especially through specialist online agents, is growing all the time as consumers become more confident at travelling 'unpackaged' and the prices represent better value for money. Thus, it is estimated that direct sales will grow from 22 per cent in 1997 to 30 per cent of total online sales in 2002 (Poon 2001). For small independents, however, the costs of setting up this new technology are very high and it may be difficult to raise the necessary finance. At the same time, the profits are low and, consequently, independents are being challenged by the domination of the multiples and the new online specialist travel agents.

Moreover, a further feature of distribution concerning travel agents is the trend towards disintermediation. Disintermediation is the term used to describe the process whereby the ability of principals in the tourism distribution chain to use information technology to communicate with consumers in their homes or in other public places may, ultimately, cut out the travel agent. However, in order to completely eliminate travel agents, a number of obstacles, encompassing social, economic and political, as well as technological, factors would need to be surmounted (Bennett 1995). Indeed, it can be argued that travel agents will continue to have an important role in reducing the complexity of the communication network, as they are experienced in finding out information from the increased information available (van Heijden 1996). Moreover, Bennett (1995) emphasises the importance of the travel agent as the reassuring human face of the travel industry, as consumers often seek advice which only the travel agent can provides. Travel agents can also provide the choice and help in the comparing of different companies' products. In short, the personal service travel agents provide is an invaluable part of their role and, were they to be removed from the distribution process, it could lead to a reduction in communication rates, consumer resistance to new technology, and the bias of technology owners and developments excluding other competitors. Therefore, although Inkpen (1998) argues that the Internet will lead to disintermediation as an increasing number of sophisticated sites offer on-line booking of accommodation and events, travel agents will not necessarily be marginalised by the threat of the Internet. They will, however, need to embrace it.

The Importance of Information Technology

Within the travel and tourism industry, technological developments have had a significant impact on distribution as the industry attempts to meet the demands of discerning customers who have increasingly diverse profiles. The nature of the tourism product (intangible, perishable, volatile, heterogeneous) is particularly suited to the adoption of information technology because of the dependence on the supply and exchange of information throughout the production and distribution chain. Within this distribution chain, computers have come to play an increasingly strategic and dominant role.

The dynamic nature of the tourism product is such that a mechanism is required to transmit information about products between the different sectors in the chain of distribution. Indeed, without such a mechanism, the travel and tourism industry's operational efficiency would be severely restricted. At the same time, competition between suppliers further heightens the need for efficient, reliable and accurate information regarding the products and their availability. As a result, the means of conveying information in and around the chain of production and distribution becomes virtually as important as the information itself. Therefore, it is not, perhaps, surprising that information technology is proving to be all – pervasive within the travel and tourism industry – certainly, travel agents, tour operators, airlines and hotels are all heavy users of information technology, to the extent that Poon (1988) refers to it as a 'total information system'.

Developments in information technology have undoubtedly had significant impacts on distribution, although there are disparities in the introduction of and level of development in different countries. For example, destination marketing systems have met with success in Canada, yet this is not the case in the UK or in Switzerland [see Alford (2000) for further details]. Similarly, the development of Computer Reservation Systems (CRS) has been particularly advantageous in the USA where, because of the geographical size of the country, they have become widely used for the booking of both domestic and outbound holidays. With domestic holidays, Americans are more likely to travel *via* air and so use travel agents to book flights and accommodation. Conversely, in the UK, customers are more likely to book domestic holidays direct as they tend to use their own transport and are sufficiently confidant to book their own accommodation. Other technological developments have also become more established in some countries than elsewhere, such as multi–media kiosks which provide destination specific information at the destination and, sometimes, incorporate a booking facility. In the USA, these are located in a variety of venues, including state welcome centres, hotel lobbies and tourist attractions.

Despite these national variations, information technology has undoubtedly had a significant impact on distribution, in particular in the context of outbound tourism, with the development of Computer Reservation Systems (CRS) playing a particular important role. The initiative for CRS initially came from international airlines which needed a means of selling their tickets electronically and automated seat reservations and procedures. The focus of the CRS was, therefore, on selling airline tickets. Conversely, in the UK a sophisticated leisure market had developed providing packages holidays for which the CRS was not an effective means of distribution. Therefore, tour operators in the UK developed videotext systems in order to sell their package holidays electronically. CRSs have now evolved from being airline focused to being complete global distribution systems (GDS), and now sell a range of travel products in addition to airline ticket. Over the last five years, though, new technological developments, specifically the Internet, have threatened the dominance of such distribution systems.

Existing Tourism Information Distribution Systems

The impact of information technology on distribution has been significant and there are a number of existing tourism information distribution systems. Although the increasing use of the Internet is an important part this process.

Computer Reservation Systems (CRSs) and Global Distribution Systems (GDSs)

Over the last 40 years, CRSs have emerged as the dominant technology in the travel and tourism industry, controlling the sale and distribution of a wide array of travel related services. CRS enables information to be distributed and reservations to be processed in an efficient manner and, in many markets, such as in flight only and business travel, it has become an essential business tool (Lindsay 1992). Essentially, CRS is a database that enables a tourism organisation to manage its inventory and make it accessible to its distribution channel partners. Subscribers are provided with up-to-date information on airfares and services and can book, change and cancel reservations, and issue tickets. The rapid growth of both tourism demand and supply in recent decades has demonstrated the need for these advanced computer systems.

The impetus for the development of the CRS came from the airlines in the United States. In the early 1960s, American Airlines saw the need to develop a system which automated seat reservations and the procedures of airlines. As a result, SABRE

(Semi-Automated Business Resource Environment) was then developed and introduced. To be successful, it had to:

- be a continuously operated, real-time, inquiry response system so agents could get an immediate answer to queries;
- have a large, geographically dispersed data communications network that connected all users of the reservation system to the central site (Sheldon 1997).

By the mid-1970s, not only had most other airlines followed American Airlines example (see Table 14.1 below), but also there was the increasing occurrence of direct travel agency access, into these systems *via* a dedicated terminal located at the agency itself. CRSs were developed as businesses in their own right and became extremely profitable as revenues were obtained through imposing a small charge per booking and from payments by travel agents for the right to access the system (Archdale 1991). Initially, the systems sought to manage only reservations and passenger tracking functions and provided few support features. Today, however, CRSs have evolved into GDSs as they do so much more than sell airline tickets and automate procedures. They support window functions and multi-tasking, allowing travel agents to book flights, hotels, cars and look up other information such as visa requirements, currency conversion rates, and current weather conditions.

In short CRSs have evolved into complete travel information systems and, as such, are GDSs (Poon 1993); they have multiple carrier affiliations and they all provide important electronic distribution channels for a variety of travel products. Moreover, GDSs are increasingly adapting business to include Web based products and services. The Internet reservation systems that are evolving are not necessarily a threat to GDSs as they can offer added value with services, such as theatre and restaurant bookings. Indeed, it seems inevitable that existing computer reservation systems and global distribution systems will become integrated with the Internet. At the same time, the continuing development of these communication techniques will inevitably mean that organisations involved in processing and distributing vast quantities of information will move to the Internet to facilitate these activities.

Table 14.1
Global Distribution Systems

Name	*Developed by*	*Key UK customers (1999) include*
Amadeus	Air France, Lufthansa, Iberia and Sabena	Lunn Poly. Flightbookers, Travel 2/4
Galileo	British Airways, KLM, Swissair, Austrian, Aer Lingus, Air Portugal, Olympic	BTI Hogg Robinson, Carlson Wagonlit, Portland, Gold Medal, Trailfinders, Airtours Group, Seaforths
Sabre	American Airlines	Amex, STA Travel, P&O, The Travel Co. MSW Group, Travelforce, Carlson Wagonlit, Bakers Dolphin, Phoenix
Worldspan	Delta, Northwest, TWA	Thomas Cook, Going Places, TMPL Group, Co-op Travelcare, Globepost, Crystal Holidays, Lotus Leisure, Global Travel Group, Scotway Group, Microsoft Expedia

Source: Adapted from Mintel (2000)

The Problems Associated with CRSs

Inherent Bias in CRSs

From the outset airlines saw CRSs as their own property and, as a result, there were legitimate concerns that CRSs would be biased as, in theory, the schedules of the owning airline appeared before that of the competition. At the same time, airlines that were not involved in the development of a CRS found they were expected to pay a higher fee for having a presence on the CRS. The income from these fees were then used to offer incentives to the travel agencies to ensure they booked flights with CRS owner airlines rather than the airline that was simply paying for use of the system. Revenue management systems also monitored sales and calculated fares that gave CRS owners a competitive advantage in the marketplace.

Over time, however, this inherent bias has largely been eradicated through codes of conduct implemented in US and Europe, although systems still give the airlines control cover the distribution of the travel product in the US and have been used to protect and ifncrease market share. Although rules have succeeded in eliminating display bias, incremental revenues continue to be obtained through architectural bias and from the relationship between vendor airlines and travel agencies that foster travel agency loyalty to the vendor airline (Poon 1993).

Insufficient Scope of Services

With regard to product presentation, the offers are almost exclusively limited to the owner airlines and, as a result, other service providers only have a very limited reservation rate or are not displayed at all. Fare quoting is still a complicated and confusing process, and price transparency or even price negotiations are not supported by the systems (Schulz 1997). CRS owners have also been slow to extend functions into the leisure market and this, in turn, prompted the development of videotext technologies to fulfil the need.

High Distribution Costs

The high costs of using CRSs mean that many providers, such as small to medium tourism enterprises (for example owner run hotels), avoid using the system. For smaller agencies, Internet reservation systems can be a more cost effective means of distribution as they offer a wide range of products, but are based on less restrictive contracts than CRSs and can be used as the sole source of booking for an agency.

CRSs Discrimination Against other Tourism Enterprises

CRSs are expensive, difficult to instal and maintain, and do not automatically provide hotels, airlines and other suppliers with an automatic increase in business unless they are used to their full potential. Many commercial factors inhibit non-air vendors from automating their inventories and from using electronic distribution services. Principally, these factors relate to cost, control of inventory and conflict with existing business practices. For the hotel provider, an entry on a CRS can lead to problems of commission payments, different languages and totally different standards and codes (Lindsay 1992).

Viewdata

In the UK and in Europe, agency systems' development has taken a different route from the US experience, with viewdata and videotext systems playing a major role, particularly for the leisure market (Treacey 1989).

The role of the tour operator is considerably greater in Europe than in the USA, as in Europe tour operators played an important role in the development and introduction of computerised booking of tour packages themselves (Poon 1988). Within the UK, Thomson has been active in the development of technology since the early 1980s and provides a good example of the role of UK tour operators in automating the distribution of holidays. Thomson and Olympic Holidays were amongst the first operators to launch viewdala systems in the early 1980s (Bottomley Renshaw 1998). In the UK, most packaged holidays can only be accessed through on-line viewdata terminals developed and provided by the major tour operators. This is because UK tour operators have invested in the development of their own viewdata technology while other suppliers have become partners or co-hosts in airline CRS and still others chose not to automate – using conventional telephone calls as the main vehicle for bookings. In 1998, Thomson Holidays, a leading UK travel organisation, began to move its viewdata system on to the Internet. The company will use the 'net to receive' 'incoming requests from travel agents'. Web browsers and then links up to the existing applications on Thomson's IBM mainframes'.

Destination Marketing Systems (OMS)

Destination Marketing Systems can encompass both reservations and information and can operate at national, regional and local levels (Bennett 1995), Destination marketing systems can also be referred to as destination databases (DD), destination management systems (DMS), travel information systems (TIS), and destination information systems (DIS) (Bennett 1996).

A DMS can have up to three components:

- *Product database* – of attractions, accommodation, travel information etc.;
- *Customer database* – of those using, or those who have used, the database;
- Booking and reservation system (Baker *et al.* 1996).

DMS can incorporate any number of the following features:

- product database;
- client database;
- marketing facilities;
- information retrieval;
- reservations;
- distribution.

The focus of the DMS may vary from pre-trip to post-arrival information, reservations and product databases. DMSs fill a large gap left by the GDS in the electronic distribution of destination information, as CRSs tend to favour large chain companies with high prices whilst DMSs include all types of travel products – large or small (Sheldon 1997). The trend away from packaged travel has created a demand for easily accessible information on destinations, particularly on small and medium sized enterprises which DMSs can respond to and meet the need for (Vliots-Rowe 1992). DMS tend to be destination specific and are, as such, a restricted form of distribution.

DMSs have met with varying degrees of success and failure. The funding and level of public and private sector support given to these systems have led to difficulties and insurmountable obstacles. Swissline, in Switzerland, never emerged from the planning stage due to a lack of public and private support, whilst Hi-Line in Scotland was implemented in a region where there was insufficient – volume of business and without public tourist organisation support (Sussmann 1994). DMSs can be divided into non – commercial and commercial models, where the former are supported by public funds, are an instrument of economic development and more prevalent. Speculation would suggest a brighter future for fully commercial DMS (Baker *et al.* 1996), and small to medium tourism enterprises and national tourism organisations are increasingly looking to such systems as the way forward. This is the case in Germany, Austria and Switzerland where Tiscover AG (a pioneering company) in the development of destination management systems in Europe) had provided systems to leading national and regional tourism organisations.

Video Conferencing

The integration on the Personal Computer and the Internet will see an increase in the use of video conferencing. For a relatively small investment in additional equipment, organisations can arrange meetings - without having to travel to a specific location. On the one hand, a tourism organisation can benefit from the efficiencies that might result hut, on the other hand, this may mean that the need for business travel declines.

Kiosks

In the early 1990s, kiosks were seen as a possible way forward for the distribution of tourism information, especially to the tourists seeking information about, or at, destinations. Self service multi-media kiosks have enormous potential in terms of dissemination of information and reservation purposes. Kiosks are a means of distributing information in a particularly user friendly way because they tend to use a 'touch screen' interface. People, who are intimidated by 'technology' might find using a kiosk more intuitive and less threatening than a computer terminal. Kiosks are currently used by both the private and public sector to promote tourism and provide tourist information. They can be sited in tourist areas like railway stations, airports or city streets and have the advantage of being available 24 hours a day, 365 days a year. It seems likely that kiosks will be more tightly integrated with the internet and designed to take advantages of Internet technology in the coming years.

Home Shopping

The growth of non-terrestrial television and digital television, coupled with a relaxation of government controls in this sector, will mean that home shopping will increase in the next few years. The arrival of interactive digital TV in the UK has opened up a major new front for competition among global distribution systems, as all four GDS companies see the Internet as providing a focus for advances m travel technology (Mintel 2000). By becoming the booking engine behind the Internet companies, GDSs believe they will gain massively increased exposure through interactive TV. Worldspan has links with Microsoft in the US, UK and Europe as the booking engine behind Expedia; Sabre has Travelocity in the US and UK; Amadeus has Compuserve in the UK (Mintel 2000). The takeover of Expedia, a major Internet travel agency in 2001, by American media group, USA Network, reflects the increasing importance placed on home shopping. USA

Network believes that 'using a website in competition with an interactive TV channel would put Expedia at the head of the pack when interactive digital TV takes off in Europe (Travel Trade Gazette 2001).

This is important for the tourism marketer, as it will allow tourism organisations to find another way to communicate with their customers. Currently, many TV providers and manufacturers are working on ways to integrate TV technology with the Internet. This will mean that consumers will not have to own a personal computer to access the 'net'. This has enormous implications for e-commerce and home shopping. The Internet will no longer be the preserve of the technologically advanced, who are currently a distinct but relatively small market segment, but will be accessible to anyone with a TV – which, of course, is most people.

Conclusion

Distribution is a vital component of the travel and tourism industry and it has become the primary area for seeking competitive advantage in both cost reduction and service improvement. The advantages afforded by the increasing use of information technology means that the inherent problems of the tourism product – its perishability, intangibility, heterogeneity and inseparability – can be diminished and controlled.

This chapter has shown how distribution of the tourism product primarily concerns information as consumers need to be able to access the tourism product at multiple points of sale away from the places of service production and this involves information being passed down the distribution channels. Developments in information technology are having significant impact on distribution choices being made. Direct sale is becoming ever more popular whilst it has been argued that travel agents position may well be under threat.

15
The World Tourism

Introduction

Tourism today is a global issue. Not only have international tourism arrivals more than doubled since 1983, but also the number of destinations drawn into the so-called 'pleasure periphery' (Turner and Ash 1975) has grown to the extent that there are few countries or regions worldwide which could claim to be outside the international tourism system. At the same time, many issues relating to tourism, including its role in development, its social, political and environmental consequences and its alleged position as the world's largest industry, deserve consideration at the global level. However, with the exception of figures relating to the overall volume and value of tourism, many global issues are all too frequently overlooked.

The purpose of this chapter, therefore is to assess the present state of world tourism. This will include not only a statistical analysis of current trends and flows in international tourism, but will also, firstly, address the question: why adopt a global perspective on tourism?

A Global Perspective on Tourism?

It is inevitable, perhaps, that most tourism issues are viewed primarily at a national or local level. This stems largely from the competitive nature of national and international tourism; although tourism is described as a global activity, most countries are in competition with all other countries for a share of the world tourism market. Similarly, at the national level, regions compare for their share of domestic and incoming tourism. Therefore, national and local governments or tourism organisations work primarily in the national and regional interest.

Nevertheless, there are many aspects of tourism which transcend national and regional boundaries. In other words, whilst tourism is undoubtedly a significant worldwide economic activity, there are also other aspects or issues which can, or should, be considered on a global basis. For example, sex tourism or tourism-related prostitution has, in the past, been viewed as a problem for particular destinations. However, solutions to the problem can only be found at the international level, as evidenced by the fact that some tourism generating countries, including the UK and Australia, now prosecute their nationals found guilty of such activities whilst on holiday overseas. Similarly, the challenge of sustainable tourism, by definition, demands a global perspective, as do many other inter-related issues.

Generally, however, global issues related to tourism can be addressed under three broad headings:

- Tourism and world economic development.
- Tourism and the world environment.
- Tourism, international understanding and peace.

It is with these issues that this first section is concerned.

Tourism and World Economic Development

It has long been recognised that international tourism can be used as a developmental tool. Indeed, the primary reason for developing tourism is its potential for bringing about social and economic development. It is not surprising, therefore, that 'many of the world's countries not regard tourism as an important and integral aspect of their development strategies' (Jenkins 1991: 62).

The developmental role of tourism is normally associated with the economic benefits that accrue from international tourism, such as foreign exchange earnings, employment opportunities, income generation, and direct and indirect contributions to government revenues. Moreover, tourism, as a specific economic activity, is frequently favoured over other activities as a development tool for a number of reasons:

- Tourism is, historically, arid continues to be, a growth industry.
- Much of the investment in international tourism comes from the richer, developed countries.
- International tourism is a source of hard currencies.
- Tourism is typically a labour intensive sector.
- Normally tourism does not face trade or quota restrictions.
- Many attractions (e.g. climate, culture, environment) already exist and are, in a sense, 'free'.
- Tourism encourages the expansion of other sectors of the local economy.

However, despite the apparent ease with which tourism should be developed and bring economic benefits to destination areas and, indeed, despite the continuing growth in arrivals and tourist expenditure as demonstrated by international tourism statistics, in reality the full developmental potential of tourism is rarely realised. For example, many destinations, such as The Gambia, retain a relatively small proportion of the income generated by international tourism (see Sharpley and Sharpley 1996). This suggests that the state of world tourism in terms of development may not be as healthy as the figures might indicate. Moreover, there are a number of other key characteristics and influences not generally highlighted in statistical analyses of international tourism which shape tourism's role and potential as a tool of economic development. Many of these influences relate, quite simply, to the nature of tourism and the nature of the tourism industry at a global level. These are considered below.

The Nature of Travel and Tourism

International travel and tourism, by its very nature, necessitates the movement of individuals across national boundaries (a movement which in 1999 totalled some 664 million international arrivals. By implication, therefore, if international tourism is to achieve its full developmental potential this movement of people must be made as easy as possible. However, like any other international trade, there exists a number of barrier or impediments which may negatively influence the international flow of tourists. In a general sense, these can be social, economic and physical conditions in both generating and host countries which influence travel. For example, Ascher (1984) has observed that factors deterring tourism to particular destinations include 'poor transportation and communications, work stoppages, inferior health and sanitary conditions, unpleasant food, overcrowding, and inadequate hotel and travel facilities' .

More specifically, there are a variety of other barriers to which may restrict international tourism (Figure 15.1):

(i) Government intervention:	• visa restrictions • entry/exit quotas • currency restrictions • travel/departure tax • direct tourism policy • bi-lateral agreements • travel advice • local equity requirements
(ii) Political instability:	• military regimes • coups d'état • terrorism • fundamentalism
(iii) Conflict:	• wars/war zones
(iv) Crime:	• mugging/theft • violent crime
(v) Natural disasters:	• earthquakes/hurricanes • famine • iliness

Whilst a number of these barriers to international tourism, such as natural disasters, are uncontrollable, many others can be addressed or overcome through international agreement or co-operation. Such agreement may be bi-lateral, that is, between two countries, or multi-lateral, where a number of nation states agree to certain mutual rights and obligations. For example, while visa agreements can represent a significant barrier to tourism development, particularly where numbers are restricted or where visa charges act as a disincentive to travel, the removal of such barriers is possible through international co-operation. There are many forms of international agreement which are beyond the scope of this chapter. However, the important point here is mat efforts must be made at a global level to facilitate and encourage freedom of movement to encourage the development of tourism. It is no coincidence that this is the prime purpose of organisations such as the World Tourism Organisation (WTO) and the World Travel and Tourism Council (WTTC).

Furthermore, as an international service industry, tourism is also subject to the General Agreement on Trade in Services (GATS) – an offshoot of the wide-ranging General Agreement on Tariffs and Trade (GATT). GATS operates on the principle that free market forces are the most effective way of giving customers worldwide the best choice of service products at the best prices. The purpose of GATS in relation to tourism is, therefore, to put in place a system which will progressively eliminate barriers to tourism growth, such as restrictions on the ability of tourism companies to employ foreign personnel, establish management contracts and effect international money transfers and payments (for a fuller discussion of the effect of GATS and tourism, see WTO 1994). This is, perhaps, a sign that at last there is worldwide recognition of the value of tourism and that efforts must be made to continue to facilitate its appropriate development. However, it has also been recognised that GATS may have certain detrimental effects. That is, the process of liberalisation which GATS has set in motion may well enable western-owned, multinational companies to increase their power and influence in countries where tourism is currently under-developed (see below).

The state of world tourism today is not, however, just characterised by the extent to which nation states can lower political barriers. It also relates to the flow of tourism, globally. Tourism as an activity is dominated by the richer developed Western economies and the economic benefits of tourism mainly stay within these areas.

The Nature of Tourist Flows

A further important characteristic of tourism in relation to its developmental potential is the pattern of international tourism flows. The most obvious trend has been the dramatic growth in international tourist arrivals which, since 1950, has increased by a factor of twenty four, with a corresponding increase in international tourism receipts. At the same time, tourism has also spread; in 1950, just 15 countries accounted for almost all international arrivals but, by 1999, the top 15 receiving countries saw their share decrease to less than two-thirds whilst more than 70 countries attracted over one million arrivals. Nevertheless, not all tourist destinations have benefited from tourism's growth. According to Shaw and Williams (1994: 23) international tourism flows display three distinctive patterns:

- *Polarity* – international tourism is still largely dominated by the industrial world with the major tourism flows being either between the more developed countries or from developed countries to lesser developed countries. Thus, it has been pointed out that, 'the industrialised countries receive 56 per cent of international tourism receipts, while low-income countries (including India and China) receive just 1.5 per cent of receipts' (Vellas and Bécherel 1995: 19). Therefore, although the East Asia and Pacific region has, in recent years, become an increasingly significant source of international tourists, the benefits of international tourism remain highly polarised.
- *Regionalisation* – international tourism is highly regionalised. In other words, the most significant flows of international tourists occur within well-defined regions, in particular within Europe. Other important regions include North America, with major flows between Canada and the United States and between the United States and the Caribbean, and the Japan and East Asia region.
- *European dominance* – the third major characteristic of international tourism is that it is largely concentrated within Europe. Indeed, in the early 1960s, Europe's share of world tourism represented over 70 per cent of world arrivals. This has since fallen, although a number of Eastern European countries have recently experienced rapid growth in arrival numbers.

These statistics and flows are analysed in greater detail in the latter half of this chapter. However, the important point here is that by looking at tourism statistics globally, significant discrepancies in arrivals, visitor spending and hence developmental potential, become evident. In particular, the economic benefits generated by tourism are predominantly shared between the industrialised countries – in 1997, developing countries collectively received just 30.5 per cent of international tourism receipts – although it is likely that, in future years, the East Asian region including China will play a more dominant role in international tourism flows.

The Nature of the Industry

A particular feature of the tourism industry is that it is diverse, fragmented and multi-sectorial. That is, it comprises a large number of predominantly small, private organisations in sectors as diverse as accommodation, retail, entertainment and transport. However, the major players within the industry are large multinational corporations such as airlines, hotel chains and tour operators, and it is no coincidence that the majority of these are based in the major tourism-generating countries. For example, the United States remains the world's largest generator of international tourism and 8 out of 10 top hotel chains are American.

This feature has major implications for tourism development because these organisations are able to influence styles of tourism, levels of investment and tourist flows. In some cases, this may lead to destinations becoming dependent on the continued support of overseas organisations, particularly where there is heavy reliance on one major generating market. In Cyprus, for example, up to 50 per cent of tourists come from the UK and it could be argued that it is the influence of some UK tour operators which has led to the current state of tourism development on the island. What this means is that, although tourism appears to be a powerful vehicle for global development, not only does much of the influence come from the major tourism generating countries, but also much of the earnings from tourist activity remain with, or are repatriated to, those countries.

A further characteristic of tourism in the context of global economic development is that tourism, perhaps more than any other economic activity, can lead to serious social and environmental consequences for destination areas. In many cases, these negative impacts may outweigh the economic benefits of tourism. This suggests that, as discussed in the next section, the environmental aspects of tourism must also be considered on a global basis. However, to conclude this section, tourism and world economic development can be looked at from different points of view but, given the general process of worldwide economic development, no country today – developed or developing – can view their economy, or any aspect of it, in isolation from the rest of the world. All nation-states are now part of an interdependent global village where increasing emphasis is being placed on international, as opposed to domestic, production and consumption and where an industry's growth potential is assessed within the context of a global marketplace. Tourism is no exception to this process of globalisation.

Tourism and World Environment

Reflecting the dramatic growth tourism during the latter half of the twentieth century, in particular the emergence of international mass tourism, there has been an ever-increasing concern for its effect on the environment. It is now generally recognised that any tourism development has to take into account not only economic benefits of tourism but also its environmental and social consequences. Equally the study of tourism would not be complete without an understanding of the socio-cultural and environmental aspects of tourism.

Although most tourism textbooks address the topic, the point to be emphasised here is that the environmental aspects of tourism development must be considered on a global basis. This is not to say that sustainable environmentally-friendly approaches to the planning and management of tourism at the micro, destination level are not important. On the contrary, appropriate forms of tourism development must start at the local level and there have been many examples from the 1970s onwards, where a sustainable approach to tourism has been successfully put into practice (see Eber 1992: Inskeep and Kallenberger 1992; Harrison and Husbands 1996).

However, as important as these local initiatives are, tourism is a global phenomenon; therefore, environmentally appropriate planning must also be global. To do otherwise would be to simply shift the so-called problem of tourism (normally associated with mass tourism) from one destination to another. In other words, where a destination adopts strict environmental policies for tourism development, such as restricting numbers or promoting niche-type tourism products (e.g. eco-tourism), it is likely that the tourism industry or tourists may switch their allegiance to less restrictive or expensive destinations.

In general, it has been recognised that environmental issues can only be addressed on the global stage. For example, the Earth Summit at Rio de Janeiro in 1992 represented a significant step towards global policies for the environment, although more recent events have demonstrated that there are many difficulties to be overcome before this will be achieved. Nevertheless, truly sustainable tourism will only occur if an holistic global approach is adopted and nowhere is the much-used adage 'think global, act local' more relevant than in the context of tourism (but see Sharpley 2000).

Tourism, International Understanding and World Peace

A number of international bodies have suggested that tourism has the potential to contribute to international understanding and world peace (see Var *et al.* 1994). For example, not only does the WTO consider its fundamental role to be to 'develop tourism in order to contribute to economic expansion, international understanding, peace and prosperity', but also, in 1980, it went as far as to proclaim tourism as 'a vital force for world peace' (WTO 1980). Similarly, a number of commentators support the idea that, as a worldwide social activity that brings different societies and cultures together, tourism should foster greater international harmony and understanding.

However, this potential role of tourism has been the subject of some debate. Furthermore other general assumptions about the extent of the relationship between tourism, international understanding and world peace have also been called into question. Three points in particular deserve consideration:

Tourism and International Understanding

Var *et al.* (1998) consider that there are two related aspects of tourism which contribute to world peace: 'the promotion of cultural exchange as a means of breaking down the barriers between individuals or people of different nations . . . [and] . . . the development of greater understanding between individuals or people of different nations resulting from this exchange'. In other words, it is the contribution which tourism can make to the attainment of international understanding which will promote and safeguard peace. A number of specific schemes, such as student exchange programmes, have been specially designed in recognition of this.

However, international understanding takes place at a number of different levels, including political, individual and corporate, and is by no means an inevitable outcome of the development of tourism in general. Indeed, it could be argued that due to both the nature of the current tourism system, which is dominated by western generating markets, and the differing personal motivations for international travel, tourism can serve merely to underline existing divisions and prejudices between diverse cultural and ethnic groups. As Ap and Var (1990) observe, there is little evidence to suggest that tourism generates international understanding or strong inter-cultural relationships, it being more likely reinforce stereotypic images between peoples of different nations. This supports the findings of a number of other studies, for example Milman *et al.* (1990) and Pizam *et al.* (1991).

However, it is still possible that 'tourism, properly designed and developed, can help bridge the psychological and cultural distances that separate people of diverse races, colours, religions, and stages of social and economic development' (D' Amore 1988). Although empirical research to date has established only tenuous evidence of tourism's role as a contributor to world peace, any improvement in the state of international understanding as a result of tourism is clearly to be encouraged and, therefore, further research as to how this may be achieved would be desirable.

Tourism as Peace-broker

Perhaps the most ambitious perspective that we might take regarding the power of tourism to promote peace is the hypothesis that tourism can help to resolve existing conflicts and prejudices between unfriendly nations. Pizam (1996) attempted to test this theory by interviewing first-time tourists before and after visits to one of four destinations: Israelis visiting Egypt, Americans visiting the USSR, Greeks travelling to Turkey and Turks travelling to Greece. It was found that tourism did not contribute to positive attitudinal changes nor to perceived reduction of ethnic and nationality differences. In fact, most of the opinion changes which took place were in a negative direction. However, Pizam concludes that part of the reason for this was the fact that the tourist experiences of all four groups comprised escorted bus tours with little opportunity for meaningful interaction with local people.

Clearly, many forms of tourism, however benign, cannot support the claim of organisations, such as the WTO, that tourism is an effective means of achieving global peace and harmony. Exceptions to this might be, for example, where tourists engage in cultural exchange programmes or where individuals travel with the specific purpose of meeting with and developing an understanding of local people and cultures. However, these meetings generally take place only a small scale. Therefore, it is important to work towards developing a deeper understanding of tourist-host relationships and the potential for tourism as a broker of peace worldwide.

Peace as a Pre-condition for Tourism

In addition to addressing the role of tourism as a means of achieving greater worldwide peace and harmony, it is also important here to consider the tourism-peace relationship from the opposite viewpoint. That is, it is necessary to assess the extent to which peace (*i.e.* peaceful conditions in destination areas) is a pre-condition for successful tourism development. Reference has already been made to the fact that political upheaval or conflict represents a barrier to tourism development and events, such as the war in former Yugoslavia, the 1991 Gulf Conflict and the massacre of international tourists at Luxor in Egypt in 1997, serve to highlight the fragility of tourism as an international industry and its dependence on world peace (see Ryan 1991). Much is often made of flight cancellations, the exodus of tour operators and the effects on the tourism-dependent regions affected. However, scant attention is given to the ability of the international tourism industry to cope with continuing or recent conflict and political tensions in destination areas or to its ability to recover from these setbacks. For example, despite evidence of on-going conflict or attacks against tourists in a number of destinations, tourism has proved to be remarkably resilient. Sri Lanka is one such destination.

Peace in itself is a difficult concept to define and this makes its relationship with tourism all the more difficult to analyse. Does it mean absence of war, absence of conflict or, more generally a safe environment for tourism? Can, for example, a country with a poor record of human rights be said to be 'at peace'? Again, Sri Lanka is a good example of an area that has experienced internal conflict and whose tourism industry has fluctuated with events, but survived. Moreover, some tourists have been known to positively seek conflict as part of the 'travel' experience there is even a guide for travellers to 'The World's Most Dangerous Places' (Pelton 1997) or are willing to travel through 'risky' regions. Nevertheless, whatever definition of peace is used, the evidence suggests that, for the most part, countries will only attract significant numbers of tourists where, firstly an aura of peace is evident and second, where tourists perceive that they will not personally be at risk. Thus, the degree to which individual countries or regions may be considered peaceful is an important element in assessing the state of world tourism.

Features of Global Tourism

Having outlined various issues relating to the analysis of the state of world tourism at the global level, this second section of the chapter now considers current trends and flows in international tourism. Two points should be empathised here. Firstly, any statistical analysis of tourism should be undertaken within the context of the issues outlined above. Secondly, as we shall now consider, all tourism statistics should be approached and used with caution.

Tourism Statistics

The need for tourism statistics on a local, national and international scale is widely recognised. Statistics not only provide the basis for comparison and a measure of success in tourism, but also they provide a foundation for investment, political intervention and marketing strategies.

In short, it is statistical data that provide the empirical evidence of the growth and development of tourism.

One of the roles of the WTO is to collect and collate world tourism statistics on an annual basis. For example, according to the WTO, world receipts from tourism in 1999 totalled some $ 455 billion which, as we shall see shortly, is evidence of the continuing growth in international tourism (WTO 2000). However, 'it is not so much the size of this figure which is so impressive, but the fact that anybody should know its value or be able to work it out' (Cooper *et al.* 1993: 57). In other words, tourism statistics are notoriously difficult to measure; not only is the collection of reliable and accurate statistical information fraught with difficulties owing to the complex nature of the tourism industry, but also many countries do not have the facilities, or are unwilling to commit scarce resources to in-depth data collection. Therefore prior to examining international tourism statistics in more detail, it is important to outline why such statistics should be used with care. There are two broad areas of concern:

Definitions

A pre-requisite to any form of data collection is the need to set the parameters for the research - it is impossible to measure or count things before it is know who, or what, is to be counted. In other words, it is necessary to define different types of tourists, their activities and relevant measurement criteria (e.g. length of stay, purpose of trip, etc.) prior to any attempt to collect information. Unfortunately, however, although attempts have been made by the WTO and other organisations to produce universally acceptable definitions of tourism, not all countries adhere to them. Moreover, there is still considerable confusion surrounding tourism definitions. For example, different destinations may or may not include business travellers and day visitors in their tourist arrival statistics and generally, what, should, in theory, be a simple process is, in practice, rather complex.

The important point is, in order to be effective statistical parameters, definitions must be simple, understandable and perhaps most important universally applicable. Unfortunately, however, 'a review of any of the statistics published by the UN/WTO points up the innumerable footnotes to the data indicating national variations, differences in data collection methodology and significant diversity in terminology standards' (Theobald 1998: 11).

Measurement Techniques

The measurement of tourism can be broadly divided into the collection of statistics relating both volume and value. Volume statistics include, for example, arrivals figures and, or the number of nights a tourist in the destination, whilst value statistics are used to show the level of tourists' expenditure during their visit. The latter usually includes any payments for transport components owned by the host (destination) country and, typically, most tourism statistics include both measures. However, problems frequently emerge as a result of different data collection methods in different destinations, thereby making comparisons less meaningful.

These different collection methods include:

- counting total arrivals and/or departures at frontiers;
- sample surveys of arrivals/departures; and
- accommodation records.

In each of these cases, certain difficulties may arise. For example, there is a danger of double-counting the same visitor at border crossings, particularly in the case of landlocked countries used as a route to and from the final destination. Statistics based on accommodation records may also be inaccurate, especially where only registered accommodation returns are used and, therefore visits to friends or relatives or non-registered accommodation are not counted. There are also inherent dangers in sample surveys, mainly relating to the size or selection of the samples.

Despite these problems, it is trends and changes rather than absolute values which are of most importance. Therefore, although statistical data may not always be accurate, they are often the best available estimates and they do provide a useful source of information regarding trends and changes in demand and a basis for marketing, planning and forecasting.

The Growth of International Tourism

The growth in international tourism has been a major phenomenon of the latter half of the twentieth century. Since 1950, international tourist arrivals have increased from 25 million to over 625 million by 1998, with the preliminary 1999 figure totalling 664 million (see Table 15.1). This represents an overall growth factor of 24, whilst average annual growth has been between four and eight per cent. This suggests that international tourism has been, and remains, reasonably resilient to external factors, although a number of significant world events have temporarily halted its growth. In particular:

- *Conflict in the Middle East and Vietnam in the late 1960s.* These conflicts had a significant effect on the economies of major generating countries and were a contributing factor in the brief downturn in worldwide tourism growth in this period.

Table 15.1
International Tourist Arrivals and Receipts, 1950 – 1998

Year	*Arrivals (000s)*	*Receipts (US$mn)*	*Year*	*Arrivals (000s)*	*Receipts (US$mn)*
1950	25,282	2,100	1991	463,951	277,568
1960	69,320	6,867	1992	503,356	315,103
1965	112,863	11,604	1993	519,045	324,090
1970	165,787	17,900	1994	550,471	353,998
1975	222,290	40,702	1995	565,495	405,110
1980	285,997	105,320	1996	596,524	435,594
1985	327,188	118,084	1997	610,763	435,981
1990	458,229	268,928	1998	625,236	444,741

Source: Adapted from WTO (1999).

- *The oil crises of 1973/74 and 1976* – The increase in the price of fuel and subsequent rise in transport costs brought about by the oil crises led to an inevitable fall in demand for international travel.

- *The economic recessions of the early 1980s and 1990s*– Widespread unemployment and an overall fall in disposable incomes in many countries affected people's propensity to travel. Moreover, in the early 1990s, the recession in the world's main economies was accompanied by the effects of the Gulf War in 1991 which led to an additional fall in demand for international travel.

Despite these setbacks, the figures reveal a continuing upward trend in international tourist arrivals. Moreover, as Table 15.1 also shows, the absolute value of world tourism in terms of receipts has also increased annually, as has tourism's contribution to the world's economy.

However, although the figures for tourism on a global scale are dramatic, growth has not been equitable. That is, not all parts of the world have experienced similar growth rates, Therefore it is necessary to consider who the major generators and receivers of tourism are before looking at trends and flows on a more regional basis.

Profile of International Tourism

As mentioned earlier in this chapter, although tourism is significant to a large number of countries it is, in fact, dominated by relatively few. As Table 15.2 shows, about half of all international arrivals can be accounted for by ten nations, with the top fifteen attracting over 62 per cent of global arrivals in 1999.

Table 15.2
World's Top 15 Tourism Destinations

Rank				*International Tourist Arrivals (million)*			*% change*	*Market share*
1997	*1998*	*1999*	*Country*	*1997*	*1998*	*1999*	*1998/9*	*1999*
1	1	1	France	67.3	70.0	73.0	4.3	11.0
3	2	2	Spain	43.3	47.4	51.8	9.2	7.8
2	3	3	USA	47.8	46.4	48.5	4.5	7.3
4	4	4	Iraly	34.1	34.9	36.1	3.3	5.4
6	6	5	China	23.8	25.1	27.0	7.9	4.1
5	5	6	UK	25.5	25.7	25.7	0.0	3.9
9	8	7	Canada	17.6	18.9	19.6	3.7	2.9
8	7	8	Mexico	19.4	19.8	19.2	–2.9	2.9
14	13	9	Russian Fed	15.4	15.8	18.5	17.0	2.8
7	9	10	Poland	18.8	18.8	18.0	–4.4	2.7
12	10	11	Austria	16.6	17.4	17.5	0.7	2.6
13	11	12	Germany	15.8	16.5	17.1	3.7	2.6
10	12	13	Czech Rep	16.8	16.3	16.0	–1.8	2.4
11	14	14	Hungary	17.2	15.0	12.9	–13.8	1.9
17	15	15	Greece	10.1	10.9	12.0	9.9	1.8

Source: Adapted from WTO (1999; 2000).

A similar story is evident in terms of tourism receipts (Table 15.3). The USA earns the most from tourism, over double the second placed country, whilst almost 55 per cent of the world's receipts from tourism are earned by the top ten countires.

Table 15.3
World's Top 15 Tourism Earners

Rank		*International Tourism Receipts (US$ billions)*		*% Change*	*Market Share*
	Country	*1998*	*1999*	*1998/99*	*1999*
1.	USA	71.3	74.4	4.5	16.4
2.	Spain	29.7	32.9	10.7	7.2
3.	France	29.9	31.7	5.9	7.0
4.	Italy	29.9	28.4	–5.1	6.2
5.	UK	21.0	21.0	0.0	4.6
6.	Germany	16.4	16.8	2.4	3.7
7.	China	12.6	14.1	11.9	3.1
8.	Austria	11.2	11.1	–0.9	2.4
9.	Canada	9.4	10.0	6.7	2.2
10.	Greece	6.2	8.8	41.6	1.9
11.	Russian Fed.	6.5	7.8	19.4	1.7
12.	Mexico	7.9	7.6	–3.9	1.7
13.	Australia	7.3	7.5	2.6	1.7
14.	Switzerland	7.8	7.4	-5.9	1.6
15.	China/HK	7.1	7.2	1.8	1.6

Source: WTO (2000).

Moreover, of the ten most popular destinations for itnernational tourism, five (United States, France, Italy, Austria and UK) are also ranked within the ten largest tourism generators (Table 15.4).

This pattern and concentration of world tourism has remained largely unchanged for a number of years although, more recently, this established shape of world tourism has begun to change. For example, in recent years, Japan has been fast overtaking some European countries in generating tourism, the reason for this being both its rapid increase in wealth and also the increasing desire of the Japanese to travel overseas. Indeed, the Japanese government has been positively encouraging outbound travel among its population in an attempt to redress, to some extent, the country's large trade surplus with the rest of the world.

Other countries which have shown a significant growth in international tourism expenditure since 1980 include Taiwan, Korea, Singapore and Thailand, all of which have shown an average annual growth rate of between 17 and 21 per cent during this period. This can be compared with the average growth rate of six to eight per cent for a number of the traditionally dominant tourism generators, such as Germany, UK and France, and, despite the downturn in many Asian economies during the late 1990s, this trend is likely to continue.

Table 15.4
World's Top 15 Tourism Generators

Rank		*Inrernational Tourism Expenditure (US$ bn)*		*% Change*	*Marke Share*
	Country	*1998*	*1999*	*1998/99*	*1998*
1.	US	56.1	60.1	7.1	14.8
2.	Germany	46.9	48.2	2.6	12.4
3.	Japan	28.8	32.8	13.8	7.6
4.	UK	32.3	—	—	8.5
5.	France	17.8	17.7	–03	4.7
6.	Italy	17.7	16.9	–4.2	4.7
7.	Netherlands	11.0	11.4	3.6	2.9
8.	Canada	10.8	11.3	5.0	2.8
9.	China	9.2	—	—	2.4
10.	Austria	9.5	9.2	–3.3	2.5
11.	Belgium/Lux	8.8	—	—	2.3
12.	Sweden	7.7	7.6	–2.1	2.0
11.	Russian Fed.	8.3	7.4	–10.2	2.2
14.	Switzerland	7.1	7.0	–1.8	1.9
15.	Austria	5.4	5.8	7.5	1.4

Source: WTO(2000).

Nevertheless, it is worth noting that the increasing significance of countries such as Japan, Taiwan and Singapore is based on tourism spending – the WTO has found that 'expenditure' is a more reliable measure of outbound tourism than aggregated departure statistics. In other words, the growing prominence of these countries stems not necessarily from the absolute numbers travelling but from the average spend per tourist on each trip. Table 15.3 shows the fifteen countries which produce the highest expenditure per trip.

Table 15.5
Top Ten Countries with Highest Expenditure Per Trip Aborad 1996

Rank	*Country*	*Av. expenditure per trip abroad (US$)*
1.	Venezuela	4,405
2.	Thailand	2,260
3.	Japan	2,218
4.	Macau	2,014
5.	Brazil	1,979
6.	Australia	1,948
7.	Singapore	1,857
8.	Belgium	1,752
9.	Iceland	1,631
10.	Slovakia	1,581
11.	Republic of Korea	1,497
12.	Mauritius	1,491
13.	Papua New Guinea	1,480
14.	Bermuda	1,480
15.	Norway	1,461

Source : WTO (1988).

Interestingly, neither the major European generating countries nor the United States feature in the top twenty in this league table, whilst the greatest spenders per trip, with the exception of Japan, are not normally considered to be major tourism generators. To illustrate this point, Venezuelans, for example, spent an average of $ 4,405 per trip in 1996 (latest available figures) while German travellers spent, on average, $ 657 per trip. However, Venezuela was responsible for roughly 511,000 international departures in 1996 as compared with around 77 million from Germany. Consequently, not only must statistics generally be treated with some caution, but care must also be taken in judging the relative importance of different markets on a worldwide scale.

However, it is not only changing markets for tourism which are responsible for influencing trends in global tourism flows. Although the world's four most popular destinations remained the same in 1998 as in 1980 (i.e. France, United States, Spain and Italy), many emering destinations are gaining an ever-increasing share of international arrivals. China, Hongi-Kong, Turkey, South Africa, Indonesia and Thailand have, amongst others, experienced significant average annual growth rates in arrivals of between 12 and 15 per cent since 1980.

In terms of earnings from tourism, these countries have also experienced significant rates of increase. For example, Hong Kong has broken into the top fifteen of tourism earners in the world, while China, Singapore, Thailand and Indonesia as well as Australia and Poland, have all moved into the top twenty tourism earning destinations since 1980.

It is apparent, then, that while the major worldwide economies continue to dominate global tourism, this traditional position is now being challenged. Moreover, it is also evident that there are large differences in the geographical distribution of arrival and receipts and that a definite regional pattern of growth and stagnation is emerging. Therefore, it is important to consider global tourism from a regional perspective in order to:

- identify major inter-regional and intra-regional tourist flows ;
- assess regional growth potential;
- illustrate the regional nature of international tourist flows.

Regional Trends in Global Tourism

For analytical purposes, the WTO has divided the world into six regions: Europe, The Americas, Middle East, South Asia, East Asia and Pacific and Africa. Broadly speaking, it is the East Asia

Pacific region which has experienced the most significant growth in terms of its share of international tourist arrivals over the last decade, whilst most other regions, although continuing to attract greater numbers of tourists, have seen their share of world tourism decline. More specifically, each region has faced particular challenges and opportunities. These are outlined below.

EUROPE

As Table 15.6 illustrates, Europe receives the greatest proportion of international tourism each year – three times as many as its nearest 'rival', the Americas.

Europe's dominant position results from a number of factor. The region:

- is made up of a large number of small, geographically close nation states;
- is densely populated, with relatively high disposable incomes and a high priority placed on foreign holidays, particularly within France, Germany and the UK;
- has established communication networks and a large tourism industry and infrastructure; and
- is climatically, geographically and culturally diverse.

Table 15.6
International Tourism Arrivals and Receipts by Region, 1998

Region	*Tourist arrivals (million)*	*% share of world arrivals*	*Tourism receipts (US$Bn)*	*% share of world receipts*
Europe	383.8	60.3	232.5	52.7
Americas	119.9	18.8	118.0	26.8
East Asia Pacific	87.4	13.7	67.8	15.4
Mrica	24.9	3.9	9.8	2.2
Middle East	15.3	2.4	8.6	1.9
South Asia	5.2	0.8	4.3	1.0
World	636.6	100	441.0	100

Source: Adapted from WTO (2000).

With the exception of 1980, 1981 and 1991, international tourist arrivals in Europe have grown every year and, since 1970, have more than tripled from 113 million visits in 1970 to over 383 million in 1998. However, despite the growing number of arrivals in the region, Europe's share of world tourism is gradually declining. There are a number of inter-related reasons for this:

- increasing competition from 'new' destinations outside Europe;
- the growing propensity for Europeans to travel to other areas of the world for holiday/business purposes;
- the perception that many European tourism destinations are expensive in comparison with destinations elsewhere;
- the growing maturity of the tourist market in Europe and the tourism industry; and
- the downturn in some generating economies, particularly Germany.

The main problem facing tourism in Europe in recent years has been a lack of world competitiveness, exacerbated by the over-reliance on tourists from within the region. For example, although in 1991, over 80 per cent of international tourism in Europe was generated internally, this proportion had fallen by 1995. During the same period, the proportion of travellers from the European region arriving in South Asia, Africa and the Middle East increased by 6 to 8 per cent. Should this trend continue, it is most likely that these hardest hit would be western and southern European countries, such as France, Spain and Italy, which have traditionally accounted for the largest per centage of both arrivals and receipts in the region.

Europe's proportion of world earnings from tourism has also declined correspondingly, although the figures have tended to fluctuate. For example, in 1990, Europe's share of international receipts was 54.4 per cent, reached a low point at 50 per cent in 1993, but has recovered to around 52 per cent in the late 1990s. However, the general trend is downwards, a fact which is even more concerning given that tourism is an increasingly important sector in the economies of Europe. In 1995, earnings from tourism represented 8.7 per cent the region's export earnings, compared with 6.4 per cent in 1985.

THE AMERICAS

The Americas region, which includes North, Central and South America as well as the Caribbean is, after Europe, the second most important tourism-receiving region of the world. In 1998, it accounted for 18.8 per cent of international tourist arrivals and almost 27 per cent of world tourism receipts. However, the extent of tourism within this region is much greater than the figures would suggest. Whilst the United States, Canada, Mexico and Brazil receive the majority of international arrivals in the area, they also have highly developed domestic tourism industries, a fact that is not accounted for in the WTO statistics.

The main tourist flows in the Americas come from within the region; 74 per cent of arrivals are generated internally – half of these come from the United States and Canada – followed by European arrivals (14.6 per cent). Despite the dominance of the internal market, arrivals from both Europe and East Asia Pacific (EAP) are increasing, particularly from the UK and Japan. The reason for this can be attributed, in part, to the competitively priced nature of the tourism product in the region. Not surprisingly, the US attracts both the highest number of arrivals in the region (39 per cent) and the greatest proportion of receipts (63 per cent). Indeed, the US tops the list of the world's highest tourism earners. However, the Caribbean accounts for a surprisingly large proportion of international tourism in the region – 13.1 per cent of arrivals and 12.7 per cent of receipts. Conversely, despite their large populations and geographical size, both South and Central America attract a relatively low proportion of international tourists (12.6 per cent and 3.3 per cent respectively in 1999). This is largely because of economic and political difficulties.

AFRICA

In contrast to the Americas and despite its geographical size, the African region enjoys a relatively low proportion of international tourism. In 1998, the region accounted for just 3.9 per cent of all international arrivals and 2.2 per cent of receipts. These low figures can be explained by a number of factors, including:

- there are many developing countries in the region lacking tourism infrastructure, investment and tourism development policies;

- many countries have suffered severe political and economic difficulties; and
- intra-African tourism remains under-developed; in 1995, only 42 per cent of arrivals were from within the region, compared with almost 35 per cent from Europe alone.

Of the European arrivals, the highest number come from France, followed by Germany and the UK, the pattern of tourist flows undoubtedly being influenced by historical colonial ties. For example, the majority of international tourist arrivals in The Gambia are from Britain, whilst the former French colony of Senegal attracts almost exclusively French tourists. Arrivals from the Americas remain low, partially as a result of a lack of international air routes.

Despite the overall low number of arrivals in the region, some individual countries have successfully exploited their tourism potential. For example, both Tunisia and Morocco have become popular destinations, making use of their proximity to the major European markets. Tunisia is the region's second most popular destination with over 4.7 million arrivals in 1998, followed by Morocco which attracted 3.2 million tourists in the same year. However, as a result of its more settled political climate, South Africa has rapidly increased its share of arrivals and is now the highest tourism earner and attracts the greatest number of international tourists within the region. In 1998, South Africa accounted for 27.8 per cent of receipts and 23.4 per cent of arrivals in the region.

Other countries have also begun to develop tourism industries including Zimbabwe, Mauritius, Namibia and Tanzania, but still twenty African countries still receive fewer than 100,000 visitors a year and thirteen of these attract less than 50,000. Nevertheless, the region possesses a great deal of potential for further tourism development and tourism is becoming an increasingly important part of the region's economy. For example, the contribution of tourism to Africa's export earnings increased from 4.9 per cent in 1985 to 8 per cent in 1995. However, for this to continue, significant levels of investment in tourism infrastructure and promotion, combined with a more stack political and economic environment, will be required.

THE MIDDLE EAST

Between 1994 and 1996, tourist arrivals in the Middle East grew more quickly than in any other region and, in 1999, achieved the world's fastest growth rate of 16 per cent. Such a growth rate is surprising, particularly since the Gulf War in 1991 seriously impacted upon tourism in the area. However, as early as 1992, tourist arrivals had surpassed pre-Gulf War levels and, by 1996, total arrivals in the region had increased by 70 per cent since 1990. Similarly, the region's share of world tourism arrivals has grown every year since 1991, although it remains low at just 2.7 per cent.

The main destinations within the Middle East are Saudi Arabia with over 3.3 million arrivals in 1998, followed by Egypt (3.2 million) and Dubai (2.2 million). More generally, tourist flows to the region tend to be erratic, primarily as a result of political events and upheavals. For example, the massacre of tourists at Luxor in Egypt in 1997 had a significant impact on arrivals (although provisional 1999 figures point to a remarkable recovery, the country attracting almost 4.5 million visitors), whilst the tourism industries in many other countries suffer from the region's tendency towards political instability. Nevertheless, tourism does remain surprisingly resilient; this can be explained, in part, by the region's unique cultural and religious attractions.

SOUTH ASIA

This region comprises those countries encircling and including the Indian sub-continent, such as Pakistan, Bangladesh, Nepal and Sri Lanka, and accounts for the smallest share of world tourism arrivals. Moreover, only 23 per cent of international arrivals are generated within the region, partially as a result of the under-developed transport infrastructure and partly as a result of political tensions between countries in the region. The largest proportion (over 45 per cent) of international arrivals come from Europe, with the UK representing the single largest generating country, although the Americas is an increasingly important market for the region.

Just under two thirds of all international arrivals in the region are shared by India and Pakistan. Indeed, India is the main destination with 45 per cent of arrivals and 68 per cent of receipts in 1998. However, a number of other countries, including

Nepal, Sri Lanka and the Maldives, are all highly dependent on tourism. Nevertheless, tourism remains very under-developed in many parts of South Asia. Military conflict, political upheavals and human rights issues have discouraged tourism in countries such as Afghanistan, Myanmar (Burma) and Iran, and, whilst arrivals in general are increasing annually, the area has not matched the remarkable growth of the neighbouring East Asia Pacific region.

EAST ASIA/PACIFIC

Of all the regions identified by the WTO, the EAP area has experienced the most significant and sustained growth. Between 1990 and 1997, international arrivals increased by 70 per cent, from 53 million to 90 million. During the same period, receipts from tourism have more than doubled.

This remarkable growth was, until the financial crisis in the late 1990s, fuelled by the increasing strength of the economies in the EAP region. As a result, intra-regional tourism has been very strong; in 1995, almost 80 per cent of international arrivals were generated from within the region. Japan, South Korea and Taiwan, in particular, have contributed to this trend. Conversely, Europe supplied just 12 per cent. At the same time, many of these countries have been developing and investing heavily in their tourism industries. Thailand, Malaysia, South Korea, Hong Kong, Singapore and Indonesia have all undertaken development and promotional programmes. Therefore, international tourism in the region has benefited from both the growth in business-related tourism and more traditional types of tourism.

The main destinations in the region are China, Hong Kong, Malaysia, Thailand, Singapore and Indonesia, all of which have shown significant growth in tourist arrivals and receipts in the last fifteen years; they also achieved significant growth in 1999 following the region's economic turmoil in 1997/1998. However, new destinations, such as Vietnam and Cambodia, are also developing their tourism industries with some success, whilst Australia is also becoming more popular. Arrivals there rose from less that one million in 1980 to over 7.3 million in 1998, partially because of increased charter flights from Europe. At the same time, tourism to the tiny island states of Polynesia, Melanesia and Micronesia is also increasing, despite their geographical isolation. The attraction of these destinations lies in their quality tourism image and their proximity to New Zealand and Australia.

However, the future growth prospects for the region are uncertain. The economic crisis of 1997 indicated a lack of economic stability and, although arrivals figures as a whole have bounced back (partly because devaluation of many South East Asian currencies, making the countries relatively cheap to visit), longer-term growth remains less certain.

Bibliography

Aaker, D.A. (1992) *Strategic Market Management.* New York: John Wiley.

Abegg, B. (1996) *Klimaänderung und Tourismus–Klimafolgenforschung am Beispiel des Wintertourismus in den Schweizer Alpen*. Zurich: VDF Hochschulverlag der ETH Zurich.

Abegg, B. *et al.* (1997) Climate impact assessment in tourism. *Die Erde,* 128: 105 – 16.

Abell, D.F. (1980) *Defining the Business: The Starting Point of Stratigic Planning*. Englewood Cliffs, NJ: Prentice Hall.

Adams D.L (1973) Uncertainty in nature, cognitive dissonance, and the perceptual distortion of environmental information: weather forecasts and New England beach trip decisions. *Economic Geography,* 4: 287 – 97.

Aderhold, P. (1999) *Kurzfassung der Reiseanalyse* '99. Hamburg: Forschungs-gemeinschaft Urlaub und Reisen.

Airey, D. and Butler, R. (1999) *Tourism at the Pegional Level,* Portoroz, Slovenia, International Association of Scientific Experts in Tourism, Reports, 41, pp. 71 – 90.

Alford, P. (2000), *E-business in the Travel Industry*, London: Travel & Tourism Intelligence.

Analysis of the Changing World of International Airline Alliances. *Tourism Management,* 22, 229–243.

Anon. (1998) Malediven – Bedroht durch wörmeres Kiima, *Fremdenvekehrs-wirtschaft International,* 26: 88.

Arthur, W.B. (1996) Increasing Returns and the New World of Business. *Harvard Business Review,* 74, July/August, 100 – 111.

ATOL, (2001a), *ATOL Business,* Issue 18 (August), London: CAA.

ATOL (2001b), *A brief history of consumer protection for customers of air travel organisers*, www.atol.org.uk/atol/student/history12.htm.

Baden-Fuller; C. And Stopford, J. (1992) *Rejuvenating the Muture Business.* Oxford: Routledge.

Bennett, M.M. (1997) Strategic Alliances in the World Airline Industry. *Progress in Tourism and Hospitality Research,* 3, 212 – 223.

Blamey, R. and Hatch D. (1996) *Profiles and Motivations of Nature-Based Tourists Visiting Australia.* Occasional Paper No. 25. Canberra: Bureau of Tourism Research.

Blamey, R.K. (I995) *The Nature of Ecotourism.* Occasional Paper No.21. Canberra: Bureau of Tourism Research.

Bocock, R. (1993), *Consumption,* London: Routledge.

Bottomley Renshaw, M. (1997), *The Travel Agent, 2nd Edition,* Sunderland: Business Education Publishers.

Braun. O.L. and Lohmann, M. (1989) *Die Reiseentscheidung Fleuge Ergebnisse zum Stand der Forschung.* Starnberg: Studienkreis fur Tourismus.

Braun. O.L., Lohmann, M. *et al.* (1999) Potential impact of climate change effects on references for tourism destination: a psychological pilot study. *Climate Research,* 11 (April): 247 – 54.

Bray. D. (1998) Visioning Event Horizons – Global Warming, the German Coastal Region and Tourism, Abschlussbericht zum Projekt Klimawandelund Küstentourismus. Hamburg (Meteorologisches Institut der Universitat Hamburg) (unpublished).

Buerki, R. (2000) Climate change – adaptation of tourists and tourism managers. Paper presented to the International Millennium Conference: Tourism and Hospitality in the 21st century, University of Surrey, Guildford, England, 11 – 14 January 2000.

Buerki, R. and Elsasser, H. (1999) Nachfragetrends und Umwelturändenungen an der Schwelle zum 21. Jahrhundert – Das Beispiel Wintertourismus in den Alpen. Manuscript (Zurich).

Buhalis, D. And Cooper, C. (1998) Competiton or Co-operation? Small and Medium Sized Tourism Enterprises at the Destination, in E. Laws, B. Faulkner and G. Moscardo (eds), *Embracing and Managing Change in Tourism – International Case Studies.* London: Routledge.

Campbell, D., Stonehouse, G. and Houston, B. (1999) *Businews Strategy: An Introduction.* Oxford: Butterworth–Heinemann.

Canadian Tourism Human Resource Council (CTHRC) (1996) *National Occupational Standards for the Canadian Tourism Industry: Heritage Interpreter.* Ottawa.: CTHRC. .

Cannadine, D. (1980) *Lords and Landlords: the Aristocracy and the Towns, 1774 – 1967*. Leicester: Leicester University Press.

Chakravarthy, B. (1997) A New Strategy Framework for Coping with Turbulence. *Sloan Management Review,* Winter, pp. 69 – 82.

Christiansen, T. (1997) 1st Sylt noch zu retten?, *Kieler Nachrichten*, 12 June.

Clawson, M. (1966) The influence of weather on outdoor recreation. In W. Sewell (ed.), *Human Dimensions of Weather Modification.* Department of Geography, University of Chicago, Research Paper No.105, pp. 183 – 93.

Confederation of British Industry (1999) The New Regional Dimension to Tourism Delivery. Seminar, London, 30 September 1999.

Cooper, C., Fletcher, J., Gilbert, D., Shepherd, R. and Wanhill, S. (1998), *Tourism: Principles and Practice, 2nd Edition,* Harlow: Longman.

Cotterill, D. (1996) Developing a sustainable ecotourism business. In H. Richins, J. Richardson and A. Crabtree (eds), *Taking the Next Steps.* Brisbane: Ecotourisn Association of Australia, pp. 135 – 40.

Coulter, M. (2002) *Strategic Management in Action,* 2nd edn. Englewoodk Cliffs, NJ: Prentice Hall.

D'Aveni, R.A. (1994) *Hypercompetition: Managing the Dynamics of Strategic Manoeuvring.* New York: Free Press.

Dale, C. (2000), The UK tour-operating industry: a competitive analysis, *Journal of Vacation Marketing* 6(4): 357 – 367.

Dann, G. (1977), Anomie, ego–enhancement and tourism, *Annals of Tourism Research* 4(4): 184 – 194.

Dann, G. (1981), Tourist motivation : an appraisal, *Annals of Tourism Research* 8(2) : 187 – 219.

Dann, G.J.S. (1996) *The Language of Tourism. A Sociolinguistic Perspective :* Wallingford, UK, CAB International.

De Freitas, C.R. (1990) Recreation climate assessment. *International Journal of Climatology,* 10: 89 – 103.

Department for Culture, Media and Sport (1999) *Tomorrow's Tourism,* London: DCMS.

Dev, C.S. and Klein, S. (1993) Strategic Alliances in the Hotel Industry. *Cornell Hotel and Restaurant Administration Quarterly,* February, pp 43 – 45.

Donne, M. (2000) The Future of International Airline Alliances. *Travel and Tourism Analyst,* 6, 3 – 21.

ECES, Egyptian Centre for Economic Studies (1998) Egypt: The Tourism Cluster, Final Report, Phase 1.

Emery, F. (1981), Alternative futures in tourism, *International Journal of Tourism Management* (1): 241 – 255.

Edwards, A. and Graham A. (1997) *International Tourism Forecasts to* 2010. London: Travel & Tourism Intelligence. (http://www.t-ti.com/publications.htm)

Evans, N. (2001a) Collaborative Strategy : an Analysis of the Changing World of International Airline Alliances. *Tourism Management*, 22, 229 – 243.

Evans, N. (2001b) Alliances in the International Travel Industry: Sustainable Strategic Options? *International Journal of Hospitality and Tourism Administration*, 2(1), 1 – 26.

Feige, M., Seidel, A., Kirchhoff, M. and Smetan. C. (1999) Entwicklungspfade des Küstentourismus. Abschlussbericht zum Projekt Klimawandel und Küstentourismus, Berlin: (DWIF, Deutsches Wirtschaftswissenschaftliches Institut für Fremdenverkehr) (unpublished).

Finlay, P. (2000) *Strategic Management: An Introduction to Business and Corporate Strategy*. Harlow: Pearson Education.

Geva, A. and Goldman A. (1991) Satisfaction measurement in guided tours. *Annals of Tourism Research*, 18 (2): 177 – 85.

Gilbert, D. (1991), An examination of the consumer behaviour process related to tourism, in C. Cooper (ed.) *Progress in Tourism, Recreation and Hospitality Managment. Volume III*, London: Bellhaven Press: 78 – 105.

Gilbert, D. and Joshi, I. (1992), Quality management and the tourism and hospitality industry, in C. Cooper and A. Lockwood (eds.) *Progress in Tourism, Recretation and Hospitality Management, Volume 4*, London: Belhaven Press.

Ginter, P. and Duncan, J. (1990) Macro–environmental analysis. *Long Range Planning*, December, 91 – 100.

Go, F.M. and Pine, R. (1995) *Globalisation Stragtegy in the Hotel Industry*. London: International Thomson Business Press.

Go, F.M. and Appelman, J. (2001) Achieving Global Competitiveness in SMEs by Building Trust in Interfirm Alliances, in S. Wahab and C. Cooper (eds), *Tourism in the Age of Globalisation*. London: Routledge.

Goodall, B. (1991), Understanding holiday choice, in C. Cooper (ed.) *Progress in Tourism, Recreation and Hospitality Management, Volume III*, London: Bellhaven Press 58 – 77.

Haberberg, A. and Rieple, A. (2001) *The Strategic Management of Organisations*. Harlow Pearson Education.

Ham, S.H. (1982) Familiarity and adaptation: A study of family attendance at interpretive activities. Ph.D. dissertation, University of Idaho. USA.

Ham, S. and Krumpe, E. (1996) Identifying audiences and messages for nonformal environmental education: a theoretical framework for interpreters. *Journal of Interpretation Research,* 1(i): 111 – 23.

Hamel G. and Prahalad, C.K. (1989) Strategic intent. *Harvard Business Review* (67(3), 63 – 76.

Hamel, G. and Prahalad, C.K. (1994) *Competing for the Future.* Cambridge, MA: Harvard Business School Press.

Hansen, J. (1997) A warming world needs human remedy now. *International Herald Tribune,* 19 June, p. 10.

Hassemann, K. (1997) Die Launen der Medien. *Die Zeit,* Nr. 32, 1 August, p. 311.

Heeley, J. (1975) A study of organisations concerned with tourism in the UK. MSc thesis, Scottish Hotel School Glasgow, University of Strathclyde.

Heeley, J. (1980) Tourism and local government, with special reference to the county of Norfolk. PhD thesis, Centre for East Anglian Studies, Norwich, University of East Anglia.

Heeley, J. (1981) Planning for tourism in Britain: an historical perspective. *Town Planning Review (Journal of the Royal Town Planning Institute),* 52 (1): 61 – 79.

Heene, A and Sanchez, R. (1997) *Competence-based Strategic Management.* New York: John Wiley.

Helms, M.M. and Wright, P. (1992) External Considerations: Their Influence on Future Strategic Planning. *Management Decision,* 30(8), 4 – 16.

Holloway, J.C. (1994) *The Business of Tourism,* London: Pitman.

Holloway, J.C. (1998), *The Business of Tourism, 5th Edition,* Harlow: Longman.

Holloway, S. (1998) *Changing Planes: A Strategic Management Perspective on an Industry in Transition.* Aldershot: Ashgate.

Hope, C. and Muhlemann, A. (1998), Total quality, human resource managment and tourism, *Tourism Economics* 4(4): 367 – 386.

Houghton, J.T., Meira Filho, L.G., Callander, B.A., Harris, N., Kattenberg, A. and Maskell, K. (eds) (1996) *Climate Change* 1995. *The Science of Climate Change.* Cambridge: Cambridge University Press.

IHK Kiel (1998) *Wirtschaftslage und Erwartungen in Schleswig-Holstein: Tourismuswirtschaft Sommersaison* 1998. Kiel: Industrie–und Handels–kammer.

Ioannides, D. (1998), Tour operators: the gatekeepers of tourism, in D. Ioannides and K. Debbage (eds) *The Economic Geography of the Tourist Industry: A Supply-side Analysis,* London: Routledge: 139 – 158.

Jafari, J. (1987), Tourism models: the sociocultural aspects, *Tourism Management* 8(2): 152 – 159.

Jebb, M. (1986), *Walkers,* London: Constable.

Jeffreys, E. (1999) England – a new framework for action. *Tourism,* Issue 102.

Johnson, G. And Scholes, K. (2002) *Exploring Corporate Strategy,* 6th edn. Harlow: Pearson Education.

Kay, J. (1993) *Foundations of Corporate Success.* Oxford: Oxford University Press.

Knapp, D. and Barrie. E. (1998) Ecology. versus issue interpretation: the analysis of two different messages. *Journals of Interpretation Research,* 3 (1): 21 – 38.

Know es. T. (1996) *Corporate Strategy for Hospitality,* Harlow: Longman.

Krippendorf, J. (1987), *The Holiday Makers,* Oxford: Heinemann.

Krupp, C. (1995) *Klimaänderungen und die Folgen.* Berlin: Herausgegeben vom Wissenschaftszentram Berlin für Sozialforschung.

Laws, E. (1997) *Managing Packaged Tourism,* London: International Thomson Business Press.

Lean, G. (1999) They're going under. *The Independent,* 13 June, p. 15.

Lim, C. (1997) Review of international tourism demand models. *Annals of Tourism Research.* 24 (4): 835 – 49.

Lohmann, M. and Kaim, E. (1999) Weather and holiday preference – image, attitude and experience, *Revue de Tourisme.* 2: 54 – 64.

Lohmann, M., 'Kierchhoff, H.W. *et al.* (1998) Entwicklungspfade des Tourismus unter Einfluss des Klimawandels, Abschlussericht zum Projekt Klimawandel und Küstentourismus. Kiel, NIT (unpublished).

Lury, C. (1996), *Consumer Culture,* Cambridge: Polity Press.

Lynch R. (2000) *Corporate Strategy.* Harlow: Pearson Education.

Lynch, R. (2000) *Corporate Strategy,* 2nd edn. Harlow: Pearson Education.

Matthews, R. (1989) *Marketing Bureaux.* London: English Tourist Board (Insights).

Maxeiner, D. (1997) Die Launen der Sonne. *Die Zeit,* Nr. 31, 25 July. p. 38.

McCarthy, M. (1999) Beachy Head cliff collapses into the sea. *The Independent,* 12 January. p. 5.

McGahan, A.M. and Porter, M.E. (1997) How Much Does Industry Matter, Really? *Strategic Management Journal,* 18 (Summer special issue) 15 – 30.

Middleton, V. (2001), *Marketing in Travel and Tourism, 3rd Edition,* Oxford: Butterworth.

Middleton, V.T.C. and Clarke, J. (2001) *Marketing in Travel and Tourism,* 3rd edn. Oxford: Butterworth-Heinemann.

Mill, R. and Morrison, A. (1985) *The Tourism System,* New Jersey: Prentice Hall International.

Mintel (2000), *Inclusive Tours,* London: Mintel International Group Limited.

Mullins. G.W. and Hanna, J.W. (1981) Participation in interpretive activity subgroups. *Journal of Interpretation.* 6 (1): 25 - 31.

Munt, I. (1994), The 'other' postmodern tourism: culture, travel and the new middle classes, *Theory, Culture and Society* 11(3): 101 – 123.

Neale, R.S. (1981) *Bath : A Social History 1680 – 1850 or a Valley of Pleasure, yet a Sink of Iniquity.* London: Routledge and Kegan Paul.

Olsen, M.D. (1993) International Growth Styrategies of Major US Hotel Companies. *Travel and Tourism Analyst,* 3, 51 – 64.

ONT (2001), *Social Trends 31,* London: Office for National Statistics.

Oum, T.H., and Park J.H. (1997) Airline Alliances: Current Status, Policy Issues, and Future Directions. *Journal of Air port Managment,* 3(3), 133 – 144.

Parasuraman. A., Zeithaml, V. and Berry, L. (1985), A conceptual model service quality and its implications for future research, *Journal of Marketing* 49(4): 41 – 50.

Parrinello, G. (1993), Motivation and anticipation in post-industrial tourism, *Annals of Tourism Research* 20(2): 233 – 249.

Pearce, P. (1992), Fundamentals of tourism motivation, in D. Pearce and R. Butler (eds.) *Tourism Research: Critiques and Challenges,* London: Routledge: 113 – 134.

Pearce, P. and Caltabiano, M. (1983) Inferring travel motivation from travellers' experiences, *Journal of Travel Research* 22: 16 – 20.

Pearce, P.L. and Caltablano, M.L. (1983) Inferring travel motivation from travellers, experiences. *Journal of Travel Research,* 22: 16 – 20.

Pender, L. (2001), *Travel Trade and Transport: An Introduction,* London: Continuum.

Peng, Li (1997) Opening address to Pacific Asia Travel Association Annual Conference, Beijing, China.

Pizam, A. and Calantone, R. (1987), Beyond psychographics – values as determinants of tourist behaviour, *International Journal of Hospitality Management* 6(3): 177 – 181.

Poon, A, (2001), Travel distribution: the future of travel agents, *Travel and Tourism Analyst,* No. 3, 57 – 80.

Porter, M.E. (1979) How Competitive Forces Shape Strategy. *Harvard Business Review,* March/April.

Porter, M. E. (1980), *Competitive Strategy: Techniques for Analysing Industries and Competitors,* New York: The Free Press.

Porter, M.E. (1985) *Competitive Adventage.* New York: Free Press.

Porter, M.E. (1990) *The Competitive Advantage of Nations.* London: Macmillan.

Prahalad, C.K. and Hamel, G. (1990) The Core Competence of the Organisation. *Harvard Business Review* 68(3), 79 – 93.

Reynolds, P. (1999) Mother Nature's wrath. *Time,* 22 February, p. 54.

Rhoades, D.L., and Lush, H. (1997) A Typology of Strategic Alliances in the Airline Industry: Propositions for Stability and Duration. *Journal of Air Transport Management,* 3(3), 109 – 114.

Rokeach, M. (1973), *The Nature of Human Values,* New York: The Free Press.

Rumelt, R.P. (1991) How Much Does Industry Matter? *Strategic Management Journal,* 12(3), 167 – 186.

Sharpley, R. (1999), *Tourism, Tourists & Society, 2nd Edition,* Huntingdon: Elm Publications.

Shaw, G. and Williams, A. (1977), *The Rise and Fall of British Coastal Resorts: Cultural and Economic Perspectives,* London: Mansell Publishing.

Sheldon, P. (1997), *Tourism Information Technology,* Wallingford: CAB International.

Sigaux, G. (1966), *History of Tourism,* London: Leisure Arts Ltd.

Simonian, H. (1996) Star Parts for Bit Players, *Financial Times,* 28 October.

Smeral, E. (1996) Globalisation and Changes in the Competitiveness of Tourism Destinations, in *Globalisation and Tourism, Editions AIEST,* St Gallen, Switzerland: Editions AIEST.

Smith, S.L.J. (1995) *Tourism Analysis: A Handbook,* 2nd edn. Harlow: Longman.

Solomon, M. (1994), *Consumer Behaviour : Buying, Having and Being, 2nd Edition,* Needham Heights, Mass.: Allyn and Bacon.

Stehr, N. and von Storch, H. (1995) The social construct of climate and climate change. *Climate Research,* 5: 99 – 105.

Sterr, H. (1997) Die Problematik des Klimawandels für das integrierte Küstenzonen Management. *Schriftenreihe für Landschaftspftege und Naturschutz* 52: 87 – 98.

Stevenson, H.H. (1989) Defining Corporate Strengths and Weaknesses, in D. Asch and C. Bowman (eds.) *Readings in Strategic Management.* Basingstoke: Macmillan in association with The Open University.

Stonehouse, G., Hamill, J., Campbell, D.J. and Purdie, A. (2000) *Global and Transnational Business – Management and Strategy.* Chichester: John Wiley.

Strebel, P. (1992) *Breakpoints.* Cambridge MA: Harvard Business School Press.

Tenbrock, C. (1997) Die Swnde der Schwarzmaler. *Die Zeit,* Nr. 43, 17 October, p. 23.

Thomas, H. and Thomas, R. (1998) The implications for tourism of shifts in British local governance, *Progress in Tourism and Hospitality Research*, 4: 295 – 306.

Tourism Training Australia (1999) TTA Web site: http://www.tourism training.com.au.

Towner, J. (1985), The Grand Tour: a key phase in the history of tourism, *Annals of Tourism Research* 12(3): 297 – 333.

Towner, J. (1994), The history and development of tourism, in P. Callaghan, P. Long and M. Robinson (eds.) *Travel & Tourism, 2nd Edition,* Sunderland: Business Education Publishers: 7 – 23.

Towner, J. (1996), *An Historical Geography of Recreation and Tourism in the Western World 1540 - 1940,* Chichester: John Wiley & Sons.

Turner, I. (1996) Working with Chaos. *Financial Times,* 4 October.

Wahab, S. and Cooper, C. (2001) Tourism, Globalisation and the Competitive Advantage of Nations, in S. Wahab and C. Cooper (eds),

Tourism in the Age of Globalisation. Lonond: Routledge.

Walton, J.K. (1978) *The Blackpool Landlady*: a *Social History*, Manchester: Manchester University Press.

Walton, J. (1983), *The English Seaside Resort: A Social History, 1750-1914,* Leicester: Leicester Unviersity Press.

Walton, J. (2000), *The British Seaside: Holidays and resorts in the twentieth century,* Manchester: Manchester University Press.

Walvin, J, (1978) *Beside the Seaside,* London: Allen Lane.

Weiler, B. and Crabtree, A. (forthcoming) Assessing ecotour guide performance: findings from the fired. Proceedings of the 1998 Heritage Interpretation International Conference, Sydney.

Weiler, B. and Ham. S. (2000) Tour guides and interpretation in ecotourism. In D. Weaver (ed.). *The Encyclopaedia of Ecotourism.* Wallingford. U.K: CAB International.

Wheeller, B. (1992), Eco or ego tourism: new wave tourism. *ETB Insights. Vol III*, London: English Tourist Board: D 41 – 44.

Wickham, P.A. (2000) *Financial Times Corporate Strategy Casebook.* Harlow: Pearson Education.

World Tourism Organisation (1996) *Towards New Forms of Public-Private Sector Partnerships: The Changing Role, Structure and Activities of National Tourism Administrations.* A Special Report for the World Tourism Organisation. Madrid: WTO.

World Tourism Organisation (1999) *Tourism Highlights* 1999. Revised preliminary estimates. Madrid: WTO.

World Tourism Organisation On-line Statistical Database Service, World Tourism. WTO. (http://www.world-tourism.org/wtich.htm)

World Travel & Tourism Council (1998) *Progress & Priorities - Annual Report* 1998. London: WTTC.

www.whitbread.co.uk

Yale, P. (1995), *The Business of Tour Operations,* Harlow, Longman.

York Visitor and Conference Bureau (1990) Annual Report for the year ended 30 June 1990.

Young G. (1973), *Tourism: Blessing or Blight?,* Harmondsworth: Penguin.